THE MUTE
CHRISTIAN
under the Smarting Rod

Paul
Kamau

by
Thomas Brooks

THE MUTE CHRISTIAN

under the Smarting Rod

Thomas Brooks

1608-1680
English Puritan
Preacher of the Word
London

Originally Published

1659

2011 Edition

From the 1866 Edition
Edited, Updated, & Corrected

by

Hail & Fire
www.hailandfire.com

"The Mute Christian under the Smarting Rod," by Thomas Brooks, is herein edited, updated, corrected, and reprinted by Hail & Fire.

ISBN-10 0982804334
ISBN-13 978-0-9828043-3-9

Hail & Fire is a resource for Reformed and Gospel Theology in the works, exhortations, prayers, and apologetics of those who have maintained the Gospel and expounded upon the Scripture as the Eternal Word of God and the sole authority in Christian doctrine. "By manifestation of the truth commending ourselves to every man's conscience in the sight of God." 2 Corinthians 4:2

www.hailandfire.com

For the Saints

"The Lord is in his holy temple: let
all the earth keep silence before him."
Habakkuk 2:20

❦ CONTENTS ❧

❧ INTRODUCTION ❧
to the 1866 Edition

The 'Mute Christian' was originally published in 1659. A 2nd edition—though not so designated—was immediately called for and appeared in 1660. Thereafter few books were more in demand, being next to the 'Precious Remedies.' The earlier portion of the title (as in above two editions) was 'The Silent Soul with Sovereign Antidotes,' etc. Our text is taken from 'the eighth edition, corrected,' collated with the original and subsequent intervening editions. Its title-page is given below.—G.

THE

MUTE CHRISTIAN

UNDER THE SMARTING ROD:

WITH SOVEREIGN ANTIDOTES

Against the Most Miserable Exigents:[1]

or,

A Christian with an Olive Leaf in his mouth, when he is under the greatest afflictions, the sharpest and sorest trials and troubles, the saddest and darkest Providences and Changes, with Answers to divers Questions and Objections that are of greatest importance; all tending to win and work Souls to be still, quiet, calm and silent under all changes that have, or may pass upon them in this World, etc.

The *Eighth Edition,* Corrected.

By THOMAS BROOKS, late Preacher of the Word at St. Margaret New-Fish-Street, London.

"The Lord is in his Holy Temple: Let all the Earth keep silence before him." Hab. 2:20

LONDON, Printed for John Hancock, and are to be sold at the *Three Bibles,* over against the *Royal Exchange* in *Cornhill.*

1684

---

1. Urgencies.—H&F.

❧ THE ❧
EPISTLE
DEDICATORY

**To all afflicted and distressed, dissatisfied, disquieted,
and discomposed Christians throughout the world.**

The choicest saints are "born to troubles as the sparks fly
upwards," Job 5:7. "Many are the troubles of the righteous";[1]
if they were many, and not troubles, then, as it is in the
proverb, the more the merrier; or if they were troubles and
not many, then the fewer the better cheer. But God, who is
infinite in wisdom and matchless in goodness, has ordered
troubles, yea, many troubles to come trooping in upon us
on every side. As our mercies, so our crosses seldom come
single; they usually come treading one upon the heels of
another; they are like April showers, no sooner is one over
but another comes. And yet, Christians, it is mercy, it is rich
mercy, that every affliction is not an execution, that every
correction is not a damnation. The higher the waters rise,
the nearer Noah's ark was lifted up to heaven; the more
your afflictions are increased, the more your heart shall be
raised heavenward.

Because I would not hold you too long, I shall only
endeavor two things: first, to give you the reasons of my

---

1. "Many are the afflictions of the righteous: but the Lord delivereth
him out of them all," Ps. 34:19; also Ps. 88:3-4. *Qui non est Crucianus non
est Christianus.* Luther. ["Whoever suffers no affliction, is no Christian." A
reference to Rom. 8:16-17, "The Spirit itself beareth witness with our spirit,
that we are the children of God: And if children, then heirs; heirs of God,
and joint-heirs with Christ; if so be that we suffer with him, that we may be
also glorified together."—H&F.]

appearing once more in print; and secondly, a little counsel and direction that the following tract may be to your soul's advantage. The true reasons of my sending this piece into the world, such as it is, are these:

The afflicting hand of God has been hard upon me, and upon my dearest relations in this world and upon many of my precious Christian friends, whom I much love and honor in the Lord, which put me to studying the mind of God in that Scripture that I have made the subject-matter of the following discourse. Luther could not understand some Psalms until he was afflicted; the Christ-cross is no letter in the book, and "yet," says he, "it has taught me more than all the letters in the book." Afflictions are a golden key by which the Lord opens the rich treasure of his Word to his people's souls; and this in some measure, through grace, my soul has experienced. When Samson had found honey, he gave some to his father and mother to eat, Judges 14:9-10; some honey I have found in my following text: and therefore I may not, I cannot be such a churl as not to give them some of my honey to taste, who have drunk deep of my gall and wormwood.[1] Augustine observes on that place, "Come and hear, all ye that fear God, and I will declare what he hath done for my soul," Ps. 66:16, "He does not call them," says he, "to acquaint them with speculations—how wide the earth is, how far the heavens are stretched out, what the number of the stars is, or what is the course of the sun—but come and I will tell you the wonders of his grace, the faithfulness of his promises, the riches of his mercy to my soul." Gracious experiences are to be communicated. *Lilmod lelammed,* "we therefore learn that we may teach," is a proverb among the Rabbins.[2] And I do therefore "lay in and lay up," say the heathen, that I may draw forth again and lay out for the good of many. When God has dealt bountifully with us, others should reap some noble good by us. The family, the town, the city, the country, where a man lives, should fare the better for his faring well. Our mercies and experiences should be as a running spring

---

1. Some have accounted nothing their own that they have not communicated to others.
2. Obsolete: Rabbinate.—H&F.

at our doors, which is not only for our own use, but also for our neighbors', yea, and for strangers too.[1]

Litera scripta manet, "what is written is permanent" and it spreads itself further by far—in time, in place, and among persons—than the voice can reach. The pen is an artificial tongue; it speaks as well to absent as to present friends; it speaks to them afar off as well as those that are near; it speaks to many thousands at once; it speaks not only to the present age but also to succeeding ages. The pen is a kind of image of eternity; it will make a man live when he is dead, Heb. 11:4. Though "the prophets do not live forever," yet their labors may, Zec. 1:5. A man's writings may preach when he cannot, when he may not, when, by reason of bodily weakness, he dare not, and yea, more, when he *is* not.[2]

Few men, if any, have iron memories. How soon is a sermon preached and forgotten, when a sermon written remains! Augustine writing to Volusian, says, "That which is written is always at hand to be read, when the reader is at leisure."[3] Men do not easily forget their own names, nor their father's house, nor the wives of their bosoms, nor the fruit of their loins, nor to eat their daily bread, and yet, how easily do they forget that Word of grace, that should be dearer to them than all! Most men's memories, especially in the great concernments of their souls, are like a sieve or boulter,[4] where the good corn and fine flour goes through, but the light chaff and coarse bran remain behind; or like a strainer, where the sweet liquor is strained out, but the dregs left behind; or like a grate that lets the pure water run through, but if there is any straws, sticks, mud, or filth that it holds, as it were, with iron hands. Most men's memories are very treacherous, especially in good things; few men's memories

---

1. "Behold, a king shall reign in righteousness, and princes shall rule in judgment. And a man shall be as an hiding place from the wind, and a covert from the tempest; as rivers of water in a dry place, as the shadow of a great rock in a weary land," Isa. 32:1-2.—H&F.
2. There are here, as elsewhere in Brooks, reminiscences of Thomas Adams, who was a prime favorite of our author.—G.
3. Augustine Ep. i. ad. Volus.
4. 'Sifter.'—G.

are as a holy ark, a heavenly storehouse or magazine[1] for their souls, and therefore they stand in more need of a written word. But,

Another reason for this work is its marvelous suitableness and usefulness under these great turns and changes that have passed upon us. As every wise husbandman observes the fittest seasons to sow his seed—some he sows in the autumn when the leaves fall, some in the spring of the year, some in a dry season and some in a wet season, some in a moist clay and some in a sandy dry ground, Isa. 28:25—so every spiritual husbandman must observe the fittest times to sow his spiritual seed. He has heavenly seed by him for all occasions and seasons, for spring and fall; for all grounds, heads, and hearts. Now whether the seed sown in the following treatise be not suitable to the times and seasons wherein we are cast, is left to the judgment of the prudent reader to determine; if the author had thought otherwise, this effort would had been stifled in the womb.

Another reason is the good acceptance that my other weak labors have found. God has blessed them, not only to the conviction, the edification, confirmation, and consolation of many, but also to the conversion of many, "As it is written, To whom he was not spoken of, they shall see: and they that have not heard shall understand." Rom. 15:21.[2] God is a free agent to work by what hand he pleases, and sometimes he takes pleasure to do great things by weak means that "no flesh may glory in his presence." God will not "despise the day of small things"; and who or what are you that you dare despise that day? The Spirit breathes upon whose preaching and writing he pleases, and all prospers according as that wind blows, Joh. 3:8.[3]

Another reason is that all afflicted and distressed Christians may have a proper salve for every sore, a proper remedy

---

1. Storage room, especially for munitions.—H&F.
2. Also 1 Cor. 1:17-18, 2:9-10; and, "I am not ashamed of the Gospel of Christ: for it is the power of God unto salvation to every one that believeth," Rom. 1:16.—H&F.
3. "The wind bloweth where it listeth, and thou hearest the sound thereof, but canst not tell whence it cometh, and whither it goeth," Joh. 3:8.—H&F.

against every disease, at hand. As every good man, so every good book is not fit to be the afflicted man's companion; but this is. Here he may see his face, his head, his hand, his heart, his ways, his works; here he may see all his diseases discovered, and proper remedies proposed and applied; here he may find arguments to silence him, and means to quiet him, when it is at worst with him; in every storm here he may find a tree to shelter him; and in every danger, here he may find a city of refuge to secure him; and in every difficulty, here he may have a light to guide him; and in every peril, here he may find a buckler to defend him; and in every distress, here he may find a cordial[1] to strengthen him; and in every trouble, here he may find a staff to support him.[2]

I send this book into the world also to satisfy some bosom friends and some faithful friends. Man is made to be a friend, and he is fitted for friendly offices. He that is not friendly is not worthy to have a friend, and he that has a friend and does not show himself friendly, is not worthy to be accounted a man. Friendship is a kind of life, without which there is no comfort of a man's life. Christian friendship ties such a knot that great Alexander cannot cut.[3] Summer friends I value not, but winter friends are worth their weight in gold; and who can deny anything to such, especially in these days, wherein real, faithful, constant friends are so rare to be found? The friendship of most men in these days is like Jonah's gourd, now very promising and flourishing, and soon fading and withering; it is like those plants in the water, which have broad leaves on the surface of the water, but scarce any root at all; their expressions are high, but their affections are low; they speak much, but do little.[4] As drums, and trumpets, and ensigns in a battle make a great noise and a fine show, but do not themselves take action, so these counterfeit friends will compliment highly, bow handsomely, speak plausibly, and promise lustily, and

---

1. A cheering; a comforting that gladdens and strengthens.—H&F.
2. "A word fitly spoken is like apples of gold in pictures of silver." Pro. 25:11.
3. The 'Gordian Knot' is alluded to.—G.
4. "Oh my friends. I have never a friend," said Socrates. "A friend is a very mutable creature," said Plato.

yet have neither a hand nor heart to perform anything cordially or faithfully. From such friends it is a mercy to be delivered, and therefore King Antigonus was wont[1] to pray to God that he would protect him from his friends; and when one of his council asked him why he prayed so, he returned this answer, "Every man will shun and defend himself against his professed enemies, but from our professed or pretended friends, of whom few are faithful, none can safe-guard himself, but has need of protection from heaven." But for all this, there are some that are real friends, faithful friends, active friends, winter friends, bosom friends, fast friends; and for their sakes, especially those among them that have been long, very long, under the smarting rod and in the fiery furnace, and that have been often poured from vessel to vessel, have I once more appeared in print to the world.

There has not been any authors or author come to my hand, that has handled this subject as I have done; and therefore I do not know but it may be the more gratefully received and acceptable to the world; and if by this essay others that are more able shall be provoked to do more worthily upon this subject, I shall therein rejoice. I shall only add, that though much of the following matter was preached upon the Lord's visitation of my dear yoke-fellow, myself, and some other friends, yet there are many things of special concernment in the following tract, that yet I have not upon any account communicated to the world. And thus I have given you a true and faithful account of the reasons that have prevailed with me to publish this treatise to the world and to dedicate it to the reader.

The second thing promised was, the giving to you of a little good counsel, that you may so read the following discourse, as that it may turn much to your soul's advantage; for, as many fish and catch nothing, so, many read good books and get nothing, because they read them over cursorily, slightly, superficially; but he that would read to profit, must then also:

---

1. Accustomed or habituated.—H&F.

Read and look up for a blessing: "Paul may plant, and Apollos may water," but all will be to no purpose, except "the Lord give the increase," 1 Cor. 3:6-7. God must do the deed, when all is done, or else all that is done will do you no good. If you would have this work successful and effectual, you must look away from man and look up to God, who alone can make it a blessing to you. As without a blessing from heaven, your clothes cannot warm you, nor your food nourish you, nor a physic[1] cure you, nor friends comfort you, Mic. 6:14; so without a blessing from heaven, without the precious influences of the Spirit, what here is done will do you no good, it will not turn to your account in the day of Christ; and therefore cast an eye heavenwards, Hag. 1:6.[2] It is Seneca's observation, that the husbandmen in Egypt never look up to heaven for rain in the time of drought, but look after the overflowing of the banks of the Nile as the only cause of their plenty. Ah, how many are there in these days, who, when they go to read a book, never look up, never look after the rain of God's blessing, but only look to the Nile; they only look to the wit, the learning, the arts, the parts,[3] the eloquence, etc., of the author, they never look so high as heaven; and hence it comes to pass, that though these read much, yet they profit little.

He that would read to profit must read and meditate. Meditation is the food of your souls; it is the very stomach and natural heat whereby spiritual truths are digested. A man shall as soon live without his heart, as he shall be able to get good by what he reads, without meditation. Prayer, says Bernard, without meditation, is dry and formal, and reading without meditation is useless and unprofitable.[4] He that would be a wise, a prudent, and an able experienced

---

1. Medicine or the art of healing.—H&F.
2. "Ye have sown much, and bring in little; ye eat, but ye have not enough; ye drink, but ye are not filled with drink; ye clothe you, but there is none warm; and he that earneth wages earneth wages to put it into a bag with holes. Thus saith the Lord of hosts; Consider your ways. Ye looked for much, and, lo, it came to little; and when ye brought it home, I did blow upon it. Why? saith the Lord." Hag. 1:6-9.—H&F.
3. Powers; accomplishments.—H&F.
4. *Lectio sine meditatione arida est; meditatio sine lectione erronea est; oratio sine meditatione livida est.* Augustine.

statesman, must not hastily ramble and run over many cities, countries, customs, laws, and manners of people, without serious musing and pondering upon such things as may make him an expert statesman; so he that would get good by reading, that would complete his knowledge and perfect his experience in spiritual things, must not slightly and hastily ramble and run over this book or that, but ponder upon what he reads, as Mary pondered the saying of the angel in her heart. "Lord!" says Augustine, "the more I meditate on you, the sweeter you are to me." So the more you shall meditate on the following matter, the sweeter it will be to you. They usually thrive best who meditate most. Meditation is a soul fattening duty; it is a grace strengthening duty, it is a duty-crowning duty. Gerson calls meditation the nurse of prayer; Jerome calls it his paradise; Basil calls it the treasury where all the graces are locked up; Theophylact calls it the very gate and portal by which we enter into glory; and Aristotle, though a heathen, places felicity in the contemplation of the mind. You may read much and hear much, yet without meditation you will never be excellent, you will never be eminent Christians.

Read, and test what you read; take nothing upon trust, but all upon trial, as those noble Bereans did, Act. 17:10-11. You will try and tell[1] and weigh gold, though it is handed to you by your fathers; and so should you all those heavenly truths that are handed to you by your spiritual fathers. I hope that upon trial you will find nothing but what will hold weight in the balance of the sanctuary; and though all is not gold that glisters,[2] yet I judge that you will find nothing here that sparkles that will not be found upon trial to be true gold.

Read and do, read and practice what you read, or else all your reading will do you no good. He that has a good book in his hand, but not the lesson of it in his heart or life, is like that ass that carries burdens and feeds upon thistles.[3]

---

1. 'Count.'—G.
2. 'Glistens.'—H&F.
3. "Wherefore is there a price in the hand of a fool to get wisdom, seeing he hath no heart to it?" Pro. 17:16.—H&F.

In divine account, a man knows no more than he practices. Profession without practice will but make a man twice told[1] a child of darkness;[2] to speak well is to sound like a cymbal,[3] but to do well is to act like an angel. He that practices what he reads and understands, God will help him to understand what he understands not. There is no fear of knowing too much, though there is much fear in practicing too little; the most doing man shall be the most knowing man; the mightiest man in practice will in the end prove the mightiest man in Scripture. "For whosoever hath, to him shall be given, and he shall have more abundance: but whosoever hath not, from him shall be taken away even that he hath," Mat. 13:12, and Ps. 119:98-100.[4]

Theory is the guide of practice, and practice is the life of theory. Salvian relates how the heathen did reproach some Christians, who by their lewd lives made the Gospel of Christ to be a reproach. "Where," said they, "is that good law which they do believe? Where are those rules of godliness which they do learn? They read the holy Gospel, and yet are unclean; they read the Apostles' writings, and yet live in drunkenness; they follow Christ, and yet disobey Christ;[5] they profess a holy law, and yet do lead impure lives."[6] Ah! How may many preachers take up sad complaints against many readers in these days! They read our works, and yet in their lives they deny our

---

1. A reference to Jud. 1:12, "Clouds they are without water, carried about of winds; trees whose fruit withereth, without fruit, twice dead, plucked up by the roots."—H&F.

2. "Add to your faith virtue; to virtue knowledge; to knowledge temperance; to temperance patience; to patience godliness; to godliness brotherly kindness; and to brotherly kindness charity. For if these things be in you, and abound, they make you that ye shall neither be barren nor unfruitful in the knowledge of our Lord Jesus Christ. But he that lacketh these things is blind," 2 Pet. 1:5-9.—H&F.

3. 1 Cor. 13:1.

4. "Thou through thy commandments hast made me wiser than mine enemies: for they are ever with me. I have more understanding than all my teachers: for thy testimonies are my meditation. I understand more than the ancients, because I keep thy precepts," Ps. 119:98-10.

5. "Why call ye me, Lord, Lord, and do not the things which I say?" Luk. 6:46.—H&F.

6. Salvianus de G. D. l. iv.

works; they praise our works, and yet in their conversations they reproach our works; they cry up our labors in their discourses, and yet they cry them down in their practices. Yet, I hope better things of you into whose hands this treatise shall fall. The Samaritan woman did not fill her pitcher with water, that she might talk of it, but that she might use it. The application is easy. But,

Read and apply. Reading is but the drawing of the bow, application is the hitting of the mark. The choicest truths will no further profit you than they are applied by you; you would have done as well not to read, as not to apply what you read.[1] No man attains to health by reading of Galen or knowing Hippocrates and his aphorisms, but by the practical application of them; all the reading in the world will never make for the health of your souls except you apply what you read. The true reason why many read so much and profit so little is, because they do not apply and bring home what they read to their own souls. But,

Read and pray. He that does not make it a matter of conscience to pray over what he reads will find little sweetness or profit in his reading. No man makes such gain of his reading, as he that prays over what he reads. Luther professed that he profited more in the knowledge of the Scriptures by prayer, in a short space, than by study in a longer. As John, by weeping, got the sealed book open, so certainly men would gain much more than they do by reading good men's works, if they would but pray more over what they read.[2] Ah, Christians! Pray before you read, and pray after you read, that all may be blessed and sanctified to you; when you have done reading, close with this:

> So let me live, so let me die,
> That I may live eternally.

And when you are in the mount for yourselves, bear him upon your hearts, who is willing to "spend and be spent" for your sakes, for your souls, 2 Cor. 12:15. Oh! Pray for

---

1. The plaster will not heal if it is not applied.
2. Prayer is *porta coeli, clavis paradise.* ["The door of heaven, the key of paradise."—H&F.]

me, that I may more and more be under the rich influences and glorious pouring out of the Spirit; that I may "be an able minister of the New Testament, not of the letter, but of the Spirit," 2 Cor. 3:6; that I may always find an everlasting spring and an overflowing fountain within me, which may always make me faithful, constant, and abundant in the work of the Lord; and that I may live daily under those inward teachings of the Spirit that may enable me to speak from the heart to the heart, from the conscience to the conscience, and from experience to experience; that I may be a "burning and a shining light," that everlasting arms may be still under me; that while I live, I may be serviceable to his glory and his people's good; that no discouragements may discourage me in my work; and that when my work is done, I may give up my account with joy and not with grief. I shall follow these poor labors with my weak prayers, that they may contribute much to your internal and eternal welfare, and so rest.

Your soul's servant in our dearest Lord,

Thomas Brooks

THE MUTE CHRISTIAN

under the Smarting Rod

❧ THE ❧
MUTE CHRISTIAN
under the Smarting Rod

**"I was dumb, I opened not my mouth;
because thou didst it."
Ps. 39:9**

Not to trouble you with a tedious preface, wherein usually is a flood of words and only a drop of matter,

This Psalm consists of two parts, the first exegetical or narrative, the second eutical[1] or precative.[2] Narration and prayer take up the whole. In the former, you have the prophet's disease discovered, and in the latter, the remedy applied. My text falls in the latter part, where you have the way of David's cure, or the means by which his soul was reduced to a still and quiet temper. I shall shed a little light on the words, and then come to the point that I intend to stand upon.

"I was dumb." The Hebrew word signifies to be mute,

---

1. A misspelling of 'euctical'; supplicatory; 'eucharistical;' prayer and the giving of thanks.—H&F.
2. Supplicatory.—G.

tongue tied,[1] or dumb. The Hebrew word signifies to bind, as well as to be mute and dumb, because they that are dumb are as it were tongue tied; they have their lips stitched and bound up. Ah! The sight of God's hand in the afflictions that was upon him makes him lay a law of silence upon his heart and tongue.

"I opened not my mouth, because thou didst it," Ps. 39:9. He looks through all secondary causes to the first cause, and is silent: he sees the hand of God in all, and so sits mute and quiet. The sight of God in an affliction is of an irresistible efficacy to silence the heart, and to stop the mouth of a gracious man. In the words you may observe three things:

The person speaking, and that is, David—David a king, David a saint, David "a man after God's own heart," David a Christian—and here we are to look upon David, not as a king, but as a Christian, as a man whose heart was right with God.

The action and carriage of David under the hand of God, in these words—"I was dumb, and opened not my mouth."

The reason for this humble and sweet carriage of his, in these words—"because thou didst it."

---

1. Tongue tied in the sense of being bound not to speak rather than being incapable of reply; willingness to remain silent, as one who is bound not to answer back but to stand in awe: "Stand in awe, and sin not; be still, and put your trust in the Lord," Ps. 4:4-5.—H&F.

❧ THE PROPOSITION ❧

That it is the great duty and concernment of gracious souls to be mute and silent under the greatest afflictions, the saddest providences, and sharpest trials that they meet with in this world.

For the opening and clearing up of this great and useful truth, I shall inquire: I. What this silence is that is here pointed at in the proposition. II. What a gracious and a holy silence includes. III. What a gracious and a holy silence does not exclude. And, IV. The reasons why Christians must be mute and silent under the greatest afflictions, the saddest providences, and the sharpest trials. And then, bring home all through application to our own souls.

I.
What is the silence here meant?

I answer that there is a sevenfold silence:

There is a stoical silence.

The stoics of old thought it altogether below a man that has reason or understanding either to rejoice in any good or to mourn for any evil; but this stoical silence is such a sinful insensibility as is very provoking to a holy God, Isa. 26:10-11. God will make the most insensible sinner sensible either of his hand here or of his wrath in hell. It is a heathenish and a horrid sin to be without natural affections, Rom. 1:31.

And of this sin Quintus Fabius Maximus seems to be foully guilty, who, when he heard that his mother and wife, whom he dearly loved, were slain by the fall of an house and that his younger son, a brave hopeful young man, died at the same time in Umbria, he never changed his countenance, but went on with the affairs of the commonwealth as if no such calamity had befallen him. This carriage of his spoke out more stupidity than patience, Lam. 2:17-19 and Isa. 57:10.

And so Harpalus was not at all appalled when he saw two of his sons laid ready dressed in a charger, when Astyages had bid him to supper. This was a sottish[1] insensibility. Certainly, if the loss of a child in the house be no more to you than the loss of a chick in the yard,[2] your heart is base and sordid, and you may well expect some sore awakening judgment.[3] This age is full of such monsters, who think it below the greatness and magnanimity of their spirits to be moved, affected, or afflicted with any afflictions that befall them. I know none so ripe and ready for hell as these.

Aristotle speaks of fishes, that though they have spears thrust into their sides, yet they awake not. God thrusts many a sharp spear through many a sinner's heart, and yet he feels nothing, he complains of nothing. These men's souls will bleed to death. Seneca, Ep. x, reports of Senecio Cornelius, who minded his body more than his soul and his money more than heaven; when he had all the day long

---

1. Senseless; very foolish.—H&F.
2. Even of the life of a beast: "A righteous man regardeth the life of his beast," Pro. 12:10. So also, the reaction of David at the taking of the cherished ewe that "was as a daughter" to the poor man in Nathan's tale; David's "anger was greatly kindled" so that he would have the transgressor repay fourfold *and* die, "because he did the thing, and because he had no pity," 2 Sam. 12:1-6.—H&F.
3. "Strangers have devoured his strength, and he knoweth it not: yea, gray hairs are here and there upon him, yet he knoweth not. And the pride of Israel testifieth to his face: and they do not return to the Lord their God, nor seek him for all this," Hos. 7:9-10.—H&F.

waited on his dying friend, and his friend was dead, returns to his house, sups merrily, comforts himself quickly, goes to bed cheerfully. His sorrows were ended and the time of his mourning expired before his deceased friend was interred. Such stupidity is a curse that many a man lies under. But this stoical silence, which is but a sinful sullenness, is not the silence here meant.

There is a politic silence.

Many are silent out of policy. Should they not be silent, they should lay themselves more open either to the rage and fury of men, or else to the plots and designs of men; to prevent which they are silent and will lay their hands upon their mouths that others might not lay their hands upon their estates, lives, or liberties: "And Saul also went home to Gibeah, and there went with him a band of men, whose hearts God had touched. But the children of Belial said, How shall this man save us? And they despised him, and brought him no presents; but he held his peace," or was as though he had been deaf, 1 Sam. 10:26-27. This new king being but newly entered upon his kingly government and observing his condition to be but mean[1] and low, his friends but few, and his enemies many and potent, sons of Belial, *i.e.* men without yoke,[2] as the word signifies, men that were desperately wicked, that were marked out for hell, that were even incarnate devils, who would neither submit to reason nor religion, nor be governed by the laws of nature or of nations, nor yet by the laws of God. Now, this young prince, to prevent sedition and rebellion, blood and destruction, prudently and politically chooses rather to lay his hand upon his mouth than to take a wolf by the ear or a lion by the beard; wanting neither wit nor will to be mute;

---

1. Obscure birth; wanting dignity.—H&F.
2. Who cannot be brought into service.—H&F.

he turns a deaf ear to all they say, his unsettled condition requiring silence.[1]

Henry the Sixth, emperor of Germany, used to say, *Qui nescit tacere, nescit loqui,* "He that knows not how to be silent, knows not how to speak." Saul knew this was a time for silence; he knew his work was rather to be an auditor than an orator. But this is not the silence the proposition speaks of.

There is a foolish silence.

Some fools there be that can neither do well nor speak well, and because they cannot word it either as they would nor as they should, they are so wise as to remain silent: "Even a fool, when he holds his peace, is counted wise, and he that shutteth his lips is esteemed a man of understanding," Pro. 17:28. As he cannot be wise that speaks much, so he cannot be known for the fool he is if he says nothing. There are many wise fools in the world; there are many silly fools, who, by holding their tongues, gain the credit and honor of being discreet men. He that does not expose his want of wisdom by foolish babbling is accounted wise, though he may be otherwise. Silence is so rare a virtue, where wisdom regulates it, that it is accounted a virtue where folly imposes it. Silence was so highly honored among the old Romans, that they erected altars to it. That man shall pass for a man of understanding, who so far understands himself as to hold his tongue. For though it be a great misery to be a fool, yet it is a greater that a man cannot be a fool but he must needs show it. But this foolish silence is not the silence here meant.

---

1. "Hear, see, and be silent, if you will live in peace." French Proverb.

There is a sullen silence.

Many, to gratify a humor, a lust, are sullenly silent; these are troubled with a dumb devil,[1] which was the worst devil of all the devils you read of in the Scripture, Mar. 9:17-28. There is a generation amongst us, who, when they are under the afflicting hand of God, are as men who have no mouths to plead with God, no lips to praise God, nor tongues to justify God. These are possessed with a dumb devil. This dumb devil had possessed Ahab for a time, "And Ahab came into his house, heavy and displeased, and laid him down upon his bed, and turned away his face, and would eat no bread," 1 Kin. 21:4. Ahab's ambitious humor and his covetous humor being crossed, he is resolved to starve himself and to die of sullenness. A sullen silence is both a sin and a punishment. No devil frets and vexes, wears and wastes the spirits of a man, like this dumb devil, like this sullen silence.

Some write of a certain devil, whom they call *Hudgin,* who will not, they say, hurt anyone, except he is wronged. I cannot speak so favorably of a sullen silence, for that wrongs many at once, God and Christ, bodies and souls. But this is not the silence here meant.

---

1. The current editor disagrees—there is no reason to account a sullen silence a devil rather than the motions of a man's heart, as noted, 'to gratify a humor.' A man may be sullenly silent in a design to armor himself against all assault of conscience or law or reproof. Consider the sullen silence of him who would draw others to duty beyond duty or reason—so Ahab desired of Naboth in order to gain the mastery over him; consider the sullen silence of a child who would have its way. "The wicked are estranged from the womb, etc., they are like the deaf adder that stoppeth her ear; which will not hearken to the voice of charmers, charming never so wisely," Ps. 58:3-5. Again, "They refused to hearken, and pulled away the shoulder, and stopped their ears, that they should not hear. Yea, they made their hearts as an adamant stone, lest they should hear the law, and the words which the Lord of hosts hath sent in his Spirit by the former prophets, etc." Zec. 7:11-12.—H&F.

There is a forced silence.

Many are silent per[1] force. He that is under the power of his enemy, though he suffer many hard things, yet he is silent under his sufferings, because he knows he is liable to worse; he that has taken away his liberty, may take away his life; he that has taken away his money, may take off his head; he that has let him bleed from the foot, may let him bleed from the throat if he will not be still and quiet. This works silence by force. So, when many are under the afflicting hand of God, conscience tells them that now they are under the hand of an enemy, and the power of that God whom they have dishonored, whose Son they have crucified, whose Spirit they have grieved, whose righteous laws they have transgressed, whose ordinances they have despised, and whose people they have abused and opposed; and that he that has taken away one child, may take away every child; and he that has taken away the wife, might have taken away the husband; and he that has taken away some part of the estate, might have taken away all the estate; and that he who has inflicted some distempers upon the body, might have cast both body and soul into hellfire forever; and he that has shut him up in his chamber, may shut him out of heaven at pleasure. The thoughts and sense of these things makes many a sinner silent under the hand of God; but this is but a forced silence.[2] And such was the silence of Philip the Second, King of Spain, who, when his invincible Armada, that had been three years in fitting, was lost, gave command that all over Spain they should give thanks to God and the saints that it was no more grievous. As the stick forces the dog to be quiet and still, and the rod forces the child to be silent and mute, so the apprehensions of what God has done and of what God may do, forces many a soul to be silent, Jer. 3:10 and 1 Kin. 14:5-18. But this is

---

1. By force.—H&F.
2. *Oculos quos peccatum claudit, poena aperit,* Gregory, "The eye that sin shuts, affliction opens."

not the silence here meant: a forced silence is no silence in the eye of God.

There is a despairing silence.

A despairing soul is *Magormissabib*, a terror to himself; he has a hell in his heart and horror in his conscience. He looks upwards and there he beholds God frowning, and Christ bleeding; he looks inwards and there he finds conscience accusing and condemning of him;[1] he looks on the one side of him, and there he hears all his sins crying out, "We are thine, and we will follow thee; we will go to the grave with thee, we will go to judgment with thee, and from judgment we will go to hell with thee." He looks on the other side of him and there he sees infernal fiends in fearful shapes, amazing and terrifying to him, and waiting to receive his despairing soul as soon as it shall take its leave of his wretched body; he looks above him and there he sees the gates of heaven shut against him; he looks beneath him and there he sees hell gaping for him; and under these sad sights, he is full of secret conclusions against his own soul. There is mercy for others, says the despairing soul, but none for me; grace and favors for others, but none for me; pardon and peace for others, but none for me; blessedness and happiness for others, but none for me: there is no help, "there is no help, no," Jer. 2:25 and 18:12.[2] This seems to be the case of him who died with this desperate saying in his mouth, *Spes et fortuna valete*, "Farewell, life and hope together."[3] Now, under these dismal apprehensions and sad conclusions about its present and future condition, the despairing soul sits silent, being filled with amazement and

---

1. Ps. 94:7 & 28:1.
2. "They said, There is no hope: but we will walk after our own devices, and we will every one do the imagination of his evil heart." Jer. 18:12.
3. As that despairing Pope said, the cross could do him no good, because he had so often sold it.

astonishment: "I am so troubled that I cannot speak," Ps. 77:4. But this is not the silence here meant. But,

There is a prudent silence.

Lastly, there is a prudent silence, a holy, a gracious silence; a silence that springs from prudent principles, from holy principles, and from gracious causes and considerations; and this is the silence here meant. And this I shall fully discover in my answers to the second question, which is this:

II.
What does a prudent, a gracious, and a holy silence under affliction include?

These eight things:

A gracious silence includes an acknowledgment of God as the author of all the afflictions that come upon us.

It includes *a sight of God, and an acknowledgment of God as the author of all the afflictions that come upon us.* And this you have plain in the text: "I was dumb, I opened not my mouth; because thou didst it." The Psalmist looks through secondary causes to the first cause, and so sits mute before the Lord. There is no sickness so little, but God has a finger in it, though it is but the aching of the little finger. As the scribe is more properly said and seen to write than the pen; and he that makes and keeps the clock, is more properly said to make it go and strike, than the wheels and weights that hang upon it; and as every workman is more seen and properly said to effect his works, rather than the tools which he uses as his instruments. So the Lord, who is the chief agent and mover in all actions, and who has the greatest hand in all our afflictions, is more to be seen and owned than any inferior or subordinate causes whatsoever.[1] So Job, who beheld God in all: "The Lord gave, and the Lord hath taken away," Job 1:21. Had he not seen God in the affliction, he would have cried out: "Oh, these wretched Chaldeans, they have plundered and spoiled me; these wicked Sabeans, they have robbed and wronged me!" Job discerns God's commission in the Chaldeans' and the Sabeans' hands, and then lays his own hand upon his mouth. So Aaron, beholding the hand of God in the untimely death of his two sons, holds his peace, Lev. 10:3. The sight of God in this sad stroke is a bridle both to his mind and mouth, he neither mutters nor murmurs. So Joseph saw the hand of God in his brethren's selling of him into Egypt, Gen. 45:8, and that silences him.

Men that see not God in an affliction are easily cast into a feverish fit, they will quickly be in a flame and when their passions are up and their hearts on fire, they will begin to be saucy, and make no bones of telling God to his teeth, that they "do well to be angry," Jon. 4:8-9. Such as will not acknowledge God to be the author of all their afflictions, will be ready enough to fall in with that mad principle of the Manichees, who maintained the devil to be the author of all calamities; as if there could be any "evil of affliction in the city" and the Lord have no hand in it, Amo. 3:6. Such as can see the ordering hand of God in all their afflictions, will, with David, lay their hands upon their mouths, when the rod of God is upon their backs, 2 Sam. 16:11-12. If God's hand be not seen in the affliction, the heart will do nothing but fret and rage under affliction.

A gracious apprehension of the majesty, sovereignty, dignity, authority, & presence of God.

It includes and takes in *some holy, gracious apprehensions of*

---

1. In second causes, many times a Christian may see much envy, hatred, malice, pride, etc. But in the first cause, he can see nothing but grace and mercy, sweetness, and goodness.

the majesty, sovereignty, dignity, authority, and presence of that God under whose afflicting hand we are: "But the Lord is in his holy temple: let all the earth be silent," or, as the Hebrew reads, "Be silent, all the earth, before his face," Hab. 2:20. When God would have all the people of the earth to be hushed, quiet, and silent before him, he would have them to behold him in his temple, where he sits in state, in majesty, and glory: "Hold thy peace at the presence of the Lord God," Zep. 1. Chat not, murmur not, repine not, quarrel not; whist,[1] stand mute, be silent, lay your hand on your mouth, when his hand is upon your back, who is *totus oculus,* "all eye" to see, as well as all hand to punish. As the eyes of a well-drawn picture are fastened on you which way so ever you turn, so are the eyes of the Lord and therefore, you have cause to stand mute before him.

Thus Aaron had an eye to the sovereignty of God and that silences him. And Job had an eye upon the majesty of God, and that stills him. And Eli had an eye upon the authority and presence of God, and that quiets him.[2] A man never comes to humble himself, nor to be silent under the hand of God, until he comes to see the hand of God to be a mighty hand: "Humble yourselves therefore under the mighty hand of God," 1 Pet. 5:6. When men look upon the hand of God as a weak hand, a feeble hand, a low hand, a mean hand, their hearts rise against his hand. "Who is the Lord," says Pharaoh, "that I should obey his voice?" Exo. 5:2. And until Pharaoh came to see the hand of God as a mighty hand, and to feel it as a mighty hand, he would not let Israel go. When Tiribazus, a noble Persian,[3] was arrested, at first he drew out his sword and defended himself; but when they charged him in the King's name and informed him that they came from the King and were commanded to bring him to the King, he yielded willingly. So when afflictions

---

1. Be silent or still.—H&F.
2. Lev. 10:3; Job 37:13-14; & 1 Sam. 3:11-19.
3. The favorite of Artaxerxes II.—G.

arrest us, we shall murmur and grumble, and struggle, and strive even to the death, before we shall yield to that God that strikes, until we come to see his majesty and authority, until we come to see him as the King of Kings, and Lord of Lords. It is such a sight of God as this that makes the heart to stoop under his almighty hand, Phi. 2:9-12. The Thracians, being ignorant of the dignity and majesty of God, when it thundered and lightening was seen, used to express their madness and folly in shooting their arrows against heaven threatening-wise.[1] As a sight of his grace cheers the soul, so a sight of his greatness and glory silences the soul. But,

A gracious silence includes a holy quietness & calmness of mind & spirit under the afflicting hand of God.

A gracious and a prudent silence, takes in *a holy quietness and calmness of mind and spirit under the afflicting hand of God.* A gracious silence shuts out all inward heat, murmuring, fretting, quarreling, wrangling, and boiling of heart: "Truly my soul keepeth silence unto God, or is silent or still," Ps. 62:1, that is, "my soul is quiet and submissive to God;" all murmuring and repining, passions and turbulent affections, being allayed, tamed, and subdued. This also is clear in the text and in the former instances of Aaron, Eli, and Job. They saw that it was a Father that put those bitter cups in their hands, and love that laid those heavy crosses upon their shoulders, and grace that put those yokes about their necks; and this caused much quietness and calmness in their spirits. Marius bit in his pain when the chirurgeon[2] cut off his leg.[3] Some men, when God cuts off this mercy and that mercy from them, they bite in their pain, they hide and conceal their grief and trouble; but could you but look

---

1. Herodotus.
2. Surgeon.—H&F.
3. Query, M. Marius, the friend of Cicero?—G.

into their hearts, you will find all in an uproar, all out of order, all in a flame; and however they may seem to be cold without, yet they are all in a hot burning fever within. Such a feverish fit David was once in, Ps. 39:3. But certainly a holy silence allays all tumults in the mind, and makes a man "in patience to possess his own soul," Luk. 21:19, which, next to his possession of God, is the choicest and sweetest possession in all the world. The law of silence is both upon that man's heart and mind, as it is upon his tongue, who is truly and divinely silent under the rebuking hand of God.[1] As tongue-service separated from heart-service is no service in the account of God; so tongue-silence separated from heart-silence is no silence in the esteem of God. "This people draw near me with their mouth, and with their lips do honour me, but have removed their heart far from me, and their fear toward me is taught by the precept of men," Isa. 29:13 and Mat. 15:8-9. A man is then graciously silent when all is quiet within and without.[2]

Terpander,[3] a harpist and a poet, was one that, by the sweetness of his verse and music, could allay the tumultuous motions of men's minds, as David by his harp did for Saul. When God's people are under the rod, he makes by his Spirit and Word such sweet music in their souls, as allays all tumultuous motions, passions, and perturbations, Ps. 94:17-19 and Ps. 119:49-50, so that they sit, Noah-like, quiet and still, and in peace possess their souls.

---

1. "Be not rash with thy mouth, and let not thine heart be hasty to utter any thing before God: for God is in heaven, and thou upon earth: therefore let thy words be few," Ecc. 5:2.—H&F.

2. "Surely I have behaved and quieted myself, as a child that is weaned of his mother: my soul is even as a weaned child," Ps. 131:2.—H&F.

3. Of Lesbos, the father of Greek music.—G.

*A gracious silence includes a clearing & acquitting of
God of all blame in all afflictions he brings upon us.*

A prudent and a holy silence encompasses *a humble,
justifying, clearing and acquitting of God of all blame, rigor,
and injustice, in all the afflictions he brings upon us:* "That thou
mayest be justified when thou speakest, and be clear when
thou judgest," Ps. 51:4, that is, when you correct. God's
judging his people is God's correcting or chastening of his
people: "For if we would judge ourselves, we should not be
judged. But when we are judged, we are chastened of the
Lord, that we should not be condemned with the world,"
1 Cor. 11:31-32. David's great care, when he was under the
afflicting hand of God, was to clear the Lord of injustice.
"Ah! Lord," says he, "there is not the least show, spot, stain,
blemish, or mixture of injustice, in all the afflictions you
have brought upon me; I desire to take shame to myself and
to set to my seal that the Lord is righteous and that there
is no injustice, no cruelty, nor any extremity in all that the
Lord has brought upon me." And so, in that Ps. 119:75, 137,
he sweetly and readily subscribes unto the righteousness of
God in those sharp and smart afflictions that God exercised
him with. "I know, Oh Lord, that thy judgments are right,
and that thou in faithfulness hast afflicted me. Righteous
art thou, Oh Lord, and righteous are thy judgments."
God's judgments are always just; he never afflicts but in
faithfulness. His will is the rule of justice and therefore, a
gracious soul dares not cavil nor question his proceedings.
The afflicted soul knows that a righteous God can do
nothing but that which is righteous; it knows that God is
not to be controlled and therefore, the afflicted man puts
his mouth in the dust and keeps silence before him. Who
dare say, "Wherefore hast thou done so?"

The Turks, when they are cruelly lashed, are compelled to
return to the judge that commanded it, to kiss his hand,
give him thanks, and pay the officer that whipped them,

and so clear the judge and officer of injustice. Silently to kiss the rod, and the hand that whips with it, is the noblest way of clearing the Lord of all injustice.

The Babylonian captivity was the sorest, the heaviest affliction that ever God inflicted upon any people under heaven; witness that 1 Sam. 12 and Dan. 9:12, etc. Yet, under those smart afflictions, wisdom is justified of her children: "Thou art just in all that is brought upon us, for thou hast done right, but we have done wickedly," Neh. 9:33; "The Lord is righteous, for I have rebelled against him," Lam. 1:18. A holy silence shines in nothing more than in an humble justifying and clearing of God from all that which a corrupt heart is apt enough to charge God with in the day of affliction. God, in that he is good, can give nothing nor do nothing, but that which is good; "Others do frequently, he cannot possibly," says Luther, on Ps. 120.

A holy silence includes gracious, blessed, & soul quieting conclusions about the events of the afflictions that are upon us.

A holy silence takes in *gracious, blessed, soul quieting conclusions about the issues and events of those afflictions that are upon us,* Lam. 3:27-33. In this choice Scripture you may observe these soul stilling conclusions:

Afflictions shall work for their good.

1. First, that they shall work for their good. "It is good for a man that he bear the yoke in his youth," Lam. 27. A gracious soul secretly concludes, as stars shine brightest in the night, so God will make my soul shine and glisten like gold, whilst I am in this furnace, and when I come out of the furnace of affliction: "He knoweth the way that I take;

and when he hath tried me, I shall come forth as gold," Job 23:10.[1]

Surely, as the tasting of honey did open Jonathan's eyes, so this cross, this affliction, shall open my eyes; by this stroke I shall come to have a clearer sight of my sins and of myself, and a fuller sight of my God, Job 33:27-28, 40:4-5, and 42:1-7.

Surely this affliction shall issue in the purging away of my dross,[2] Isa. 1:25.

Surely as plowing of the ground kills the weeds and harrowing[3] breaks hard clods, so these afflictions shall kill my sins and soften my heart, Hos. 5:15. "Come, and let us return unto the Lord: for he hath torn, and he will heal us; he hath smitten, and he will bind us up," Hos. 6:1, etc.

Surely as the plaster draws out the core,[4] so the afflictions that are upon me shall draw out the core of pride, the core of self-love, the core of envy, the core of earthliness, the core of formality, the core of hypocrisy. "Before I was afflicted I went astray: but now have I kept thy Word. Thou art good, and doest good; teach me thy statutes, etc." Ps. 119:67-71.

Surely by these the Lord will crucify my heart more and more to the world, and the world to my heart, Gal. 6:14 and Ps. 131:1-3.

---

1. "I will bring the third part through the fire, and will refine them as silver is refined, and will try them as gold is tried: they shall call on my name, and I will hear them: I will say, It is my people: and they shall say, The Lord is my God," Zec. 13:9.—H&F.
2. Worthless matter that is separated from a precious metal when it is refined in a furnace.—H&F.
3. A harrow is a tool drawn over plowed ground to break the clods and level the ground and to cover the seed after it is sown.—H&F.
4. The inner portion of an ulcer or boil.—H&F.

Surely by these afflictions the Lord will hide pride from my soul, Job 33:14-21.

Surely these afflictions are but the Lord's pruning-knives, by which he will prune my heart, and make it more fertile and fruitful; they are but the Lord's portion, by which he will clear me and rid me of those spiritual diseases and maladies, which are most deadly and dangerous to my soul.

Affliction is such a medicine, as will carry away all ill humors better than all the *benedicta medicamenta*,[1] as physicians call them, Zec. 13:8-9.

Surely these shall increase my spiritual experiences, Rom. 5:3-5.

Surely by these I shall be made more to partake of God's holiness, Heb. 12:10. As black[2] soap makes white clothes, so does sharp afflictions make holy hearts.

Surely by these God will communicate more of himself to me, Ps. 119:24-25, 50, 61, 67-71.

Surely by these afflictions the Lord will draw out my heart more and more to seek him, Isa. 26:16-17. Tatianus told the heathen Greeks, that when they were sick, then they would send for their gods to be with them,[3] as Agamemnon did at the siege of Troy, send for his ten councilors. "In their afflictions they will seek me early," Hos. 5:15, or, as the Hebrew has it, "they will search for me early in the morning." In times of affliction, Christians will industriously, speedily, and early seek the Lord.

Surely by these trials and troubles the Lord will fix my soul

---

1. Beneficial or good medicine.—H&F.
2. Black soap is made using wood ash as the source of lye.—H&F.
3. In his *Pros Hellenas, Oratio adversus Graecos*.—G.

more than ever upon the great concernments of another world, Joh. 14:1-3, Rom. 8:17-18, and 2 Cor. 4:16-18.

Surely by these afflictions the Lord will work in me more tenderness and compassion towards those that are afflicted, Heb. 10:34 and 13:3. As that Tyrian Queen[1] said,

> Evils have taught me to bemoan,
> All that afflictions make to groan.

The Romans punished one that was seen looking out his window with a crown of roses on his head in a time of public calamity. Bishop Bonner was full of guts, but empty of bowels; I am afraid this age is full of such Bonners.

Surely these are but God's love-tokens: "As many as I love, I rebuke and chasten," Rev. 3:19. Seneca persuaded his friend Polybius to bear his affliction quietly, because he was the emperor's favorite, telling him that it was not lawful for him to complain while Caesar was his friend. So says the holy Christian, "Oh my soul! Be quiet, be still; all is in love, all is a fruit of divine favor. I see honey upon the top of every twig, I see the rod is but a rosemary branch, I have sugar with my gall, and wine with my wormwood; therefore be silent, oh my soul!" And this general conclusion, that all should be for good, had this blessed effect upon the church: "He sitteth alone, and keepeth silence, because he hath borne it upon him," Lam. 3:28.[2]

Affliction abases the loveliness of the world that might entice us; it abates the lustiness of the flesh within, which might otherwise ensnare us! And it abets[3] the spirit in

---

1. Dido in Virgil, *Nec ignara mali, miseris succurrere disco.*—Ed.

2. Some say, if a knife or needle be touched with a loadstone of an iron color, it will cut or enter into a man's body without any sense of pain at all; so will afflictions when touched with the loadstone of divine love.

3. Previous editions: 'abate.' We have changed this is our text, as the context proves an error in the edition: the meaning is 'abet,' to assist and strengthen, rather than 'abate.'—H&F.

its quarrel against the flesh and the world; by all which it proves a mighty advantage to us.

Affliction will keep the Christian humble & low.

2. They shall keep them humble and low: "He putteth his mouth in the dust; if so be there may be hope. He giveth his cheek to him that smiteth him: he is filled full with reproach. For the Lord will not cast off for ever," Lam. 3:29-31. Some say that these words are an allusion to the manner of those that, having been conquered and subdued, lay their necks down at the conqueror's feet to be trampled upon, and so lick up the dust that is under the conqueror's feet. Others of the learned looked upon the words as an allusion to poor petitioners, who cast themselves down at princes' feet that they may draw forth their pity and compassion towards them. As I have read of Aristippus, who fell on the ground before Dionysius and kissed his feet when he presented a petition to him and, being asked the reason, answered, *Aures habet in pedibus,* "He has his ears in his feet." Take it whatever way you will, it holds forth this to us, that holy hearts will be humble under the afflicting hand of God. When God's rod is upon their backs, their mouths will be in the dust. A good heart will lie lowest when the hand of God is lifted highest, Job 42:1-7 and Act. 9:1-9.

The Lord will not cast off forever.

3. The third soul quieting conclusion you have in Lamentations 3:31, "For the Lord will not cast off forever." The rod shall not always lie upon the back of the righteous. "At even-tide, lo there is trouble, but before morning it is gone," Isa. 17:12-14. As Athanasius said to his friends when they came to bewail his misery and banishment, *Nubecula est, citò transibit,* "It is but a little cloud," said he, "and it will quickly be gone." There are none of God's afflicted ones that have not their *lucida intervalla,* "their intermissions,

respites, breathers-whiles."[1] Yea, so small a while does the hand of the Lord rest upon his people that Luther cannot get diminutives enough to extenuate it, for he calls it a very little little cross that we bear: "Come, my people, enter thou into thy chambers, and shut thy doors about thee: hide thyself as it were for a little moment (or for a little space, a little while), until the indignation be overpast," Isa. 26:20. The indignation does not *transire*, but *pertransire*, that is, it does not pass, but over-pass.[2] The sharpness, shortness, and suddenness of the saints' afflictions is set forth as being like the travail of a woman, Joh. 16:21, which is sharp, short, and sudden.[3]

Though the Lord cause grief, yet he will have
compassion, according to the multitude of his mercies.

4. The fourth soul silencing conclusion you have in Lamentations 3:32, "But though he cause grief, yet will he have compassion, according to the multitude of his mercies." In wrath God "remembers mercy," Hab. 3:2. "For his anger endureth but a moment; in his favour is life: weeping may endure for a night, but joy cometh in the morning," Ps. 30:5. Their mourning shall last but until morning. God will turn their winter's night into a summer's day, their sighing into singing, their grief into gladness, their mourning into music, their bitter into sweet, their wilderness into a paradise. The life of a Christian is filled up with interchanges of sickness and health, weakness and strength, want and wealth, disgrace and honor, crosses and comforts, miseries and mercies, joys and sorrows, mirth and mourning. All honey would harm us, all wormwood would undo us, but a composition of both is the best way in the world to keep our souls in a healthy constitution. It is best

---

1. Breathing-space or 'breathers.'—H&F.
2. Or pass over (us).—H&F.
3. A little storm, as he said of Julian's persecution, and an eternal calm follows.

and most for the health of the soul that the south wind of mercy and the north wind of adversity do both blow upon it; and though every wind that blows shall blow good to the saints, yet certainly their sins die most and their graces thrive best when they are under the drying, nipping north wind of calamity, as well as under the warm, cherishing south wind of mercy and prosperity.

The Lord does not willingly afflict nor
grieve the children of men.

5. The fifth soul quieting conclusion you have in Lamentations 3:33, "For he doth not afflict willingly" (or, as the Hebrew has it, "from his heart"), nor grieve the children of men." The church concludes that God's heart was not in their afflictions, though his hand was. He takes no delight to afflict his children, it goes against the hair[1] and the heart. It is a grief to him to be grievous to them, a pain to him to be punishing them, a bereavement to him to strike them; he has no will, no motion, no inclination, no disposition to the work of afflicting his people. Therefore, he calls it his "work, his strange work," Isa. 28:21. Mercy and punishment, they flow from God, as the honey and the sting from the bee. The bee makes honey of its own nature, but it does not sting except when it is provoked. God takes delight in showing mercy, Mic. 7:18,[2] and he takes no pleasure in giving his people up to adversity, Hos. 11:8. Mercy and kindness flow from him freely and naturally. He is never severe, never harsh, he never stings, he never terrifies us, but when he is sadly provoked by us. God's hand sometimes may lie very hard upon his people, when his heart, his bowels, at those very times may be yearning towards his people, Jer.

---

1. Against the hair falling in a certain direction: the grain.—H&F.
2. "Who is a God like unto thee, that pardoneth iniquity, and passeth by the transgression of the remnant of his heritage? He retaineth not his anger for ever, because he delighteth in mercy," Mic. 7:18.—H&F.

31:18-20.[1] No man can tell how the heart of God stands by his hand: his hand of mercy may be open to those against whom his heart is set, as you see in the poor rich fool and Dives[2] in the Gospel, and his hand of severity may lie hard upon those on whom he has set his heart, as you may see in Job and Lazarus. And thus you see those gracious, blessed, soul quieting conclusions about the issues and events of afflictions that a holy and a prudent silence includes.

A holy silence includes the charge that conscience lays upon the soul to be quiet & still.

A holy and prudent silence includes and takes in *a strict charge, a solemn command, that conscience lays upon the soul to be quiet and still.*[3] "Rest in the Lord" (or as the Hebrew has it, "be silent to the Lord"), "and wait patiently for him," Ps. 37:7. I charge thee, oh my soul, not to mutter, nor to murmur; I command thee, oh my soul, to be dumb and silent under the afflicting hand of God. As Christ laid a charge, a command, upon the boisterous winds and the roaring raging seas—Mat. 8:26, "Be still; and there was a great calm"—so conscience lays a charge upon the soul to be quiet and still: "Wait on the Lord; be of good courage, and he shall strengthen thy heart: wait, I say, on the Lord," Ps. 27:14. Peace, oh my soul! Be still, leave off your muttering, leave off your murmuring, leave off your

---

1. "I have surely heard Ephraim bemoaning himself thus; Thou hast chastised me, and I was chastised, as a bullock unaccustomed to the yoke: turn thou me, and I shall be turned; for thou art the Lord my God. Surely after that I was turned, I repented; and after that I was instructed, I smote upon my thigh: I was ashamed, yea, even confounded, because I did bear the reproach of my youth. Is Ephraim my dear son? Is he a pleasant child? For since I spake against him, I do earnestly remember him still: therefore my bowels are troubled for him; I will surely have mercy upon him, saith the Lord," Jer. 31:18-20.—H&F.

2. This is a reference to the rich man, which tradition names Dives, in the story of Lazarus and the rich man, Luk. 16:19-31.—H&F.

3. The heathen could say, *A recta conscientia ne latum quidem unguem discedendum,* "Man may not depart a hair's breadth all his life long from the dictates of a good conscience." [Seneca in Epist. and *De Vita Beata.*—G.]

complaining, leave off your chafing and vexing, and lay your hand upon your mouth and be silent. Conscience allays and stills all the tumults and uproars that are in the soul, by such like reasoning as the clerk of Ephesus stilled that uproar: "For we are in danger to be called in question for this day's uproar, there being no cause whereby we may give an account of this concourse," Act. 19:40. Oh my soul! Be quiet, be silent, or else you will one day be called in question for all those inward mutterings, uproars, and passions that are in you, seeing no sufficient cause can be produced why you should murmur, quarrel, or wrangle under the righteous hand of God.

A holy silence includes resigning ourselves to God under his afflicting hand.

A holy and prudent silence includes *a surrendering, a, resigning up of ourselves to God, while we are under his afflicting hand.* The silent soul gives himself up to God.[1] The secret language of the soul is this: "Lord, here am I; do with me what you please, write upon me as you please: I give up myself to be at your disposal."

There was a good woman, who, when she was sick, being asked whether she were willing to live or die, answered, "Whichever God pleases." "But," said one that stood by, "If God should refer it to you, which would you choose?" "Truly," she said, "if God should refer it to me, I would even refer it to him again." This was a soul worth gold. "Well!" says a gracious soul, "the ambitious man gives himself up to his honor, but I give up myself unto you; the voluptuous man gives himself up to his pleasures, but I give up myself to you; the covetous man gives himself up to his bags,[2] but I give up myself to you; the wanton gives himself up to his

---

1. Ps. 27:8; Jam. 4:7; 1 Sam. 3:18; & Ps. 119:24-25, 50, 61, 67-71.
2. As in money bags.—H&F.

minion,[1] but I give up myself to you; the drunkard gives himself up to his cup, but I give up myself to you; the papist gives up himself to his idols, but I give myself to you; the Turk gives up himself to his Mahomet, but I give up myself to you; the heretic gives up himself to his heretical opinions, but I give up myself to you. Lord! Lay what burden you will upon me, only let your everlasting arms be under me."[2] Strike, Lord, strike and spare not, for I am lain down in your will, I have learned to say amen to your amen; you have a greater interest in me than I have in myself, and therefore I give up myself unto you and am willing to be at your disposal, and am ready to receive whatever impression you shall stamp upon me. Oh blessed Lord! Have you not again and again said unto me, as once the King of Israel said to the King of Syria, "I am thine, and all that I have," 1 Kin. 20:4. "I am thine," says the Lord, "Oh soul! To save you; my mercy is yours to pardon you; my blood is yours to cleanse you; my merits are yours to justify you; my righteousness is yours to clothe you; my Spirit is yours to lead you; my grace is yours to enrich you; and my glory is yours to reward you." "Therefore," says a gracious soul, "I cannot but resign myself unto you. Lord! Here I am, do with me as seems good in your own eyes. I know that the best way to have my own will is to resign up myself to your will and to say amen to your amen."

I have read of a gentleman, who, meeting with a shepherd on a misty morning, asked him what weather it would be? It will be, said the shepherd, what weather pleases me. And upon being courteously asked to express his meaning said, "Sir, it shall be what weather pleases God, and what weather pleases God pleases me." When a Christian's will is molded into the will of God, he is sure to have his will. But,

---

1. His darlings or whomever gains his favor through flattery.—H&F.
2. Martin Luther.

A holy silence includes a patient waiting upon the Lord for deliverance.

Lastly, a holy and prudent silence includes a *patient waiting upon the Lord under our afflictions until deliverance comes:* "My soul, wait thou only upon God, for my expectation is from him," Ps. 62:5, Ps. 40:1-3, and, "It is good that a man should both hope, and quietly (or as the Hebrew has it, silently) wait for the salvation of the Lord," Lam. 3:26. The husbandman patiently waits for the precious fruits of the earth, the mariner patiently waits for wind and tide, and so does the watchman for the dawning of the day; and so does the silent soul in the night of adversity, patiently wait for the dawning of the day of mercy, Jam. 5:7-8.[1] The mercies of God are not styled *the swift*, but *the sure* mercies of David, and therefore a gracious soul waits patiently for them. And thus you see what a gracious, a prudent silence includes.

III.
What does a prudent, a gracious, and a holy silence under affliction not exclude?

Now there are several things that a holy patience does not exclude:

A holy silence under affliction does not exclude a sense & feeling of our afflictions.

A holy and prudent silence under affliction does not exclude and shut out *a sense and feeling of our afflictions.* Although he "was dumb, and laid his hand upon his mouth," yet he was very sensible of his affliction, Ps. 39:9. "Remove thy stroke

---

1. "Be patient therefore, brethren, unto the coming of the Lord. Behold, the husbandman waiteth for the precious fruit of the earth, and hath long patience for it, until he receive the early and latter rain. Be ye also patient; stablish your hearts: for the coming of the Lord draweth nigh," Jam. 5:7-8.—H&F.

away from me; I am consumed by the blow of thine hand. When thou with rebukes dost correct man for iniquity, thou makest his beauty to consume away like a moth: surely every man is vanity," Ps. 39:10-11. He is sensible of his pain as well as his sin, and having prayed off[1] his sin in the former verses, he labors here to pray off his pain. Diseases, aches, sicknesses, and pains are all the daughters of sin and he that is not sensible of them as the fruits and products of sin, does but add to his sin and provoke the Lord to add to his sufferings, Isa. 26:9-11. No man shall ever be charged by God for feeling his burden, if he neither fret nor faint under it. Grace does not destroy nature, but rather perfects it. Grace is of a noble offspring; it neither turns men into stocks nor stoics. The more grace, the more sensible of the tokens, frowns, blows, and lashes of a displeased Father. Though Calvin, under his greatest pains, was never heard to mutter nor murmur, yet he was heard often to say, "How long, Lord, how long?" A religious commander being shot in battle, when the wound was searched and the bullet cut out, to some standing by and pitying his pain, he replied, "Though I groan, yet I bless God, I do not grumble."[2] God allows his people to groan, though not to grumble. It is a God-provoking sin to be stupid and senseless under the afflicting hand of God. God will heat that man's furnace of affliction sevenfold hotter, who is in the furnace that feels it not: "Who among you will give ear to this? Who will hearken and hear for the time to come? Who gave Jacob for a spoil, and Israel to the robbers? Did not the Lord, he against whom we have sinned? For they would not walk in his ways, neither were they obedient unto his law. Therefore he hath poured upon him the fury of his anger, and the strength of battle: and he hath set him on fire round about, yet he knew not; and it burned him, yet he laid it not to

---

1. 'Prayed off,' a prayer for relief, as the Psalmist says, "Cast thy burden upon the Lord, and he shall sustain thee: he shall never suffer the righteous to be moved," Ps. 55:22.—H&F.
2. Sir Philip Sydney perhaps.—G.

heart," Isa. 42:23-25. Stupidity lays a man open to the greatest fury and severity.

The physician, when he finds that the medicine that he has given his patient will not work, he seconds it with one more violent; and if that will not work, he gives another yet more violent. If a gentle plaster will not serve, then the chirurgeon[1] applies that which is more corrosive; and if that will not do, then he makes use of his cauterizing knife. So when the Lord afflicts and men feel it not; when he strikes and they grieve not; when he wounds them and they awake not, then the furnace is made hotter than ever; then his fury burns, then he lays irons upon irons, bolt upon bolt, and chain upon chain, until he has made their lives a hell. Afflictions are the saints' diet-drink,[2] and where do you read in all the Scripture that any of the saints ever drank of this diet-drink and were not sensible of it.

A holy silence does not shut out prayer for deliverance.

A holy and prudent silence does not shut out *prayer for deliverance out of our afflictions.* Though the Psalmist lays his hand upon his mouth in the text, yet he prays for deliverance: "Remove thy stroke away from me," ver. 10, and ver. 11-12, "Hear my prayer, oh Lord! And give ear unto my cry; hold not thy peace at my tears; for I am a stranger with thee, and a sojourner, as all my fathers were. Oh spare me, that I may recover strength, before I go hence and be no more." "Is any among you afflicted? Let him pray," Jam. 5:13. "Call upon me in the day of trouble: I will deliver thee, and thou shalt glorify me," Ps. 1:15. Times of affliction, by God's own injunction, are special times of supplication.[3]

---

1. Surgeon.—H&F.
2. A drink prepared with medicinal ingredients.—H&F.
3. It is an old saying, *Qui nescit orare, discat navigare,* "He that would learn to pray, let him go to sea." ["They that go down to the sea in ships, that do business in great waters; These see the works of the Lord, and his wonders

David's heart was more often out of tune than his harp, but then he prays and presently cries, "Return to thy rest, oh my soul," Ps. 116:7. Jonah prays in the whale's belly and Daniel prays when among the lions, and Job prays when he sat among ashes, and Jeremiah prays when in the dungeon, etc. Yea, the heathen mariners, as stout as they were, when in a storm, they cry, every man to his god, Jonah 1:5-6. To call upon God, especially in times of distress and trouble, is a lesson that the very light and law of nature teaches. The Persian messenger, though a heathen, as Aeschylus observes, speaks thus: "When the Grecian forces hotly pursued our host, and we must needs venture over the great water Strymon, frozen then, but beginning to thaw, when a hundred to one we had all died for it, with my eyes I saw, says he, many of those gallants whom I had heard before so boldly maintain there was no God, every one upon his knees and devoutly praying that the ice might hold until they got over."[1] And shall blind nature do more than grace? If the time of affliction be not a time of supplication, I know not what is.

As there are two kinds of antidotes against poison, viz. hot and cold, so there are two kinds of antidotes against all the troubles and afflictions of this life, viz. prayer and patience: the one hot, the other cold; the one quenching, the other quickening. Chrysostom understood this well enough when he cried out: "Oh! It is more bitter than death to be spoiled of prayer," and thereupon he observes that Daniel chose rather to run the hazard of his life than to lose his prayer.

---

in the deep. For he commandeth, and raiseth the stormy wind, which lifteth up the waves thereof. They mount up to the heaven, they go down again to the depths: their soul is melted because of trouble. They reel to and fro, and stagger like a drunken man, and are at their wits' end. Then they cry unto the Lord in their trouble, and he bringeth them out of their distresses. He maketh the storm a calm, so that the waves thereof are still. Then are they glad because they be quiet; so he bringeth them unto their desired haven. Oh that men would praise the Lord for his goodness, and for his wonderful works to the children of men!" Ps. 107:23-31.—H&F.]

1. Cf. Aeschylus, *Suppl.* 258; *Agam.* 192.—G.

Well, this is the second thing. A holy silence does not exclude prayer. But,

A holy silence does not exclude our being afflicted with our sins as the cause of our suffering.

A holy and prudent silence does not exclude *men's being affected and afflicted with their sins as the meritorious cause of all their sorrows and sufferings.*[1] "Wherefore doth a living man complain, a man for the punishment of his sin? Let us search and try our ways, and turn again to the Lord," Lam. 3:39-40; "Behold, I am vile, what shall I answer thee? I will lay my hand upon my mouth. Once have I spoken, but I will not answer; yea, twice, but I proceed no further," Job 40:4-5; "I will bear the indignation of the Lord, because I have sinned," Mic. 7:9. In all our sorrows we should read our sins, and when God's hand is upon our backs, our hands should be upon our sins.

It was a good saying of one, "I hide not my sins, but I show them; I wipe them not away, but I sprinkle them; I do not excuse them, but accuse them. The beginning of my salvation is the knowledge of my transgression."[2] When some told Prince Henry, that *deliciae generis humani,* that "darling of mankind,"[3] that the sins of the people brought that affliction on him, "Oh no!" said he, "I have sins enough of my own to cause that." "I have sinned, saith David, but what have these poor sheep done?" 2 Sam. 24:17. When a Christian is under the afflicting hand of God, he may well say, "I may thank this proud heart of mine, this worldly heart, this froward heart, this formal heart, this dull heart,

---

1. Read Ezr. 9, Neh. 9, Dan. 9:5-15, with Job 7. "I have sinned; what shall I do unto thee, Oh thou preserver of men? Why hast thou set me as a mark against thee, so that I am a burden to myself?" Job 7:20.

2. [Joh. Lud.] Vivaldus.

3. Son of James I, whose death was married to immortal verse by George Chapman.—G.

this backsliding heart, this self-seeking heart of mine; for that this cup is so bitter, this pain so grievous, this loss so great, this disease so desperate, this wound so incurable; it is my own self, my own sin, that has caused these floods of sorrows to break in upon me."[1] But,

A holy silence does not exclude teaching & instructing others while we are afflicted.

A holy and prudent silence does not exclude *the teaching and instructing of others when we are afflicted.* The words of the afflicted stick close; many times they work strongly, powerfully, strangely, savingly, upon the souls and consciences of others. Many of Paul's epistles were written to the churches when he was in bonds, viz., Galatians, Ephesians, Philippians, Colossians, Philemon; he begot Onesimus in his bonds, Phi. 10. And many of the brethren in the Lord waxed bold and confident by his bonds, and were confirmed, and made partakers of grace by his ministry, when he was in bonds, Phi. 1:7, 13-14. As the words of dying persons do many times stick and work gloriously, so many times do the words of afflicted persons work very nobly and efficaciously. I have read of one Adrianus, who, seeing the martyrs suffer such grievous things for the cause of Christ, asked what that was which enabled them to suffer such things, and one of them named the verse from 1 Cor. 2:9, "Eye hath not seen, nor ear heard, neither have entered into the heart of man, the things which God hath prepared for them that love him." This word was "like apples of gold in pictures of silver," Pro. 25:11, for it made him not only a convert, but a martyr too. And this was the means of Justin Martyr's conversion, as he himself confesses. Doubtless, many have been made happy by the words of the afflicted. The tongue of the afflicted has

---

1. "Be afflicted, and mourn, and weep: let your laughter be turned to mourning, and your joy to heaviness. Humble yourselves in the sight of the Lord, and he shall lift you up," Jam. 4:9-10.—H&F.

been to many as choice silver. The words of the afflicted many times are both pleasing and profitable; they please the ear and they win the heart; they slide insensibly into the hearers' souls and work efficaciously upon the hearers' hearts: "The words of a wise man's mouth are gracious," Ecc. 10:12, or 'grace,' as the Hebrew has it; and so Jerome reads it, *Verba oris sapientis gratia,* "The words of the mouth of a wise man are grace." They minister grace to others and they win grace and favor from others. Gracious lips make gracious hearts; gracious words are a grace, an ornament to the speaker, and they are a comfort, a delight, and an advantage to the hearer.

Now, the words of a wise man's mouth are never more gracious than when he is most afflicted and distressed. Now, you shall find most worth and weight in his words; now his lips, like the spouse's, are like a thread of scarlet; they are red with talking much of a crucified Christ, and they are thin like a thread, not swelled with vain and unprofitable discourses. Now his "mouth speaks of wisdom, and his tongue speaks judgment, for the law of the Lord is in his heart," Ps. 37:30; now his lips "drop as honeycombs," Son. 4:11; now his tongue is a tree of life,[1] whose leaves are medicinal, Pro. 12:18. As the silver trumpets sounded most joy to the Jews in the day of their gladness, so the mouth of a wise man, like a silver trumpet, sounds most joy and advantage to others in the days of his sadness, Num. 10:10.

The heathen man could say, *Quando sapiens loquitur, aulae animi aperit,* "When a wise man speaks, he opens the rich treasure and wardrobe of his mind"; so may I say, when an afflicted saint speaks, oh the pearls, the treasures that he scatters! But,

---

1. Pro. 15:4.—H&F.

A holy silence does not exclude mourning or weeping under affliction.

A holy and prudent silence does not exclude *moderate mourning or weeping under the afflicting hand of God.* "And Hezekiah wept sore," Isa. 38:3, or, as the Hebrew has it, "wept with great weeping."[1] But was not the Lord displeased with him for his great weeping? No, ver. 5, "I have heard thy prayers, I have seen thy tears: behold, I will add unto thy days fifteen years." God had as well a bottle for his tears, as a bag for his sins, Ps. 56:8. There is no water so sweet as the saints' tears, when they do not overflow the banks of moderation. Tears are not mute, they have a voice and their oratory is of great prevalency[2] with the almighty God. And therefore the weeping prophet called out for tears: "Their heart crieth unto the Lord, oh wall of the daughter of Zion, let tears run down like a river day and night: give thyself no rest; let not the apple of thine eye cease," Lam. 2:18, or, as the Hebrew has it, "let not the daughters of your eye be silent."[3] That which we call the ball or apple of the eye, the Hebrews call the daughter of the eye, because it is as dear and tender to a man as an only daughter; and because therein appears the likeness of a little daughter. Upon which words, said Bellarmine, *Clames assidue ad Deum, non lingua, sed oculis, non verbis sed lachrymis, ista enim est oratio, quae pacare solet:* cry aloud to God, not with your tongue, but with your eyes; not with your words, but with your tears; for that is the prayer that makes the most forcible entry into the ears of the great God of heaven. When God strikes, he looks that we should tremble; when his hand is lifted high, he looks that our hearts should stoop low; when he has the rod in his hand, he looks that we should have tears in our eyes, as you

---

1. Ps. 6:6, 39:1; Jer. 9:1-2; Lam. 1 & 2:11-18.
2. Influence and efficaciousness.—H&F.
3. And the Greeks call the apple of the eye, the damsel of the eye, the girl of the eye; and the Latins call it the babe of the eye.

may see by comparing these Scriptures together, Ps. 55:2, 38:6 and Job 30:26-32. Good men weep easily, says the Greek poet,[1] and the better any is the more he is inclined to weeping, especially under affliction: as you may see in David, whose tears, instead of gems, were the common ornaments of his bed, Jonathan, Job, Ezra, Daniel, etc. How, says one, shall God wipe away my tears in heaven, if I shed none on earth? And how shall I reap in joy, if I sow not in tears? I was born with tears, and I shall die with tears; and why then should I live without them in this valley of tears?

There is a time to weep, as well as there is a time to laugh; and a time to mourn, as well as a time to dance, Ecc. 3:4. The mourning garment among the Jews was the black garment, and the black garment was the mourning garment: "Why go ye mourning?" Ps. 43:2. The Hebrew word *Kedar* signifies black. Why do you go in black? Sometimes Christians must put off their gay ornaments, and put on their black, their mourning garments, Exo. 33:3-6. But,

A gracious & a prudent silence does not exclude groaning under our afflictions.

A gracious and prudent silence does not exclude *sighing, groaning, or roaring under afflictions*.[2] A man may sigh and groan, and roar under the hand of God, and yet be silent. It is not sighing, but muttering; it is not groaning, but grumbling; it is not roaring, but murmuring, that is opposite to a holy silence: "And the children of Israel sighed by reason of the bondage," Exo. 2:23. "For my sighing cometh before I eat," Job 3:24, or, as the Hebrew has it, "before my meat." His sighing, like bad weather, came unsent for

---

1. Cf. Seneca de Consolatione ad Polybium, iv. § 2, and Juvenal, xv. 133.—G.
2. You may see much of this by comparing the following Scriptures: Ps. 31:10; Jer. 45:3; Exo. 2:24; Job 23:2; & Ps. 6:6.

and unsought: so, "Lord, all my desire is before thee; and my groaning is not hid from thee," Ps. 38:9. "By reason of the voice of my groaning, my bones cleave to my skin," Ps. 102:5. "And my roarings are poured out like the waters," Job 3:24. "I am feeble and sore broken; I have roared by reason of the disquietness of my heart," Ps. 38:8. "My God! My God! Why hast thou forsaken me? Why art thou so far from helping me, from the words of my roaring?" Ps. 22:1. "When I kept silence, my bones waxed old, through my roarings all the day long," Ps. 32:3. He roars, but does not rage; he roars, but does not repine. When a man is in extremity, nature prompts him to roar and the law of grace is not against it; and though sighing, roaring, groaning, cannot deliver a man out of his misery, yet they do give some ease to a man under his misery. When Solon wept for his son's death, one said to him, "Weeping will not help." And he answered, "Alas! Therefore do I weep, because weeping will not help." So a Christian many times sighs, because sighing will not help; and he groans, because groaning will not help; and he roars, because roaring will not help. Sometimes the sorrows of the saints are so great, that all tears are dried up, and they can get no ease by weeping; and therefore for a little ease they fall to sighing and groaning; and this may be done, and yet the heart may be quiet and silent before the Lord. Peter wept and sobbed, and yet was silent. Sometimes the sighs and groans of a saint do in some sort tell that which his tongue can in no sort utter.[1] But,

A holy silence does not exclude the use of just means of deliverance out of our afflictions.

A holy and prudent silence does not exclude nor shut out *the use of any just or lawful means whereby persons may be*

---

1. "Likewise the Spirit also helpeth our infirmities: for we know not what we should pray for as we ought: but the Spirit itself maketh intercession for us with groanings which cannot be uttered," Rom. 8:26.—H&F.

delivered out of their afflictions.[1] God would not have his people so in love with their afflictions, as not to use such righteous means as may deliver them out of their afflictions: "But when they persecute you in this city, flee you into another," Mat. 10:23. When Peter was in prison, the saints thronged together to pray, Act. 12:5, as the original has it, ver. 12, and they were so instant and earnest with God in prayer, they did so beseech and besiege the Lord, they did so beg and bounce at heaven's gate, ver. 5, that God could have no rest until, by many miracles of power and mercy, he had returned Peter as a bosom-favor to them: "And after that many days were fulfilled, the Jews took counsel to kill him: but their laying await was known of Saul: and they watched the gates day and night to kill him. Then the disciples took him by night, and let him down by the wall in a basket," Act. 9:23-25. The blood of the saints is precious in God's eye, and it should not be vile in their own eyes. When providence opens a door of escape there is no reason why the saints should set themselves as marks and butts[2] for their enemies to shoot at.[3] The Apostles desire the brethren "to pray for them that they may be delivered from unreasonable *(atoroi,* absurd) and wicked (*poneroi,* villainous) men; for all men have not faith," 2 Th. 3:1-2. It is a mercy worth seeking, to be delivered out of the hands of absurd, villainous, and troublesome men.

Afflictions are evil in themselves and we may desire and endeavor to be delivered from them, Jam. 5:14-15 and Isa. 38:18-21; both inward and outward means are to be used for our own preservation. Had not Noah built an ark, he had been swept away with the flood, though he had been with Nimrod and his crew on the tower of Babel, which

---

1.   2 Kin. 5:14-15; Mat. 4:6-7; Act. 25:7-11; 1 Cor. 7:21; & Luk. 13:11-17; Num. 35:22-25; & Act. 23:12-24.

2.   A mark to be shot at, an object of attack or ridicule.—H&F.

3.   "Give not that which is holy unto the dogs, neither cast ye your pearls before swine, lest they trample them under their feet, and turn again and rend you," Mat. 7:6.—H&F.

was raised to the height of one thousand five hundred forty-six paces, as Heylin reports.[1] Though we may not trust in means, yet we may and ought to use the means and in the use of them, eye[2] that God that can only bless them, and you do your work. As the pilot that guides the ship has his hand upon the rudder and his eye on the star that directs him at the same time, so when your hand is upon the means, let your eye be upon your God and deliverance will come. We may neglect God as well by neglecting of means as by trusting in the means: it is best to use them and in the use of them, to live above them. Augustine tells of a man that, being fallen into a pit, one passing by begins to question him as to what he made there and how he came to be there. "Oh!" said the poor man, "ask me not how I came to be here, but help me and tell me how I may get out." The application is easy. But, lastly,

A holy silence does not exclude a just & sober complaining against the authors of our affliction.

A holy and a prudent silence does not exclude *a just and sober complaining against the authors, contrivers, abettors, or instruments of our afflictions:* "Alexander the coppersmith did me much evil; the Lord reward him according to his works," 2 Tim. 4:14. This Alexander is conceived by some to be that Alexander that is mentioned in Act. 19:33, who stood so close to Paul at Ephesus that he ran the hazard of losing his life by appearing on his side.[3] Yet if glorious professors come to be furious persecutors, Christians may complain: "Of the Jews five times received I forty stripes, save one," 2 Cor. 11:24. They inflict, says Maimonides, no more than

---

1. Heylin Cosm. l. iii.
2. Look to.—H&F.
3. Calvin *in loc.* assumes this, designating him as one *martyris propinquus;* and Trapp adds, Brooks-like, "A glorious professor may become a furious persecutor."—G. [This seems to the current editor to be a far fetched assumption, nevertheless, the illustration is very useful, for example, Gal. 2:4-5.—H&F.]

forty stripes, though he be as strong as Samson, but if he be weak, they abate of that number. They scourged Paul with the greatest severity, in making him suffer so often the utmost extremity of the Jewish law, whereas they that were weak had their punishment mitigated: "Thrice was I beaten with rods," ver. 25, that is, by the Romans, whose custom it was to beat the guilty with rods.

If Pharaoh makes Israel groan, Israel may make his complaint against Pharaoh to the Keeper of Israel, Exo. 2:23-25. If the proud and blasphemous king of Assyria shall come with his mighty army to destroy the people of the Lord, Hezekiah may spread his letter of blasphemy before the Lord, Isa. 37:14-21.

It was the saying of Socrates, that every man in this life had need of a faithful friend and a bitter enemy; the one to advise him and the other to make him look about him. And this Hezekiah found by experience.

Though Joseph's bow abode in strength and the arm of his hands were made strong by the hands of the mighty God of Jacob, yet Joseph may say that the archers or the arrow-masters, as the Hebrew has it, have sorely grieved him and shot at him, and hated him, Gen. 49:23-24. And so David sadly complained of Doeg, Ps. 52. Yea, Christ himself, who was the most perfect pattern for dumbness and silence under sorest trials, complains against Judas, Pilate, and the rest of his persecutors, "They gave me also gall for my meat; and in my thirst they gave me vinegar to drink. Let their table become a snare before them, etc." Ps. 69:21-30. Yea, though God will make his people's enemies to be the workmen that shall fit them and square them for his building, to be goldsmiths to add pearls to their crown, to be rods to beat off their dust, scullions to scour off their rust, fire to purge away their dross, and water to cleanse away their filthiness, fleshliness, and earthliness, yet may they point at them and pour out their complaints to God against them, Ps. 17. This truth I might make good by more than a hundred texts of Scripture, but it is time to come to the reasons of the point.

IV.
Why must Christians be mute and silent under the greatest afflictions, the saddest providences, and sharpest trials that they meet with in this world?

I answer:

Reason 1.
Christians must be silent under afflictions that they may better hear & understand the voice of the rod.

That they may the better hear and understand the voice of the rod. As the word has a voice, the Spirit a voice, and conscience a voice, so the rod has a voice.[1] Afflictions are the rod of God's anger, the rod of his displeasure, and his rod of revenge. He gives a commission to his rod, to awaken his people, to reform his people, or else to revenge the quarrel of his covenant upon them, if they will not bear the rod and kiss the rod, and sit mute and silent under the rod: "The Lord's voice crieth unto the city, and the man of wisdom shall see thy name: hear ye the rod, and who hath appointed it," Mic. 6:9. God's rods are not mute, they are vocal, they are speaking as well as smiting; every twig[2] has a voice. Ah, soul, says one twig, you say it smarts, well, tell me, is it good to provoke a jealous God? "Thy way and thy doings have procured these things unto thee," Jer. 4:18. Ah, soul, says another twig, you say it is bitter, it reaches to your heart, but have your own doings not procured these things? "For whom

---

1. *Schola crucis est schola lucis.* ["The school of the cross is the school of light."—H&F.]
2. A branch or rod is meant: a rod of discipline.—H&F.

the Lord loveth he chasteneth, and scourgeth every son whom he receiveth," Heb. 12:6. Ah, soul, says another twig, where is the profit, the pleasure, the sweetness that you have found in wandering from God? "What fruit had ye then in those things whereof ye are now ashamed? For the end of those things is death," Rom. 6:21. Ah, soul, says another twig, was it not best with you, when you were high in your communion with God and when you were humble and close[1] in your walking with God? "He hath shewed thee, Oh man, what is good, etc." Mic. 6:8. Ah, Christian, says another twig, will you search your heart, and "try your ways, and turn again to the Lord" your God, Lam. 3:40? Ah, soul, says another twig, will you die to sin more than ever, and to the world more than ever, and to relations more than ever, and to yourself more than ever, Luk.14:26-33? Ah, soul, says another twig, will you live more to Christ than ever, and cleave closer to Christ than ever, and prize Christ more than ever, and venture further for Christ than ever? "For none of us liveth to himself, and no man dieth to himself," Rom. 14:7. Ah, soul, says another twig, will you love Christ with a more inflamed love, and hope in Christ with a more raised hope, and depend upon Christ with a greater confidence, and wait upon Christ with more invincible patience, etc.? Now, if the soul be not mute and silent under the rod, how is it possible that it should ever hear the voice of the rod, or that it should ever hearken to the voice of every twig of the rod? The rod has a voice that is in the hands of earthly fathers, but children hear it not, they understand it not, until they are hushed and quiet, and brought to sit silently under it; so also, no more shall we hear or understand the voice of the rod that is in our heavenly Father's hand, until we come to sit silently under it. But,

---

1. Tenacious.—H&F.

Reason 2.
Gracious souls should be silent under afflictions that they may distinguish themselves from the men of the world.

Gracious souls should be mute and silent under their greatest afflictions and sharpest trials *that they may differentiate and distinguish themselves from the men of the world, who usually fret and fling, mutter or murmur, curse and swagger, when they are under the afflicting hand of God:* "And they shall pass through it hardly bestead[1] and hungry: and it shall come to pass, that, when they shall be hungry, they shall fret themselves, and curse their king, and their God, and look upward. And they shall look unto the earth; and behold trouble and darkness, dimness of anguish; and they shall be driven to darkness," Isa. 8:21-22. Ah, how fretful and froward, how disturbed and distracted, how mad and forlorn, are these poor wretches under the rebukes of God! They look upward and downward, this way and that way, on this side and on that and, finding no help, no succor, no support, no deliverance, like Bedlams, yea, like incarnate devils, they fall upon cursing of God and their king: "We roar all like bears, and mourn sore like doves: we look for judgment, but there is none; for salvation, but it is far from us," Isa. 59:11.[2] They express their inward vexation and indignation by roaring like bears. When bears are robbed of their whelps, or taken in a pit, oh how dreadfully will they roar, rage, tear, and tumble! So, when wicked persons are fallen into the pit of affliction, oh how will they roar, rage, tear, and cry out! Not of their sins, but of their punishments; as Cain, "My punishment is greater than I am able to bear," Gen. 4:13. "Thy sons have fainted, they lie at the head of all the streets, as a wild bull in a net: they are full of the fury of the Lord, the rebuke of thy God," Isa.

---

1. 'Hard pressed.'—H&F.
2. The bear, as Aristotle observes, licks her whelps into form, and loves them beyond measure, and is most fierce, roaring and raging when she is robbed of them. [Cf. Pliny, *sub voce.*—G.]

51:20. When the huntsman has taken the wild bull in his toil, and so entangled him that he is not able to unwind himself, oh, how fierce and furious will he be! How will he spend himself in struggling to get out! Such wicked men are as wild bulls when they are taken in the net of affliction.

It is said of Marcellus the Roman general, that he could not be quiet, *nec victor, nec victus,* "neither conquered nor conqueror!" It is so with wicked men; they cannot be quiet, neither full nor fasting, neither sick nor well, neither in wealth nor want, neither in bonds nor at liberty, neither in prosperity nor in adversity: "And Babylon shall become heaps, a dwelling-place for dragons,[1] an astonishment, and an hissing, without an inhabitant. They shall roar together like lions: and they shall yell as lions' whelps," Jer. 51:37-38. When the lion roars, all the beasts of the field tremble, Amo. 3:8. When the lion roars, many creatures that could outrun him are so amazed and astonished at the terror of his roaring that they are not able to stir from their place.[2] Wicked men are as such roaring lions, when they are under the smarting rod: "They gnaw their tongues for pain and they blaspheme the God of heaven, because of those sores, pains, and plagues that are poured upon them; and they repented not of their deeds, to give him glory," Rev. 16:9-12. And therefore, gracious souls have cause to be silent under their sorest trials, that they may differentiate and distinguish themselves from wicked men, who are "like the troubled sea, when it cannot rest, whose waters cast up mire and dirt," Isa. 57:20. The verb in the Hebrew, signifies to make a stir, to be exceeding busy, unquiet, or troublesome. Ah, what a stir do wicked men make, when they are under the afflicting hand of God! Ah, the sea is restless and unquiet when there is no storm and it cannot stand still, but has a flux and reflux; so, it is much more restless when, by

---

1. The meaning is: a land monster, typically: a jackal.—H&F.
2. Ambrose on Amos 3:3.

tempest upon tempest, it is made to roar and rage, to foam and cast up mire and dirt. The raging sea is a fit emblem of a wicked man that is under God's afflicting hand.

Reason 3.
Gracious souls should be silent under afflictions that they may be conformable to Christ.

A third reason why gracious souls should be silent and mute under their sharpest trials is *that they may be conformable to Christ their head, who was dumb and silent under his sorest trials:* "He was oppressed, and he was afflicted; yet he opened not his mouth: he is brought as a lamb to the slaughter; and as a sheep before his shearers is dumb, so he opened not his mouth," Isa. 53:7. Christ remained mute under all his sorrows and sufferings: "For even hereunto were ye called: because Christ also suffered for us, leaving us an example, that you should follow his steps: who did no sin, neither was guile found in his mouth: who, when he was reviled, reviled not again; when he suffered, he threatened not; but committed himself to him that judgeth righteously," 1 Pet. 2:21-23.[1] Christ upon the cross did not only read us a lecture of patience and silence, but he has also set us *hupogrammon*, 'a copy' or 'pattern' of both, to be transcribed and imitated by us when we are under the smarting rod. It will be our sin and shame if we do not bear up with patience and silence under all our sufferings, considering what an admirable copy Christ has set before us. It is said of Antiochus, that going out to fight with Judas, captain of the host of the Jews, showed unto his elephants the blood of the grapes and mulberries, to provoke them the better to fight.[2] So the Holy Spirit has

---

1. Justin Martyr being asked which was the greatest miracle that our Savior Christ wrought, answered, *Patientia ejus tanta in laboribus tantis,* "His so great patience in so great trouble."

2. Macc. vi. 34.

set before us the injuries and contumelies,[1] the sorrows and sufferings, the pains and torments, the sweat and blood of our dearest Lord and his invincible patience and admirable silence under all to provoke us and encourage us to imitate the Captain of our salvation in patience and silence under all our sufferings.

Jerome having read the life and death of Hilarion—one that lived graciously and died comfortably—folded up the book saying, "Well! Hilarion shall be the champion that I will follow; his good life shall be my example, and his good death my precedent." Oh! How much more should we all say, "We have read how Christ had been afflicted, oppressed, distressed, despised, persecuted, etc. and we have read how dumb, how mute, how patient, and how silent he was under all. Oh! He shall be the copy which we shall write after, the pattern which we will walk by, the champion which we will follow." But, alas, alas! How rare is it to find a man that may be applauded with the eulogy of Salvian, *Singularis domini preclarus imitator*, "An excellent disciple of a singular master." The heathens had this notion among them, as Lactantius reports, that the way to honor their gods was to be like them;[2] and therefore some would be wicked, counting it a dishonor to their gods to be unlike them. I am sure the way to honor our Christ, is in patience and silence to be like to Christ, especially when a smarting rod is upon our backs and a bitter cup put into our hands.[3]

---

1. Reproaches and contempt.—H&F.

2. The Arabians, if their king be sick or lame, they all feign themselves so.

3. "Beloved, think it not strange concerning the fiery trial which is to try you, as though some strange thing happened unto you: But rejoice, inasmuch as ye are partakers of Christ's sufferings; that, when his glory shall be revealed, ye may be glad also with exceeding joy. If ye be reproached for the name of Christ, happy are ye; for the spirit of glory and of God resteth upon you: on their part he is evil spoken of, but on your part he is glorified," 1 Pet. 4:12-14.—H&F.

Reason 4.
***The people of God should be silent under
afflictions because it is a greater judgment &
affliction to be given up to a fretful spirit.***

The fourth reason why the people of God should be mute and silent under their afflictions, is this, because *it is ten thousand times a greater judgment and affliction, to be given up to a fretful spirit, a froward spirit, a muttering or murmuring spirit under an affliction, than it is to be afflicted.* This is both the devil's sin, and the devil's punishment. God is still afflicting, crossing, and vexing him, and he is still fretting, repining, vexing, and rising up against God. No sin to the devil's sin, no punishment to the devil's punishment. A man would do better to have all the afflictions of all the afflicted throughout the world at once upon him, than to be given up to a froward spirit, to a muttering, murmuring heart under the least affliction.

When you see a soul fretting, vexing, and stamping under the mighty hand of God, you see one of Satan's first-born, one that resembles him to the life.[1] No child can be so much like the father, as this froward soul is like to the father of lies; though he has been in chains almost this six thousand years, yet he has never lain still one day, nor one night, no nor one hour in all this time, but is still fretting, vexing, tossing, and tumbling in his chains, like a princely bedlam. He is a lion, not a lamb; a roaring lion, not a sleepy lion; not a lion standing still, but a lion going up and down; he is not satisfied with the prey he has gotten, but is restless in his designs to fill hell with souls, 1 Pet. 5:8.[2] He never lacks an apple for an Eve, nor a grape for a Noah, nor a change of raiment for a Gehazi, nor a wedge of gold for an Achan, nor a crown for an Absalom, nor a bag for a Judas,

---

1. Irenaeus calls such *ora diaboli*, "the devil's mouth."
2. "Be sober, be vigilant; because your adversary the devil, as a roaring lion, walketh about, seeking whom he may devour," 1 Pet. 5:8.—H&F.

nor a world for a Demas. If you look into one company, there you shall find Satan dishing out his meat to every palate; if you look into another company, there you shall find him fitting a last[1] to every shoe; if you look into a third company, there you shall find him suiting a garment to every back. He is under wrath and cannot but be restless. Here, with Jael, he allures poor souls in with milk and murders them with a nail; there, with Joab, he embraces with one hand and stabs with another. Here with Judas, he kisses and betrays; and there, with the whore of Babylon, he presents a golden cup with poison in it. He cannot be quiet, though his bolts[2] be always on; and the more unquiet any are under the rebukes of God, the more such resemble Satan to the life,[3] whose whole life is filled up with vexing and fretting against the Lord. "Let not any think," says Luther, "that the devil is now dead, nor yet asleep, for as he that keeps Israel, so he that hates Israel, neither slumbering nor sleeping." But in the next place,

Reason 5.
Gracious souls should be silent under afflictions because this fits them for the receipt of mercies.[4]

A fifth reason why gracious souls should be mute and silent under the greatest afflictions and sharpest trials that do befall them is that because *a holy and a prudent silence under afflictions, under miseries, does best capacitate[5] and fit the afflicted for the receipt of mercies.* When the rolling bottle lies

---

1. A form of the human foot on which the shoe is modeled.—H&F.
2. Which hold the restraining shackles or irons.—H&F.
3. That is, to the very kind of life he lives.—H&F.
4. Previous editions: 'miseries.' This has been corrected in our text: 'mercies' has been substituted for 'miseries,' as the context indicates that 'miseries' was an error in the edition; the sense is not to fit the children of God for the misery as an end in itself, but for the divine consolations and mercies that are to be received through afflictions.—H&F.
5. To endue with moral and natural power in order to make capable.—H&F.

still, you may pour into it your sweetest or your strongest waters; when the rolling, tumbling soul lies still, then God can best pour into it the sweet waters of mercy and the strong waters of divine consolation. You read of the "peaceable fruits of righteousness": "Now no chastening for the present seemeth to be joyous, but grievous; nevertheless, afterwards it yieldeth the peaceable fruits of righteousness unto them which are exercised thereby," Heb. 12:11. "And the fruit of righteousness is sown in peace, of them that make peace," Jam. 3:18. The still and quiet soul is like a ship that lies still and quiet in the harbor; you may take in what goods, what commodities you please, while the ship lies quiet and still. So when the soul is quiet and still under the hand of God, it is most fitted and advantaged[1] to take in much of God, of Christ, of heaven, of the promises, of ordinances, and of the love of God, the smiles of God, the communications of God, and the counsel of God; but when souls are unquiet, they are like a ship in a storm, they can take in nothing.[2]

Luther, speaking of God, says, God does not dwell in Babylon, but in Salem. Babylon signifies confusion, and Salem signifies peace. Now God dwells not in spirits that are unquiet and in confusion, but he dwells in peaceable and quiet spirits. Unquiet spirits can take in neither counsel nor comfort, grace nor peace, etc.: "My soul refused to be comforted," Ps. 77:2. The impatient patient will take down no cordials; he has no eye to see, nor hand to take, nor palate to relish, nor stomach to digest anything that makes for his health and welfare. When the man is sick and froward, nothing will down[3]; the sweetest music will make no melody in his ears: "Wherefore, say unto the children of Israel, I am the Lord, and I will bring you out from under

---

1. Prepared by an advantage.—H&F.
2. The angels are most quiet and still, and they take in most of God, of Christ, of heaven.
3. Soothe or mollify.—H&F.

the burdens of the Egyptians, and I will rid you out of their bondage, and I will redeem you with a stretched-out arm, and with great judgment. And I will take you to me for a people, and I will be to you a God, and ye shall know that I am the Lord your God, which bringeth you out from under the burdens of the Egyptians. And I will bring you in unto the land concerning the which I did sware to give it to Abraham, to Isaac, and to Jacob, and I will give it to you for a heritage; I am the Lord," Exo. 5:6-9. The choicest cordials and comforts that heaven or earth could afford are here held forth to them, but they have no hand to receive them. Here Moses speaks, whose lips drop honeycombs, but they can taste no sweetness. Here the best of earth and the best of heaven is set before them, but their souls are shut up and nothing will down.[1] Here is such ravishing music of paradise as might abundantly delight their hearts and please their ears, but they cannot hear. Here are soul enlivening, soul supporting, soul strengthening, soul comforting, soul raising, and soul refreshing words, but they cannot hearken to them: "And Moses spake so unto the children of Israel, but they hearkened not unto Moses, for anguish of spirit and for cruel bondage," ver. 9. They were in an anguished feverish fit and so they could neither hear nor see, taste nor take in anything that might be a mercy or a comfort to them. They were sick from impatience and discontent: and these humors having grown strong, nothing would take with them, nothing would agree with them. When persons are under strong pangs of passion, they have no ears either for reason or religion.

Reason 6.
Gracious souls should be silent under the smarting rod because it is fruitless to strive & contend with God.

A sixth reason why gracious souls should be silent under

---

1.   Soothe or mollify.—H&F.

the smarting rod is this, viz., because *it is fruitless, it is bootless[1] to strive, to contest, or contend with God.* No man has ever gotten anything by muttering or murmuring under the hand of God, except that it was more frowns, blows, and wounds. Such as will not lie quiet and still when mercy has tied them with silken cords, justice will put them in iron chains; if golden fetters will not hold you, iron shall.[2] If Jonah will vex and fret and fling, justice will fling him overboard to cool him, and quell him, and keep him prisoner in the whale's belly, until he is brought down and his spirit is made quiet before the Lord. What you get by struggling and grumbling: "Do they provoke me to anger, saith the Lord? Do they not provoke themselves to the confusion of their own faces?" Jer. 7:19. By provoking me, they do but provoke themselves; by angering me, they do but anger themselves; by vexing me, they do but fret and vex themselves: "Do we provoke the Lord to jealousy? Are we stronger than he?" 1 Cor. 10:22.

Zanchy[3] observes these two things from these words: First, that it is ill to provoke God to wrath because he is stronger than we are. And second, That though God be stronger than we are, yet there are those who provoke him to wrath; and certainly there are none that do more provoke him than those who fume and fret when his hand is upon them. Though the cup be bitter, yet it is put into your hand by your Father; though the cross be heavy, yet he that has laid it on your shoulders will bear the heaviest end of it himself; and why, then, should you mutter? Shall bears and lions take blows and knocks from their keepers, and will you not take a few blows and knocks from the keeper of

---

1. Unavailing and unprofitable.—H&F.
2. So also the Scripture: "Thou hast broken the yokes of wood; but thou shalt make for them yokes of iron," Jer. 28:13.—H&F.
3. Jerome Zanchius.—G.

Israel? Why should the clay contend with the potter[1] or the creature with his creator,[2] or the servant with his lord, or weakness with strength, or a poor nothing creature with an omnipotent God? Can stubble stand before the fire? Can chaff abide before the whirlwind? Or can a worm ward off the blow of the Almighty? A froward and impatient spirit under the hand of God will but add chain to chain, cross to cross, yoke to yoke, and burden to burden. The more men tumble and toss in their feverish fits, the more they strengthen the distemper, and the longer it will be before the cure be effected. The easiest and the surest way of cure is to lie still and quiet until the poison of the distemper be sweated out. Where patience has its perfect work,[3] there the cure will be certain and easy. When a man has his broken leg set, he lies still and quiet, and so his cure is easily and speedily wrought; but when a horse's leg is set, he frets and flings, he flounces and flies out, disjointing it again and again, and so his cure is the more difficult and tedious. Such Christians that, under the hand of God are like the horse or mule, fretting and flinging, will but add to their own sorrows and sufferings and put the day of their deliverance further off.

Reason 7.
Christians should be silent under afflictions because hereby they shall frustrate Satan's design & expectation.

A seventh reason why Christians should be mute and silent under their afflictions is because hereby they *shall cross and frustrate Satan's great design and expectation.* In all the

---

1. "Hath not the potter power over the clay, etc." Rom. 9:21. "But now, Oh Lord, thou art our father; we are the clay, and thou our potter; and we all are the work of thy hand," Isa. 64:8.—H&F.
2. "Oh house of Israel, cannot I do with you as this potter? saith the Lord. Behold, as the clay is in the potter's hand, so are ye in mine hand," Jer. 18:6.—H&F.
3. "But let patience have her perfect work, that ye may be perfect and entire, wanting nothing," Jam. 1:4.—H&F.

afflictions he brought upon Job, his design was not so much to make Job a beggar as it was to make him a blasphemer; it was not so much to make Job outwardly miserable, as it was to make Job inwardly miserable, by providing an occasion for him to mutter and murmur against the righteous hand of God that he might have had some matter of accusation against him to the Lord. He is the unwearied accuser of the brethren: "The accuser of the brethren is cast down, which accuseth them before our God day and night," Rev. 12:10. Satan is the great make-bait[1] between God and his children. He has a mint constantly going in hell, where, as a tireless mint-master, he is still coining and hammering out accusations against the saints. First, he tempts and allures souls to sin and then accuses them of those very sins he has tempted them to, that so he may disgrace them before God and bring them, if it were possible, out of favor with God; and though he knows beforehand that God and his people are, by the bond of the covenant, and by the blood of the Redeemer, so closely united that they can never be severed, yet such is his rage and wrath, envy and malice, that he will endeavor that which he knows he shall never effect. Could he but have made Job froward or fretful under the rod, he would have quickly carried the tidings to heaven, and have been so bold as to have asked God whether this was a carriage becoming such a person of whom he had given so glorious a character.[2] Satan knows that there is more evil in the least sin, than there is in all the afflictions that can be inflicted upon a person; and if he could but have caused a breach in Job's patience, ah, how he would have insulted God himself! Could he but have made Job a mutineer, he would quickly have pleaded for martial law to have been executed upon him; but Job, by remaining mute and silent under all his trials, puts Satan to a blush and spoils all his

---

1.   Tempter, furnisher of bait to tempt.—H&F.

2.   That devil that accused God to man (Gen. 3) and made out Christ to be an impostor, will scruple not to accuse the saints, when they miscarry under the rod.

projects at once. The best way to outwit the devil, is to be silent under the hand of God;[1] he that mutters is foiled by him, but he that is mute overcomes him, and to conquer a devil is more than to conquer a world.

Reason 8.
Christians should be silent under afflictions that they may be conformable to those noble patterns set before them.

The eighth and last reason why Christians should be silent and mute under their sorest trials is this, *that they may be conformable to those noble patterns that are set before them by other saints, who have been patient and silent under the smarting rod.*[2] As Aaron, Lev. 10:3; so Eli, 1 Sam. 3:18; so David, 2 Sam. 16:7-13; so Job 1:21-22; so Eliakim, Shebnah, and Joab, Isa. 36:11-21. So those saints in Act. 21:12-15, and that cloud of witnesses pointed at in Heb. 12:1. Gracious examples are more awakening, more convincing, more quickening, more provoking, and more encouraging than precepts, because in them we see that the exercise of grace and godliness is possible, though it be difficult. When we see Christians that are subject to like infirmities with ourselves, mute and silent under the afflicting hand of God, we see that it is possible that we may attain to the same noble temper of being silent under a smarting rod. Certainly, it is our greatest honor and glory in this world to be eyeing and imitating the highest and worthiest examples. What Plutarch said of Demosthenes, that he was excellent at praising the worthy acts of his ancestors, but not so at imitating them, may be said of many in these days. Oh, they are very forward and excellent at praising the patience of Job, but not at imitating it; at praising the silence of Aaron, but not at imitating it; at

---

1. "Submit yourselves therefore to God. Resist the devil, and he will flee from you," Jam. 4:7.—H&F.
2. *Praecepta docent, exempla movent*, "Precepts may instruct, but examples do persuade."—G.

praising David's dumbness,[1] but not at imitating it; at praising Eli's muteness, but not at imitating it. It was the height of Caesar's glory to walk in the steps of Alexander and of Selymus; a Turkish emperor, to walk in Caesar's steps; and of Themistocles to walk in Miltiades' steps. Oh, how much more should we account it our highest glory to imitate the worthy examples of those worthies, of whom this world is not worthy! It speaks out much of God within, when men are striving to write after the fairest copies. And thus much for the reasons of the point. I come now to the application.

V.
It is the greatest duty and concernment of Christians to be mute and silent under the greatest afflictions, the saddest providences, and the sharpest trials that they meet with in this world.

If this be so, then this truth looks sourly and wistly[2] upon several sorts of persons. As,

The truth of Christian duty looks sadly upon those who murmur under the afflicting hand of God.

This looks sourly and sadly upon murmurers, *upon such as do nothing but mutter and murmur under the afflicting hand of God*. This was Israel's sin of old,[3] and this is England's sin this day. Ah, what murmuring is there against God, what murmuring against instruments, and what murmuring against providence is to be found among us! Some murmur at what they have lost, others murmur at what they fear they shall lose; some murmur that they are no higher, others murmur because they are so low; some murmur

---

1. Muteness, as holding his peace.—H&F.
2. 'Earnestly.'—G.
3. Exo. 16:7-9; Num. 12 & 17:5-10; Exo. 15:23-24; Deu. 1:22-27; & Ps. 106:21-25.

because such a party rules, and others mutter because they themselves are not in the saddle; some murmur because their mercies are not so great as others are; some murmur because their mercies are not so many as others are; some murmur because they are afflicted, and others murmur because such and such are not afflicted as much as they are. Ah, England, England! Had you no more sins upon you, your murmuring would be enough to undo you if God did not exercise much pity and compassion towards you. But more of this later, and let this for the present suffice.

The truth of Christian duty looks sourly upon those that chafe & vex under the afflicting hand of God.

This truth looks sourly upon those that *fret, chafe, and vex when they are under the afflicting hand of God.* Many, when they feel the rod to smart, ah, how they do fret and fume! "When they were hardly bestead[1] and hungry, they fret themselves and curse their king and their God," Isa. 8:21. "The foolishness of man perverteth his way, and his heart fretteth against the Lord," Pro. 19:3. The heart may be fretful and froward when the tongue does not blaspheme. Folly brings man into misery and misery makes man to fret; man in misery is more apt to fret and chafe against the Lord than to fret and chafe against the sin that has brought him into sufferings, 2 Kin. 6:24-33 and Ps. 37:1-8. A fretful soul dares let fly at God himself. When Pharaoh was troubled and fretted he dared spit in the very face of God himself saying: "Who is the Lord, that I should obey him?" Exo. 5:2. And when Jonah is in a fretting humor, he dares tell God to his face, "that he doth well to be angry," Jon. 4:8. Jonah would have done better if he had been angry with his sin, but he did very ill to be angry with his God. God will vex every vein in that man's heart before he has finished with him who fumes and frets because he cannot

---

1. Accommodated.—H&F.

snap in sunder[1] the cords with which he is bound, Eze.
16:43. Sometimes good men are sick because of fretting,
but when they are, it costs them dearly, as Job and Jonah
found by experience. No man has ever gotten anything by
his fretting and flinging except harder blows or heavier
chains; therefore, fret not when God strikes.

The truth of Christian duty looks sourly upon those who foolishly charge God in the day of adversity.

This truth looks sourly upon those who *charge God foolishly
in the day of their adversity*. "Why doth a living man
complain, a man for the punishment of his sins?" Lam. 3:39.
He that has deserved a hanging has no reason to charge the
judge with cruelty if he escape with a whipping; and we
that have deserved a damning[2] have no reason to charge
God for being too severe[3] if we escape with a fatherly
lashing. Rather than a man taking the blame and quietly
bearing the shame of his own folly, he will put it upon God
himself, Gen. 3:12.[4] It is an evil thing when we accuse God
so that we may excuse ourselves and not blame ourselves,
that we may blame our God and lay the fault anywhere
rather than upon our own hearts and ways.[5] Job was a
man of a more noble spirit: "In all this Job sinned not, nor
charged God foolishly," Job 1:22. When God charges many

---

1. Break.—H&F.
2. "If thou, Lord, shouldest mark iniquities, Oh Lord, who shall stand?
But there is forgiveness with thee, that thou mayest be feared," Ps. 130:3-
4.—H&F.
3. Ps. 77:7; & Eze. 18:25. Some of the heathens, as Homer observes, would
lay the evils that they did incur by their own folly upon their gods: so do
many upon the true God.
4. "And the man said, The woman whom thou gavest to be with me, she
gave me of the tree, and I did eat," Gen. 3:12.—H&F.
5. "Let no man say when he is tempted, I am tempted of God: for God
cannot be tempted with evil, neither tempteth he any man: But every man is
tempted, when he is drawn away of his own lust, and enticed. Then when lust
hath conceived, it bringeth forth sin: and sin, when it is finished, bringeth
forth death," Jam. 1:13-15.—H&F.

men and drives the point home, then they presently charge God in their foolishness and they make him out to bear the brunt and blame of all; but this will be bitterness in the end. When you are under affliction, you may humbly tell God that you feel his hand heavy upon you, but you must not blame him because his hand is heavy. No man has ever yet been able to make good a charge against God, and will you be able? Surely not. By charging God foolishly in the day of your calamity, you do but provoke the Lord to charge you through and through, more fiercely and furiously with his most deadly darts of renewed misery. It is your greatest wisdom to blame your sins and lay your hand upon your mouth; for why should folly charge innocency? That man is far from being mute and silent under the hand of God, who dares charge God himself for laying his hand upon him. But,

The truth of Christian duty looks sourly upon those who will not be silent & satisfied under the afflicting hand of God.

This truth looks sourly and sadly upon such *as will not be silent nor satisfied under the afflicting hand of God,*[1] *except the Lord will give them the particular reasons why he lays his hand upon them.* Good men sometimes dash their feet against this stumbling stone: "Why is my pain perpetual, and my wound incurable, etc.?" Jer. 15:18. Though God always has reason for what he does, yet he is not bound to show us the reasons for his doings. Jeremiah's passion was up, his blood was hot, and now nothing will silence nor satisfy him but the reasons why his pain was perpetual and his wound incurable. So Job chap. 7:20, "Why hast thou set me as a

---

1. "And when the people saw that Moses delayed to come down out of the mount, the people gathered themselves together unto Aaron, and said unto him, Up, make us gods, which shall go before us; for as for this Moses, the man that brought us up out of the land of Egypt, we wot not what is become of him, etc." Exo. 32:1, 7-8.—H&F.

mark against thee, so that I am a burden to myself?" It is an evil and a dangerous thing to cavil at or to question his proceedings, who is the chief Lord of all and who may do with his own what he pleases, Rom. 9:20[1] and Dan. 4:34-37. He is unaccountable and uncontrollable, and therefore, who shall say, "What doest thou?" As no man may question his right to afflict him, nor his righteousness in the afflicting of him, so no man may question the reasons why he afflicts him. As no man can compel him to give a reason of his doings, so no man may dare to ask him the particular reasons of his doings. Kings consider themselves not bound to give their subjects a reason of their doings, and shall we bind God to give us a reason of his doings, who is the King of Kings and Lord of Lords, and whose will is the true reason and only rule of justice? Ecc. 8:2-4 and Jon. 5:22-23.[2] The general grounds and reasons that God has laid down in his Word for the reason why he afflicts his people is, namely, "for their profit," Heb. 12:10; for the purging away of their sins, Isa. 1:25;[3] for the reforming of their lives, Ps. 119:67, 71;[4] and for the saving of their souls, 1 Cor. 11:32.[5] These reasons should work upon them to bring them to be silent and satisfied under all their afflictions, though God should never satisfy their curiosity in giving them an account of some more hidden causes which may lie secret in the abysses of his eternal knowledge and infallible will.

---

1. "Nay but, Oh man, who art thou that repliest against God? Shall the thing formed say to him that formed it, Why hast thou made me thus?" Rom. 9:20.—H&F.
2. "The Father judgeth no man, but hath committed all judgment unto the Son: That all men should honour the Son, even as they honour the Father. He that honoureth not the Son honoureth not the Father which hath sent him." Joh. 5:22-23.—H&F.
3. "And I will turn my hand upon thee, and purely purge away thy dross, and take away all thy tin," Isa. 1:25.—H&F.
4. "Before I was afflicted I went astray: but now have I kept thy word, etc. It is good for me that I have been afflicted; that I might learn thy statutes," Ps. 119:67-71.—H&F.
5. "But when we are judged, we are chastened of the Lord, that we should not be condemned with the world," 1 Cor. 11:32.—H&F.

Curiosity is the spiritual drunkenness of the soul; and, as some will never be satisfied, be the cup never so deep, unless they see the bottom of it, so some curious Christians, whose souls are overspread with the leprosy of curiosity, will never be satisfied until they see the bottom and the most secret reasons of all God's dealings towards them. But they are fools in folio,[1] who affect to know more than God would have them. Did not Adam's curiosity render him and his posterity fools in folio? And what, pleasure can we take to see ourselves every day fools in print? As a man's vision, by gazing and prying into the body of the sun, may grow dark and dim, and he see less than he might otherwise, so many, by a curious prying into the secret reasons of God's dealings with them, come to grow so dark and dim that they cannot see those plain reasons that God has laid down in his Word why he afflicts and tries the children of men.

I have read of one Sir William Champney, in the reign of King Henry the Third, once living in Tower Street, London, who was the first man that ever built a turret on the top of his house, that he might the better overlook all his neighbors. But, so it fell out, that not long after, he was struck blind, so that he that could not be satisfied to see as others did see, but would see more than others, saw then nothing at all, through the just judgment of God upon him.[2] And so it is a just and righteous thing with God to strike such with spiritual blindness, who will not be satisfied with seeing the reasons laid down in the Word why he afflicts them, but they must be curiously prying and searching into the hidden and more secret reasons of his severity towards them. Ah, Christian! It is your wisdom and duty to sit silent and mute under the afflicting hand of God upon the account of revealed reasons, without making any curious inquiry into those more secret reasons that are

---

1. Of the greatest proportions.—H&F.
2. John Stow's 'Survey of London.'

locked up in the golden cabinet of God's own breast, Deu. 29:29.[1]

The truth of Christian duty looks sourly upon those who use every way to shift themselves out of their troubles.

This truth looks sourly and sadly upon those who, instead of being silent and mute under their afflictions, *use all sinful shifts and ways to shift themselves out of their troubles; who care not though they break with God, and break with men, and break with their own consciences, so they may but break off the chains that are upon them; who care not by what means the prison door is opened, so they may but escape; nor by what hands their bolts are knocked off, so they may be at liberty.* "Take heed, regard not iniquity, for this hast thou chosen rather than affliction," Job 36:21.[2] He makes but an ill choice, who chooses sin rather than suffering; and yet such an ill choice good men have sometimes made, as you may see by the proofs in the margin,[3] when troubles have compassed them round about. Though no lion roars like that in a man's own bosom—that is, his conscience—yet some, to deliver themselves from troubles without, have set that lion to roaring within. Some, to deliver themselves from outward tortures, have put themselves under inward torments. He purchases his freedom from affliction at too dear a rate, who buys it with the loss of a good name or a good conscience.

---

1. "The secret things belong unto the Lord our God: but those things which are revealed belong unto us and to our children for ever, that we may do all the words of this law," Deu. 29:29.—H&F.
2. It should be noted that Job is not guilty of this, but his friends, in searching out the cause of his calamities, would apply this to Job and find in him secret sins for which all that has befallen him is proved to be the judgement of God.—H&F.
3. 1 Sam. 21:12-15; Gen. 12:12-20, 26:7-11; Jon. 1:1-3, seq.; & 1 Sam. 28.

*Even in good men there is an aptness and
proneness to sin themselves out of affliction.*

Considerations to prevent this:

Now, because there is even in good men sometimes too
great an aptness and proneness to sin and shift themselves
out of afflictions, when they should rather be mute and
silent under them, I lay down these considerations to
prevent it.

There is more evil in the least sin
than in the greatest miseries.

Consider, that there is infinitely more evil in the least sin
than there is in the greatest miseries and afflictions that can
possibly come upon you; yea, there is more evil in the least
sin than there is in all the troubles that ever come upon the
world, yea, than there is in all the miseries and torments
of hell. The least sin is an offence to the great God, it is a
wrong to the immortal soul, it is a breach of a righteous
law; it cannot be washed away but by the blood of Jesus; it
can shut the soul out of heaven and shut the soul up a close
prisoner in hell forever and ever.[1] The least sin is rather
to be avoided and prevented than the greatest sufferings;
if this cockatrice be not crushed in the egg, it will soon
become a serpent; the very thought of sin, if but thought
on, will break out into action, and action into custom, and
custom into habit, and then both body and soul are lost
irrecoverably to all eternity. The least sin is very dangerous.

---

1. If you consider sin strictly, there cannot be any little sin, no more than
there can be a little God, a little hell, or a little damnation. ["Ye have heard
that it was said by them of old time, Thou shalt not kill; and whosoever shall
kill shall be in danger of the judgment: But I say unto you, That whosoever
is angry with his brother without a cause shall be in danger of the judgment:
and whosoever shall say to his brother, Raca, shall be in danger of the
council: but whosoever shall say, Thou fool, shall be in danger of hell fire."
Mat. 5:21-22.—H&F]

Caesar was stabbed with bodkins;[1] Herod was eaten up of lice;[2] Pope Adrian was choked with a gnat; a scorpion is little, yet able to sting a lion to death; the least spark may consume the greatest house, and the least leak sink the greatest ship; a whole arm has been *impostumated*[3] with the prick of a little finger; a little postern[4] opened may betray the greatest city; a dram of poison diffuses itself to all parts, until it strangles the vital spirits and turns out the soul from the body. If the serpent can but wriggle in through an evil thought, he will soon make a surprisal of the soul, as you see in that great instance of Adam and Eve. The trees of the forest, says one in a parable, held a solemn parliament, wherein they consulted regarding the innumerable wrongs which the axe had done them, therefore they made an act, that no tree should hereafter lend the axe an helve,[5] on pain of being cut down. The axe traveled up and down the forest, begging wood from the cedar, oak, ash, elm, even of the poplar trees, but not one would lend him a chip. At last, he desired as many as would serve him to cut down the briars and bushes, alleging that such shrubs as these did only suck away the juice of the ground and hinder the growth and obscure the glory of the fair and goodly trees. Hereupon they were all content to afford him much assistance and he pretended a thorough reformation, but behold a sad deformation, for when he had got his helve, down went both cedar, oak, ash, elm, and all that stood in his way.[6] Such are the subtle reaches of sin; it will promise to remove the briars, and business of afflictions and troubles, that hinder the soul of that juice, sweetness, comfort, delight, and content that otherwise it might enjoy. Oh, do but now

---

1. Daggers.—H&F.
2. More correctly, *'skolekobrotos,'* 'worms;' specifically 'maggots,' Act. 12:23.—H&F.
3. Latin for imposthumated: become infected.—H&F.
4. A private entrance.—H&F.
5. The wooden handle of the ax.—H&F.
6. Thomas Adams, 'The Bad Leaven.'—G.

yield a little to it and instead of removing your troubles, it will cut down your peace, your hopes, your comforts, yea, it will cut down your precious soul. What is the breaking of a vein to the bleeding of an artery, or the scratch on the hand to a stab at the heart? No more are the greatest afflictions to the least sins than the scratch to the deepest wound. Therefore, Christians, never use sinful shifts to shift yourselves out of troubles, but rather be mute and silent under them, until the Lord shall work out your deliverance from them. But,

> It is impossible for anyone to sin
> themselves out of their troubles.

Consider that *it is an impossible thing for any to sin themselves out of their troubles.* Abraham, Job, and Jonah attempted it, but could not effect it. The devils have experienced this for nearly six thousand years; they would not be now in chains if they could have sinned themselves out of their chains. If the damned could sin themselves out of everlasting burning, there would be none now roaring in that devouring unquenchable fire, Isa. 33:14. Hell would have no inhabitants, if they could but sin themselves out of it. Ah, Christians, devils and damned spirits shall as soon sin themselves out of hell, as you shall be able to sin yourselves out of your afflictions. Christians, you shall as soon stop the sun from running her course, contract[1] the sea into a nutshell, compass the earth with a span, and raise the dead at your pleasure, as ever you shall be able to sin yourselves out of your sufferings. Therefore, it is better to be silent and quiet under them than to attempt that which is impossible to accomplish. This second consideration will receive further confirmation by the next particular:

---

1. Compress.—H&F.

It is a very dangerous thing to attempt to
sin yourselves out of your troubles.

As it is an impossible thing, so it is a very prejudicial,[1] a very dangerous thing, to attempt to sin yourselves out of your troubles; for by attempting to sin yourselves out of your trouble, you will sin yourselves into many troubles, as Jonah and Jacob did; and by laboring to sin yourselves out of less troubles, you will sin yourselves into greater troubles, as Saul did; and by endeavoring to sin yourselves out from under outward troubles, you will sin yourselves into inward troubles and distresses, which are the sorest and saddest of all troubles; thus did Spira, Jerome of Prague, Bilney, and others. There have been some, who, by laboring to sin themselves out of their present sufferings, have sinned themselves into such horrors and terrors of conscience that they could neither eat, nor drink, nor sleep, but have been ready to lay violent hands upon themselves.

Cyprian, in his sermon *De Lapsis,* speaks of diverse persons who, forsaking the faith to avoid sufferings, were given over to be possessed of evil spirits and died fearfully. Oh man, you do not know what deadly sin, what deadly temptation, what deadly judgment, what deadly stroke, you may fall under, who attempt to sin yourselves out of troubles. What is it to take Venice and to be hanged at the gates thereof? It is better to be silent and mute under your afflictions than, by using sinful shifts, to sin yourself into greater afflictions.

It is a very ignoble & unworthy thing to attempt
to sin yourselves out of your troubles.

Consider that *it is a very ignoble and unworthy thing to go to sin yourselves out of your troubles and straits.* It argues a poor, a low, a weak, a dastardly, and an unmanly spirit to use base shifts to shuffle yourselves out of your troubles. Men of

---

1. Hurtful and injurious.—H&F.

noble, courageous, and magnanimous spirits will disdain
and scorn it, Dan. 3:8, 6, and Heb. 11:24. As you may see in
the three children, David, and those worthies, in that 11th
chapter of Hebrews, of whom "this world was not worthy."
Jerome writes of a brave woman, who, being upon the rack,
bade her persecutors do their worst, for she was resolved to
die rather than lie. And the prince of Conde, being taken
prisoner by Charles the Ninth, King of France, and put to
the choice whether he would go to mass or be put to death
or suffer perpetual imprisonment, his noble answer was,
that by God's help he would never choose the first, and for
either of the latter, he left to the king's pleasure and God's
providence.

A soul truly noble will sooner part with all than the peace
of a good conscience. Thus blessed Hooper desired rather
to be discharged of his bishopric than yield to certain
ceremonies.

I have read of Marcus Arethusus, an eminent servant of the
Lord in Gospel work, who, in the time of Constantine, had
been the cause of overthrowing an idol temple;[1] but Julian,
coming to be Emperor, commanded the people of that place
to build it up again. All were ready so to do, only he refused
it; whereupon his own people, to whom he had preached,
fell upon him, stripped off all his clothes, then abused his
naked body and gave it up to children and school-boys to
be lanced with their penknives; but when all this would not
do, they caused him to be set in the sun, having his naked
body anointed all over with honey, that so he might be
bitten and stung to death by flies and wasps; and all this
cruelty they exercised upon him, because he would not do
anything towards the rebuilding of that idol temple; nay,
they came so far that if he would but give one halfpenny

---

1. Lactantius speaks of many such brave spirits. I might produce a cloud
of witnesses from among the primitive Christians, who have been noble and
gallant this way.

towards the charge, they would release him, but he refused it with a noble Christian disdain, though the advancing of a halfpenny might have saved his life. And in so doing, he did but live up to that noble principle that most will commend, but few practise, viz., that Christians must choose rather to suffer the worst of torments, than commit the least of sins, whereby God should be dishonored, his name blasphemed, religion reproached, profession scorned, weak saints discouraged, and men's consciences wounded and their souls endangered. Now tell me, Christians, is it not better to be silent and mute under your sorest trials and troubles, than to labor to sin and shift yourselves out of them, and so proclaim to all the world that you are persons of very low, poor, and ignoble spirits? But,

God has always cursed sinful shifts.

Consider that sinful shifts and means God has always cursed and blasted.[1] Achan's golden wedge was but a wedge to cleave him and his garments a shroud to shroud him. Ahab purchased a vineyard with the blood of the owner, but presently it was watered with his own blood, according to the Word of the Lord. Gehazi must have the talent of silver and two changes of raiment, and that with a lie. Well, he had them and he had with them a leprosy that cleaved to him and his seed forever, 2 Kin. 5:20-27. With those very hands that Judas took money to betray his master, with those very hands he also fitted a halter[2] to hang himself. The rich and wretched glutton fared delicately and went bravely[3] every day, but the next news you hear of him is of his being in hell and crying out for a drop of water, even him who, when he was on earth, would not give a crumb. The coal carried from the altar to the nest, sets all on fire.

---

1. 2 Sam. 11; Eze. 7:13; 1 Sam. 28; 1 Kin. 21:1-19.
2. A noose.—H&F.
3. Splendidly.—H&F.

Crassus did not long enjoy the fruit of his covetousness, for the Parthians taking him, poured melted gold down his throat.

Dionysius[1] did not long enjoy the fruit of his sacrilege and tyranny, for he was glad to change his scepter into a ferule,[2] and turn schoolmaster for his maintenance. Ah, Christians, Christians, is it not far better to sit quiet and silent under your afflictions, than to use such sinful shifts and means which God will certainly blast and curse? But,

> The very attempt to sin & shift yourselves
> out of afflictions will cost you dearly.

Lastly, consider *that your very attempting to sin and shift yourselves out of troubles and afflictions, will cost you dearly.* It will cost you many prayers and tears, many sighs, many groans, many gripes, many terrors, and many horrors. Peter, by attempting to sin himself out of trouble, sins himself into a sea of sorrows: Mat. 25:75, "He went forth and wept bitterly."[3] Were Abraham, David, Jacob, and Jonah now alive, they would tell you that they have found this to be true in their own experience. Ah, Christians, it is far better to be quiet and silent under your sufferings, than to pay so dear for attempting to sin and shift yourselves out of your sufferings. A man will not buy gold at too dear a price, and why then should he buy himself out of troubles at too dear a rate?

---

1. The 'Tyrant' of Sicily.—G.
2. A flat piece of wood formerly used to strike children on the palm of the hand in school.—H&F.
3. A man may buy anything too dearly, but not Christ, grace, his own soul, and the Gospel.

❦ THE EXHORTATION ❧

Considerations to engage your souls to be mute and silent under your greatest troubles and your saddest trials.

But now I shall come to that use that I intend to stand most upon and that is, *the use of exhortation.* Seeing it is the great duty and concernment of Christians to be mute and silent under the greatest afflictions, the saddest providences, and sharpest trials that they meet with in this world. Oh, that I could prevail with you, Christians, to mind this great duty and to live up and live out this necessary truth, and I may prevail indeed if you give me leave to propound some considerations to engage your souls to be mute and silent under your greatest troubles and your saddest trials. To that purpose,

Let the greatness, sovereignty, majesty, &
dignity of God move you to silence.

Consider first, *the greatness, sovereignty, majesty, and dignity of God, and let that move you to silence,* Jer. 10:7 and 5:22: "Come, behold the works of the Lord, what desolations he hath made in the earth. He maketh wars to cease unto the end of the earth; he breaketh the bow, and cutteth the spear in sunder; he burneth the chariot in the fire. Be still, and know that I am God: I will be exalted among the heathens, I will be exalted in the earth," Ps. 46:8-10. Who can cast his eye upon the greatness of God, the majesty of God, and not sit still before him? "Hold thy peace at the presence of the

Lord God," Zep. 1:7. Oh, chat[1] not, murmur not, fret not, but stand mute before him! Shall the child be hushed before his father, the servant before the master, the subject before his prince, and the guilty person before the judge, when he majestically rises off his judgment seat, and composes his countenance into an aspect[2] of terror and severity that his sentence may fall upon the offender with the greater dread? And shall not a Christian be quiet before that God that can bathe his sword in heaven and burn the chariots on earth? Nay, shall the sheep be hushed before the wolf, birds before the hawk, and all the beasts of the field before the lion? And shall not we be hushed and quiet before him, who is the "Lion of the tribe of Judah?" Rev. 5:5. God is mighty in power, and mighty in counsel, and mighty in working, and mighty in punishing; and therefore be silent before him. It appears that God is a mighty God by the epithet that is added unto *El*, which is *Gibbon*, importing that he is a God of prevailing might; in Daniel he is called *El Elim*, the mighty of mighties. Moses, magnifying his might, says, "Who is like unto thee among the gods?" Now certainly this epithet should be a mighty motive to work souls to that which Habakkuk persuaded men to: "The Lord is in his holy Temple: let all the earth keep silence before him," Hab. 2:20. Upon this very consideration Moses commands Israel to hold their peace, Exo. 14:13-14.

It is reported of Augustus the Emperor, and likewise of Tamerlane, that warlike Scythian, that in their eyes sat such a rare majesty that many in talking with them and often beholding of them, have become dumb.[3] Oh, my brethren, shall not the brightness and splendor of the majesty of the great God, whose sparkling glory and majesty dazzles the eyes of angels and makes those princes of glory stand mute before him, move you much more to silence, to hold your

---

1. Prate or speak foolishly.—H&F.
2. Appearance.—H&F.
3. Turk. Hist., 236, 415.

peace and lay your hands upon your mouths. Surely yes. But,

All afflictions, troubles, & trials shall work for your good.

Consider, *that all your afflictions, troubles, and trials shall work for your good:* "And we know that all things shall work together for good to them that love God," Rom. 8:28. Why then should you fret, fling, and fume, seeing that God designs good for you in all? The bee sucks sweet honey out of the bitterest herbs; so God will by afflictions teach his children to suck sweet knowledge, sweet obedience, and sweet experiences, etc., out of all the bitter afflictions and trials he exercises them with.[1] That scouring and rubbing,[2] which causes others to fret, shall make his children shine the brighter; and that weight which crushes and keeps others under, shall but make his children grow better and higher; and that hammer which knocks others all in pieces, shall but knock his children the nearer to Christ, the corner stone. Stars shine brightest in the darkest night; torches give the best light when beaten; grapes yield most wine when most pressed; spices smell sweetest when pounded; vines are the better for bleeding; gold looks the brighter for scouring; juniper smells sweetest in the fire; the more you tread chamomile, the more you spread it; the salamander lives best in the heat; the Jews were best, when most afflicted; the Athenians would never mend, until they were in mourning; the Christ's cross, says Luther, is no letter in the book, and yet, says he, it has taught me more than all the letters in the book. Afflictions are the saints' best benefactors to heavenly affections; where afflictions hang heaviest, corruptions hang loosest. And grace that is hid in nature is most fragrant when the fire of affliction is put

---

1. *Afflictiones benedictiones,* "afflictions are blessings." Bernard. Doubtless Manasseh would not exchange the good he got by his iron chains, for all the gold chains that be in the world.
2. Upbraiding and reproaching.—H&F.

under to distil it out. Grace shines the brighter for scouring and is most glorious when it is most clouded.

Pliny in his Natural History[1] writes of certain trees growing in the Red Sea, which being beat upon by the waves, stand like a rock, immovable, and they are battered by the roughness of the waters. In the sea of afflictions, God will make his people stand like a rock; they shall be immovable and invincible, and the more the waves of afflictions beat upon them, the better they shall be and the more they shall thrive in grace and godliness. Now, how should this engage Christians to be mute and silent under all their troubles and trials in this world, considering that they shall all work for their good! God chastises our carcasses to heal our consciences; he afflicts our bodies to save our souls; he gives us gall and wormwood here, that the pleasures that are at his right hand may be more sweet hereafter; here he lays us upon a bed of thorns, that we may look and long more for that bed of down—even his bosom in heaven.

As there is a curse wrapped up in the best things he gives the wicked, so there is a blessing wrapped up in the worst things he brings upon his own, Ps. 25:10 and Deu. 26:16-19. As there is a curse wrapped up in a wicked man's health, so there is a blessing wrapped up in a godly man's sickness; as there is a curse wrapped up in a wicked man's strength, so there is a blessing wrapped up in a godly man's weakness;[2] as there is a curse wrapped up in a wicked man's wealth,[3] so there is a blessing wrapped up in a godly man's wants;[4]

---

1. Lib. xii. 1.9.
2. "My grace is sufficient for thee: for my strength is made perfect in weakness," 2 Cor. 12:9.—H&F.
3. "Go to now, ye rich men, weep and howl for your miseries that shall come upon you. Your riches are corrupted, and your garments are motheaten. Your gold and silver is cankered; and the rust of them shall be a witness against you, etc." Jam. 5:1-6.—H&F.
4. "But Abraham said, Son, remember that thou in thy lifetime receivedst thy good things, and likewise Lazarus evil things: but now he is comforted, and thou art tormented, etc." Luk. 16:25.—H&F.

as there is a curse wrapped up in a wicked man's honor,[1] so there is a blessing wrapped up in a godly man's reproach;[2] as there is a curse wrapped up in all a wicked man's mercies,[3] so there is a blessing wrapped up in all a godly man's crosses, losses, and changes. Why then should he not sit mute and silent before the Lord? But,

A holy silence is that excellent grace that lends a hand of support to every grace.

Consider *that a holy silence is that excellent precious grace, that lends a hand of support to every grace*, Rom. 15:4. Silence is *custos*, the keeper, of all other virtues; it lends a hand to faith, a hand to hope, a hand to love, a hand to humility, a hand to self-denial, etc. A holy silence has its influences upon all other graces that be in the soul; it causes the buds of grace to blossom and bud forth. Silence is *virtus versata circa adversa*, "a grace that keeps a man gracious in all conditions." In every condition silence is a Christian's right hand; in prosperity, it bears the soul up under all the envy, hatred, malice, and censures of the world; in adversity, it bears the soul up under all the neglect, scorn, and contempt that a Christian meets with in the world. It makes every bitter sweet, every burden light, and every yoke easy. And this the very heathen seemed to intimate in placing the image of *Angeronia*[4] with the mouth bound, upon the altar of *Volupia*[5] to show that silence under sufferings was the

---

1. "Woe unto you, when all men shall speak well of you! For so did their fathers to the false prophets," Luk. 6:26.—H&F.

2. "Blessed are they which are persecuted for righteousness' sake: for theirs is the kingdom of heaven. Blessed are ye, when men shall revile you, and persecute you, and shall say all manner of evil against you falsely, for my sake. Rejoice, and be exceeding glad: for great is your reward in heaven: for so persecuted they the prophets which were before you," Mat. 5:10-12.—H&F.

3. "But woe unto you that are rich! For ye have received your consolation. Woe unto you that are full! For ye shall hunger. Woe unto you that laugh now! For ye shall mourn and weep," Luk. 6:24-25.—H&F.

4. More accurately *Angerona*, goddess of silence.—G.

5. *Volupia*, goddess of pleasure.—G.

ready way to attain true comfort and make every bitter sweet. No man honors God, nor no man justifies God at so high a rate, as he who lays his hand upon his mouth, when the rod of God is upon his back. But,

Consider that you have deserved greater &
heavier afflictions than those you are under.

To move you to silence under your sorest and your sharpest trials, consider, _that you have deserved greater and heavier afflictions than those you are under,_ Lam. 3:39 and Mic. 7:7-9.[1] Has God taken away one mercy? You have deserved to be stripped of all. Has he taken away the delight of your eyes? He might have taken away the delight of your soul. Are you under outward wants? You have deserved to be under outward and inward together. Are you cast upon a sick bed? You have deserved a bed in hell. Are you under that ache and that pain? You have deserved to be under all aches and pains at once. Has God chastised you with whips? You have deserved to be chastised with scorpions. Are you fallen from the highest pinnacle of honor to be the scorn and contempt of men? You have deserved to be scorned and contemned by God and angels. Are you under a severe whipping? You have deserved an utter damning. Ah Christian, let but your eyes be fixed upon your demerits and your hands will be quickly upon your mouths; whatever is less than a final separation from God, whatever is less than hell, is mercy; and therefore you have cause to be silent under the sharpest dealings of God with you. But,

---

1. "Wherefore doth a living man complain, a man for the punishment of his sins?" Lam. 3:39; "I will bear the indignation of the Lord, because I have sinned against him, until he plead my cause, and execute judgment for me: he will bring me forth to the light, and I shall behold his righteousness," Mic. 7:9.—H&F.

A quiet silent spirit is of great esteem with God.

Consider that *a quiet silent spirit is of great esteem with God.* God sets the greatest value upon persons of a quiet spirit: "But let it be the hidden man of the heart, in that which is not corruptible, even the ornament of a meek and quiet spirit, which is in the sight of God of great price," 1 Pet. 3:4. A quiet spirit is a spark of the divine nature, it is a ray, a beam of glory; it is a heaven-born spirit. No man is born with a holy silence in his heart as he is born with a tongue in his mouth. This is a flower of paradise; it is a precious gem that God makes very great reckoning of. A quiet spirit speaks a man most like to God; it capacitates a man for communion with God; it renders a man most serviceable to God; and it obliges a man to most accurate walking with God. A meek and quiet spirit is an incorruptible ornament, much more valuable than gold.

A meek & a quiet spirit—what it is & what it is not.

There is a natural[1] quietness, which proceeds from a good temper and constitution of body.

There is a moral quietness, which proceeds from good education and upbringing, which flows from good injunctions, instructions, and examples.

There is an artificial quietness; some have an art to imprison their passions, and to lay a law of restraint upon their anger and wrath, when they are all in a flame within: as you may see in Cain, Esau, Absalom, and Joab, who for a time cast a close cloak over their malice, when their hearts were set on fire of hell.[2] So Domitian would seem to love them best, whom he willed least should live.

---

1. Previous editions: 'mutual.' This has been corrected in our text: 'mutual' has been changed to 'natural' as is the obvious context.—H&F.

2. "Whose hatred is covered by deceit, his wickedness shall be shewed before the whole congregation," Pro. 26:26, also Pro.10:18.—H&F.

There is a gracious quietness, which is of the Spirit's infusion, Gal. 5:22-25. Now this quietness of spirit, this spiritual frame of heart, is of great price in the sight of God. God values it above the world and therefore who would not covet it more than the world, yea, more than life itself? Certainly the great God sets a great price upon nothing but that which is of an invaluable price; what stretching, struggling, and striving is there for those things that the great ones of the earth do highly prize! Ah, what stretching of wits, interests, and consciences is there this day, to gain and hold up that which justice will cast down! How much better would it be, if all persons would in good earnest struggle and strive, even as for life, after a quiet and silent spirit, which the great and glorious God sets so great a price upon! This is a pearl of greatest price and happy is he that purchases it, though it were with the loss of all. But,

If you sit not silent under troubles & trials,
you fight against your own prayers.

Consider *that if you sit not silent and quiet under your greatest troubles and your sorest trials, you will be found fighting against your own prayers.* How often have you prayed that the will of God may be done, yea, that it may be done on the earth, as the angels, those glistering[1] courtiers, those princes of glory, do it now in heaven! Mat. 6:10. When troubles and afflictions come upon you, the will of God is done, his will is accomplished. Why then should you fret, fling, and fume, and not rather quietly rest in his will, whose will is a perfect will, a just and righteous will, a wise will, an overruling will, an infinite will, a sovereign will, a holy will, an immutable will, an uncontrollable will, an omnipotent will, and an eternal will? Certainly you will but add affliction to affliction, by fighting against your own prayers, and by vexing and fretting yourselves when the will of God is done.

---

1. Shining.—H&F.

It is sad to see a man fight against his friends, it is sadder to see him fight against his relations, it is saddest of all to see him fight against his prayers; and yet, this every Christian does who murmurs and mutters when the rod of God is upon him.[1] Some there are that pray against their prayers, as Augustine, who prayed for continence[2] with a proviso, "Lord, give me continence, but not yet." And some there are who fight against their prayers, as those who pray that the will of God may be done and yet, when his will is done upon them, they are like the troubled sea when it cannot rest, they are still fretting against the Lord. Ah, Christians, do you not have sins to fight against and temptations to fight against, and a devil to fight against, yea, a whole world to fight against? Why then should you be found fighting against your own prayers? But,

A holy silence under the heaviest burdens & the saddest providences will make all tolerable.

Consider that *a holy silence under the heaviest burdens, the greatest afflictions, the saddest providences and changes, will make all tolerable and easy to a Christian.* The silent soul can bear a burden without a burden. Those burdens and troubles that will break a froward man's back, will not so much as break a silent man's sleep; those afflictions that lie as heavy weights upon a murmurer, will lie as light as a feather upon a mute Christian, Mic. 7:7-10; that bed of sorrow, which is as a bed of thorns to a fretful soul, will be as a bed of down to a silent soul. A holy silence unstings[3] every affliction, it takes off the weight of every burden, it adds sweet to every bitter, it changes dark nights into sunshiny days, and terrible storms into desirable calms. The smallest

---

1. *Voluntas Dei necessitas rei.* Every gracious soul should say Amen to God's Amen; he should put his *fiat*, his *placet* to God's, though it go against the grain with him. [*Fiat*, "let it be so." *Placet*, "it is pleasing."—H&F.]
2. Restraint upon the passions.—H&F.
3. Disarms.—H&F.

sufferings will easily vanquish an unquiet spirit, but a quiet spirit will as easily triumph over the greatest sufferings. As little mercies are great mercies, so great sufferings are but little sufferings in the eye of a silent soul. The silent soul never complains that his affliction is too great, his burden too heavy, his cross too weighty, his sufferings too many; silence makes him victorious over all. And therefore, as ever you would have heavy afflictions light and be able to bear a burden without a burden, labor, as for life itself, after this holy silence.

A holy silence under afflictions will be your best armor against the temptations that affliction may expose you to.

Consider *that a holy silence under afflictions will be your best armor against those temptations that afflictions may expose you to.* Times of afflictions often prove times of great temptations, and therefore afflictions are called temptations:[1] "Blessed is the man which endureth temptations, for when he is tried he shall receive the crown of life, etc," Jam. 1:12. The Greek word *peirasmon*, is to be understood of temptations of probation, of afflicting temptations, and not of temptations of suggestion or of seduction; for they are not to be endured, but resisted and abhorred, Jam. 4:7 and 1 Pet. 5:9. Now,

Affliction is called temptation for these reasons:

Because, as temptation tries what metal a Christian is made of, so do afflictions.

Because, as Satan usually has a great hand in all the temptations that come upon us, so he has a great hand in all the afflictions that befall us; as you see in that great example of Job.

---

1. "Then was Jesus led up of the Spirit into the wilderness to be tempted of the devil, etc." Mat. 4:1. ['Tempted,' 'peirasthenai,'—H&F.].

Because, as temptations drive men to God, 2 Cor. 12:9-10,[1] so do afflictions, Isa. 26:16,[2] and Hos. 5:15;[3] but mainly because Satan chooses times of afflictions as the fittest seasons for his temptations. When Job was sorely afflicted in his estate, children, wife, and life, then Satan makes his fiercest assaults upon him. Now, Satan tempts him to entertain hard thoughts of God; to distrust, to impatience, to murmuring and muttering. As when Israel was feeble, faint, and weary, Amalek assaulted them and smote the hindmost of them, Deu. 25:17-18; so when Christians are most afflicted, then usually they are most tempted.[4]

Luther found this by experience when he said, "I am without set upon by all the world, and within by the devil and all his angels." Satan is a coward and loves to strike us and trample upon us when afflictions have cast us down. When besieged towns, cities, and castles are in greatest straits and troubles, then the besiegers make their fiercest assaults; so when Christians are under the greatest straits and trials, then Satan assaults them most, like a roaring lion. Now, silence under afflictions is the best antidote and preservative against all those temptations that afflictions lay us open to. Silence in afflictions is a Christian's armor of proof; it is that shield that no spear or dart of temptation can pierce. While a Christian lies under the rod, he is safe. Satan may tempt him, but he will not conquer him; he may assault him, but he cannot vanquish him. Satan may entice him to use sinful shifts to shift himself out of trouble; but

---

1. "Now I rejoice, not that ye were made sorry, but that ye sorrowed to repentance: for ye were made sorry after a godly manner, etc. For godly sorrow worketh repentance to salvation not to be repented of," 2 Cor. 7:9-10.—H&F.
2. "Lord, in trouble have they visited thee, they poured out a prayer when thy chastening was upon them," Isa. 26:16.—H&F.
3. "I will go and return to my place, till they acknowledge their offence, and seek my face: in their affliction they will seek me early," Hos. 5:15.—H&F.
4. Many saints have experienced this truth, when they have been upon their sick and dying beds.

he will choose rather to remain, yea, to die in trouble, than get out upon Satan's terms. But,

Holy silence under afflictions will give a man the quiet & peaceable possession of his own soul.

Consider *that holy silence under afflictions and trials will give a man a quiet and peaceable possession of his own soul:* "In patience possess your souls," Luk. 21:19. Next to the possession of God, the possession of a man's own soul is the greatest mercy in this world. A man may possess honors, and riches, and dear relations, and the favor and assistance of friends under his trials, but he will never come to a possession of his own soul under his troubles until he comes to be mute and to lay his hand upon his mouth. Now, what are all earthly possessions to the possession of a man's own soul? He that possesses himself possesses all; he that possesses not himself possesses nothing at all. He possesses not the use, the sweetness, the comfort, the good, the blessing of anything he enjoys, who enjoys not the possession of his own soul. That man that is not master of himself, is a master of nothing. Holy silence gives a man the greatest mastery over his own spirit; and mastery over a man's own spirit is the greatest mastery in the world, Pro. 16:32.[1] They paint the Egyptian goddess upon a rock standing in the sea, where the waves come roaring and dashing upon her, with this motto, *Semper eadem,*[2] "Storms shall not move me." A holy silence will give a man such a quiet possession of his own soul that all the storms of afflictions shall not move him; it will make him stand like a rock in a sea of troubles. Let a man but quietly possess himself, and troubles will never trouble him. But,

---

1. "He that is slow to anger is better than the mighty; and he that ruleth his spirit than he that taketh a city," Pro. 16:32. In contrast, "He that hath no rule over his own spirit is like a city that is broken down, and without walls," Pro. 25:28.—H&F.
2. Literally, "always the same."—H&F.

The instruction of God's Word is to be silent under troubles & trials.

Consider *the commands and instructions that God in his Word has laid upon you to be silent, to be mute and quiet, under all the troubles, trials, and changes that have or may pass upon you*: "Be silent, Oh all flesh, before the Lord, for he is raised up out of his holy habitation," Zec. 2:13; "Keep silence before me, Oh islands," Isa. 41:1; "The Lord is in his holy Temple; let all the earth keep silence before him," Hab. 2:20; "Therefore the prudent shall keep silence in that time, for it is an evil time," Amo. 5:13; "Be still, and know that I am God," Ps. 46:10; "Stand in awe, and sin not: commune with your own heart upon your bed, and be still," Ps. 4:4; "Fear ye not, stand still, and see the salvation of the Lord," Exo. 14:13; "Stand ye still, and see the salvation of the Lord, with you, Oh Judah, and Jerusalem," 2 Chr. 20:17; "Hearken unto this, Oh Job; stand still, and consider the wondrous works of God," Job 37:14. It is a dangerous thing for us to neglect one of his commands, who by another is able to command us into nothing or into hell at his pleasure.[1] To act or run cross to God's express command, though under pretence of revelation from God, is as much as a man's life is worth, as you may see in that sad story, 1 Kin. 13:9-24. Divine commands must be put in speedy execution, without denying or delaying, without debating or disputing the difficulties that may attend our subjection to them.[2] God's commands are spiritual, holy, just, and good; and therefore to be obeyed without muttering or murmuring. Divine commands are backed with the strongest reason, and attended with the highest encouragements. Shall the servant readily obey the commands of his master, the subject the commands of his

---

1. "But I will forewarn you whom ye shall fear: Fear him, which after he hath killed hath power to cast into hell; yea, I say unto you, Fear him," Luk. 12:5.—H&F.

2. *Obedientia non discutit Dei mandata, sed facit.* Prosper. Rom. 7:12-14.

prince, the soldier the commands of his general, the child the commands of his father, the wife the commands of her husband, and shall not a Christian as readily obey the commands of his Christ? Nay, shall vain men readily and willingly obey the sinful and senseless commands of men, and shall not we be willing to obey the commands of God? "Now Absalom had commanded his servant, saying, Mark ye now when Amnon's heart is merry with wine, and when I say unto you, Smite Amnon: then kill him, fear not: have not I commanded you? Be courageous, and be valiant. And the servants of Absalom did unto Amnon as Absalom had commanded," 2 Sam. 13:28-29. They made no bones of obeying the bloody commands of Absalom, against all law, reason, and religion.

I have read of one Johannes Abbas who willingly fetched water nearly two miles every day for a whole year together, to pour upon a dry stick, upon the bare command of his confessor.[1]

I have also read of the old kings of Peru, that they were accustomed to use a tassel or fringe made of red wool, which they wore upon their heads, and when they sent any governor to rule as viceroy in any part of their country, they delivered to him one of the threads of the tassel, and for one of those simple threads he was as much obeyed as if he had been the king himself. Now, shall one single thread be more forcible to draw infidels to obedience, than all those golden commands, last cited, shall be of force to draw you to be quiet and silent under the troubles and changes you meet with in this world? The Lord forbid!

Shall carnal and wicked persons be so ready and willing to comply with the bloody and senseless and superstitious commands of their superiors? And shall not Christians be more ready and willing to comply with the commands

---

1. Cassian. *De Instit. Renunciant.* l. iv. c. 14.

of the great God, whose commands are all just and equal, and whose will is the perfect rule of righteousness. *Prior est authoritas imperantis, quam utilitas servientis.*[1] "The chief reason of obedience is the authority of the Lord, not the utility of the servant."[2] Ah, Christians! When your hearts begin to fret and fume under the smarting rod, charge one of those commands last cited upon your hearts; and if they shall mutter, charge another of those commands upon your hearts; and if after this, they shall vex and murmur, charge another of those commands upon your hearts; and never leave charging and rubbing[3] those commands one after another upon your hearts, until you are brought to lay your hands upon your mouths and to sit silent before the Lord under your greatest straits and your sorest trials.

Mercy is nearest & deliverance is at hand when a Christian stands still & silent under the sorest trials.

Consider *that mercy is nearest, deliverance and salvation is at hand when a Christian stands still, when he sits quiet and silent under his greatest troubles and his sorest trials.*[4] In Exo. 14, they were in very great straits. Pharaoh with a mighty army was behind them, the Red Sea before them, mountains on each side of them, and no visible means to deliver them. But now they stand still to see the salvation of the Lord, ver. 13, and within a few hours their enemies are destroyed and they are gloriously delivered, ver. 24, *et seq.* David is silent, he sits mute under his sharp afflictions, Ps. 39:9; but if you look to the second and third verses of the fortieth Psalm, you shall find mercy draw near to him and work salvation for him. "He brought me up also out

---

1. Tertullian.
2. *Non parentum aut majorum authoritas, sed Dei docentis imperium,* "The commands of God must needs outweigh all authority and example of men." Jerome.
3. Awakening or stirring by reflection.—H&F.
4. Act. 12:5-11, 16:25-26; Dan. 9:20-23; & Gen. 39:20, etc.

of an horrible pit, out of the mire and clay, and set my feet upon a rock, and established my goings. And he hath put a new song into my mouth, even praise unto our God; many shall see it and fear, and shall trust in the Lord." And so when Absalom had made a great conspiracy against him and his subjects left him, and he was forced to flee for his life, his spirit was quiet and calm. "And the king said unto Zadok, Carry back the ark of God into the city: if I shall find favor in the eyes of the Lord, he will bring me again, and shew me both it and his habitation. But if he thus say, I have no delight in thee; behold, here am I, let him do to me as seemeth good unto him," 2 Sam. 15:25-26. And the same calmness and quietness of spirit was upon him when Shimei bitterly cursed him, and railed upon him, chap. 16:5-14; and within a few days, as you may see in the two following chapters, the conspirators are destroyed and David's throne more firmly established. Mercy is always nearest when a man can in quietness possess his own soul. Salvation is at hand when a Christian comes to lay his hand upon his mouth. Mercy will be upon the wing, loving-kindness will ride post[1] to put an end to that man's troubles who sits silent in the day of his sorrows and sufferings. Ah, Christians! As you would have mercy near, as you would see to the end of your afflictions, as you would have deliverance come flying upon the wings of the wind, sit mute and silent under all your troubles. As wine was then nearest when the water-pots were filled with water, even to the brim; so when the heart is fullest of quietness and calmness, then is the wine of mercy, the wine of deliverance, nearest.

Consider the heinous & dangerous nature of murmuring.

The last motive to move you to silence under your greatest trials is this: seriously consider *the heinous and dangerous*

---

1. Hastily.—H&F.

nature of murmuring. Let me propose these following particulars for your most sober consideration.

Murmuring manifests a root of bitterness
to be strong in your soul.

First, consider that murmuring *manifests a root of bitterness to be strong in your soul,* Heb. 3:12.[1] Murmuring reveals sin in its power, corruption upon its throne, Heb. 12:1.[2] As holy silence argues true grace, much grace, yea, grace in its strength and in its lively vigor, so murmuring and muttering under the hand of God argues much sin, yea, a heart full of sin; it speaks out a heart full of self-love, Exo. 15:24 and 16:7-8; and full of slavish fears, Num. 13:32-33 and 14:1-3; and full of ignorance, Joh. 6:41-42; and full of pride and unbelief, "Yea, they despised the pleasant land," or "the land of desire"—there is their pride, and "they believed not in his Word"—there is their unbelief, Ps. 106:24-25.[3] What follows? They murmured in their tents and hearkened not unto the voice of God. They were sick of the sullens[4] and preferred Egypt before Canaan, a wilderness before a paradise. As in the first chaos there were the seeds of all creatures, so in the murmurer's heart there is not only the seeds of all sin, but a lively operation of all sin. Sin is become mighty in the hearts of murmurers, and none but an almighty God can root it out. Those roots of bitterness have so spread and strengthened themselves in the hearts of

---

1. "Looking diligently lest any man fail of the grace of God; lest any root of bitterness springing up trouble you, and thereby many be defiled," Heb. 12:15.—H&F.

2. It is the evidence of bitterness within and it is defiling according to the saying of Jesus, "Those things which proceed out of the mouth come forth from the heart; and they defile the man," Mat. 15:18.—H&F.

3. Unbelief is virtually all sin.

4. A morose gloomy temper.—H&F.

murmurers, that everlasting strength must put in,[1] or they will be undone forever, Isa. 26:4.[2] But,

The Holy Spirit has set a brand of infamy upon murmurers.

Consider *that the Holy Spirit has set a brand of infamy upon murmurers. He has stigmatized them for ungodly persons:* "To execute judgment upon all, and to convince all that are ungodly among them of all their ungodly deeds which they have ungodly committed, and of all their hard speeches which ungodly sinners have spoken against him," Jud. 15-16. But who are these ungodly sinners? "They are murmurers, complainers, walking after their own lusts, etc." ver. 16. When Christ comes to execute judgment upon ungodly ones, murmurers shall be set in the front, they shall experience the fierceness of his wrath and the greatness of his wrath. The front, you know, is first assaulted and most strongly assaulted. Christ will bend all his power and strength against murmurers; his little finger shall be heavier upon them than his hand shall be upon others; other sinners shall be chastised with whips, but ungodly murmurers shall be chastised with scorpions. If you can have joy in that black character of ungodly sinners, be murmurers still; if not, cease from murmuring. Where murmuring reigns and is in its dominion, there you may speak and inscribe that person ungodly. Let murmurers make what profession they will of godliness, yet if murmuring keeps the throne in their hearts, Christ will deal with them at last as ungodly sinners. A man may be denominated ungodly, as well from his murmuring, if he lives under the dominion of it, as from, his drunkenness, swearing, whoring, lying, stealing, etc. A murmurer is an ungodly man, he is an ungodlike man; there is no man on earth more unlike God than the murmurer; and therefore, no wonder if, when Christ comes to execute

---

1. Put forth the hand of action.—H&F.
2. "Trust ye in the Lord for ever: for in the Lord Jehovah is everlasting strength," Isa. 26:4.—H&F.

judgment, he deals so severely and terribly with him. In the wars of Tamberlain,[1] one having found a great pot of gold that was hid in the earth, he brought it to Tamberlain, who asked whether it had his father's stamp upon it? But when he saw that it had not his father's stamp, but the Roman stamp upon it, he would not own it, but cast it away. The Lord Jesus, when he shall come with all his saints to execute judgment, he will not own murmurers; nay, he will cast them away forever, because they have not his Father's stamp upon them. Ah, souls, souls! If you would not go up and down[2] this world with a badge of ungodliness upon you, take heed against murmuring.

Murmuring is a sin that breeds other sins.

Consider *that murmuring is the mother-sin; it is the mother of harlots, the mother of all abominations; a sin that breeds many other sins,* viz., disobedience, contempt, ingratitude, impatience, distrust, rebellion, cursing, carnality; yea, it charges God with folly, yea, with blasphemy, Num. 16:41 and 17:10. The language of a murmuring, a muttering soul is this, "Surely God might have done this sooner, and that wiser, and the other thing better, etc." As the river Nile brings forth many crocodiles, so murmuring is a sin that breeds and brings forth many sins at once. Murmuring is like the monster hydra; cut off one head and many will rise up in its place. Oh, therefore, bend all your strength against this mother-sin. As the king of Syria said to his captains, "Fight neither with small nor great, but with the king," so say I, "Fight not so much against this sin or that, but fight against your murmuring, which is a mother-sin." Make use of all your Christian armor, make use of all the ammunition of heaven to destroy the mother and in destroying her, you

---

1. Tamerlane.—G.
2. Walk upon.—H&F.

will destroy the daughters, Eph. 6:10-11.[1] When Goliath
was slain, the Philistines fled. When a general in an army
is cut off, the common soldiers are easily and quickly
routed and destroyed. So, destroy but murmuring and you
will quickly destroy disobedience, ingratitude, impatience,
distrust, etc. Oh, kill this mother-sin, that this may never
kill your soul. I have read of Sennacherib, that after his
army was destroyed by an angel, Isa. 37:36-37, and he
returned home to his own country, he inquired of one
about him, what he thought the reason might be why
God so favored the Jews? He answered that there was one
Abraham, their father, that was willing to sacrifice his son
to death at the command of God, and that, ever since that
time, God favored that people. "Well!" said Sennacherib, "if
that be so, I have two sons, and I will sacrifice them both
to death, if that will procure their God to favor me," which,
when his two sons heard, they, as the story goes, slew their
father, Isa. 37:38, choosing rather to kill than to be killed.
So do you choose rather to kill this mother-sin than to be
killed by it, or by any of those vipers that are brought forth
by it, Ps. 137:8-9.

Murmuring is a God-provoking sin.

Consider *that murmuring is a God-provoking sin; it is a sin
that provokes God not only to afflict, but did also provoke him
to destroy[2] a people:* "How long shall I bear with this evil
congregation which murmur against me? I have heard the
murmuring of the children of Israel, which they murmur

---

1. "Finally, my brethren, be strong in the Lord, and in the power of his
might. Put on the whole armour of God, that ye may be able to stand against
the wiles of the devil," Eph. 6:10-11.—H&F.
2. The reference is to the wasting away of the generation that came out
of Egypt, which generation perished in the wilderness for their murmuring
against God: "But your little ones, which ye said should be a prey, them will
I bring in, and they shall know the land which ye have despised. But as for
you, your carcasses, they shall fall in this wilderness. And your children shall
wander in the wilderness forty years, and bear your whoredoms, until your
carcasses be wasted in the wilderness," Num. 14:31-33.—H&F.

against me. Say unto them, As truly as I live, saith the Lord, as you have spoken in mine ears, so will I do to you. Your carcasses shall fall in this wilderness, and all that were numbered of you, according to your whole number, from twenty years old and upward, which have murmured against me," Num. 14:27-29. "Neither murmur ye, as some of them also murmured, and were destroyed of the destroyer," 1 Cor. 10:10. All our murmuring does but provoke the Lord to strike us and destroy us.

I have read of Caesar that, having prepared a great feast for his nobles and friends, it so fell out that the day appointed was extremely foul, that nothing could be done to the honor of their meeting; whereupon he was so displeased and enraged that he commanded all them that had bows to shoot up their arrows at Jupiter, their chief god, in defiance of him for that rainy weather; which, when they did, their arrows fell short of heaven, and fell upon their own heads so that many of them were very sorely wounded. So all our muttering and murmuring, which are as so many arrows shot at God himself—they will return upon our pates[1] and our hearts; they do not reach him, but they will hit us; they do not hurt him, but they will wound us. Therefore, it is better to be mute than to murmur; it is dangerous to provoke a consuming fire, Heb. 12:29.[2]

Murmuring is the devil's image, sin, & punishment.

Consider *that murmuring is the devil's image, sin, and punishment.*[3] Satan is still murmuring; he murmurs at every mercy that God bestows, at every dram of grace he gives, Job 1:8-10; he murmurs at every sin he pardons, and at every soul he saves. A soul cannot receive a favorable look from heaven, nor hear a good word from heaven, nor

---

1. Heads.—H&F.
2. "For our God is a consuming fire," Heb. 12:29.—H&F.
3. Irenaeus calls murmurers *ora diaboli*, "the devil's mouth."

receive a token of love from heaven, but Satan murmurs at it; he murmurs and mutters at every act of pitying grace, and at every act of preventing grace, and at every act of supporting grace, and at every act of strengthening grace, and at every act of comforting grace that God exercises towards poor souls; he murmurs at every sip, at every drop, at every crumb of mercy that God bestows. Cyprian, Aquinas, and others conceive that the cause of Satan's banishment from heaven was his grieving and murmuring at the dignity of man, whom he beheld made after God's own image, insomuch that he would relinquish his own glory to divest so noble a creature of perfection, and rather be in hell himself than see Adam placed in paradise.[1] But certainly, after his fall, murmuring and envy at man's innocency and felicity put him upon attempting to plunge man into the bottomless gulf of sin and misery; he knowing himself to be damned and lost forever, would necessarily try every way to make happy man eternally unhappy. Mr. Howell tells it as a strange thing, that a serpent was found in the heart of an Englishman when he was dead;[2] but, alas, this old serpent was by sad experience found to have too much power in the heart of Adam while alive and while in the height of all his glory and excellency. Murmuring is the first-born of the devil; and nothing renders a man

---

1. Such a fictional anecdote is unnecessary to prove the point here—it is the glory and dignity of God that was the original cause of Satan's jealous departure from God ("I will ascend, etc., I will be like the most High," Isa. 14:14); it is the dignity and godliness of the children of God that is a provocation to Satan, and it is the uncontroverted saving of men from Satan's kingdom and control that fuels his hatred toward them: for, God "hath delivered us from the power of darkness, and hath translated us into the kingdom of his dear Son," Col. 1:13. The actual cause of Satan's banishment from heaven we need not speculate upon as some undisclosed moment in history or unrevealed fact of the Christian religion: the accuser of the brethren was "cast out" upon the earth at the death of Jesus Christ (Joh. 12:31 & Rev. 12:8-9), for which it it is said, "Therefore rejoice, ye heavens, and ye that dwell in them. Woe to the inhabiters of the earth and of the sea! For the devil is come down unto you, having great wrath, because he knoweth that he hath but a short time," Rev. 12:12.—H&F.

2. In his *Epistolae Ho-Eliane*; or, Familiar Letters. 1650.—G.

more like to him than murmuring. Constantine's sons did not more resemble their father, nor Aristotle's scholars their master, nor Alexander's soldiers their general, than murmurers resemble Satan. And as murmuring is Satan's sin, so it is his punishment. God has given him up to a murmuring spirit; nothing pleases him and all things go against him; he is perpetually muttering and murmuring at persons or things. Now, oh what a dreadful thing is it to bear Satan's image upon us, and to be given up to the devil's punishment! It would be better not to be, than to be given up to murmuring. Therefore, cease from murmuring and sit mute under your sorest trials. But,

Murmuring is a mercy-souring sin.

Consider *that murmuring is a mercy-embittering sin, a mercy-souring sin;* as putting the sweetest things into a sour vessel, sours them, or putting them into a bitter vessel, embitters them. Murmuring puts gall and wormwood into every cup of mercy that God puts into our hands. As holy silence gives a sweet taste and a delightful relish to all a man's mercies, so murmuring embitters all. The murmurer can taste no sweetness in his sweetest morsels—every mercy, every morsel, tastes like the white of an egg to him. This mercy, says the murmurer, is not toothsome,[1] or that mercy is not wholesome; here is a mercy that lacks salt, and there is a mercy that lacks sauce. A murmurer can taste no sweet, can feel no comfort; he can take no delight in any mercy he enjoys. The murmurer writes *marah,* that is, bitterness, upon all his mercies, and he reads and tastes bitterness in all his mercies. All the murmurers grapes are grapes of gall, and all their clusters are bitter. As to "the hungry soul every bitter thing is sweet," Pro. 27:7, so to the murmuring soul every sweet thing is bitter. The mute Christian can suck sweetness from every mercy, but the murmurer cries out, "Oh, it is bitter! Oh, these breasts of mercy are dry!"

---

1. Palatable.—H&F.

Murmuring is a mercy-destroying sin.

Consider *that murmuring is a mercy-destroying sin, a mercy-murdering sin.* Murmuring cuts the throat of mercy; it stabs all our mercies at the heart; it sets all a man's mercies to bleeding about him at once: "Doubtless ye shall not come into the land concerning which I sware to make you dwell therein, save Caleb the son of Jephunneh, and Joshua the son of Nun." Num. 14:30. God promises them that they should possess the holy land upon the condition of their obedience. This condition they brake; and therefore God was not foresworn though he cut them off in the wilderness, and kept them out of Canaan, Deu. 31:16-17. But what is the sin that provokes the Lord to bar them out of the land of promise and to cut them off from all those mercies that they enjoyed, which entered into the holy land? Why, it was their murmuring; as you may see in Num. 14:1-3, 26-29: "I have heard the murmurings of the children of Israel, which they murmur against me." As you love your mercies, as you would have the sweetness of your mercies, and as you would enjoy a life of mercies, take heed of murmuring. Murmuring will bring a consumption upon your mercies; it is a worm that will make all your mercies wither. As there are some that love their mercies into the grave, and others that plot their mercies into the grave, so there are some that murmur their mercies into the grave. As you would have your mercies always fresh and green, smiling and thriving, as you would have your mercies to bed and board with you, to rise up and lie down with you, and in all conditions to attend you, murmur not, murmur not. The mute Christian's mercies are most sweet and most long-lived; the murmurer's mercies, like Jonah's gourd, will quickly wither. Murmuring has cut the throat of national mercies, of domestic mercies, and of personal mercies; and therefore, oh how men should flee from it as from a serpent, as from the avenger of blood, as from hell itself!

Murmuring unfits the soul for duty.

Consider *that murmuring unfits the soul for duty,* Num. 14. A murmurer can neither hear to profit, nor pray to profit, nor read to profit, nor meditate to profit. The murmurer is neither fit to do good nor receive good.[1] Murmuring unfits the soul for the performing of duties; it unfits the soul for delighting in duties; it unfits the soul for communion with God in duties. Murmuring fills the soul with cares, fears, distractions, vexations; all which unfits a man for duty, Num. 16. As a holy quietness and calmness of spirit prompts a man to duty, as it makes every duty easy and pleasant to the soul, Pro. 3:11-17; so it is murmuring that unhinges the soul and indisposes the soul, so that it takes off the chariot wheels of the soul, that the soul cannot look up to God, nor do for God, nor receive from God, nor wait on God, nor walk with God, nor act in faith upon God, etc. Ps. 90:9-15. Oh, therefore, as you would ever be in a blessed preparedness and a blessed fitness for duty, take heed of murmuring, and sit mute and silent under the afflicting hand of God. "I have learned, in whatsoever state I am, therewith to be content. I know both how to be abased, and I know how to abound: every where and in all things I am instructed both to be full and to be hungry, both to abound and to suffer need. I can do all things through Christ which strengtheneth me," Phi. 4:11-13.

Murmuring unmans a man.

Consider *that murmuring unmans a man;* it strips him of his reason and understanding; it makes him call evil good, and good evil; it puts light for darkness and darkness for light, bitter for sweet and sweet for bitter; it calls saviors destroyers and deliverers murderers, Isa. 5:18-20; as you

---

1. "Yea, they despised the pleasant land, they believed not his word: But murmured in their tents, and hearkened not unto the voice of the Lord," Ps. 106:24-25.—H&F.

see in the murmuring Israelites, Exo. 14-16. Murmuring uncrowns[1] a man. Murmuring strips a man of all his glory; it spoils all his excellency; it destroys the nobility of man; it speaks out that he is a base ignoble creature. Murmuring clouds a man's understanding; it perverts the judgment, it puts out the eye of reason, stupefies his conscience; it sours the heart, disorders the will, and distempers the affections; it be-beasts[2] a man, yea, it sets him below the beasts that perish;[3] for it would be better that he was a beast, than to be like a beast. The murmurer is the hieroglyphic of folly; he is a comprehensive vanity; he is a man and no man; he is sottish and senseless; he neither understands God nor himself nor anything as he should; he is the man that must be sent to school, to learn of the beasts of the field, and the birds of the air, and the creeping things of the earth, how to cease from murmuring, and how to be mute, Isa. 3:5-8. Ah, sirs, as you would have the name, the honor, the reputation of being men, I say men, take heed of murmuring and sit silent before the Lord.

Murmuring is a time destroying sin.

Murmuring is a time destroying sin. Ah, the precious time that is buried in the grave of murmuring? When the murmurer should be praying, he is murmuring against the Lord; when, he should be hearing, he is murmuring against the divine providence; when he should be reading, he is murmuring against instruments. The murmurer spends much precious time in musing; in musing how to get out of such a trouble, how to get off such a yoke, how to be rid of such a burden, how to revenge himself for such a wrong, how to supplant such a person, how to reproach

---

1. Dethrones.—H&F.
2. Makes him as a brute beast.—H&F.
3. So also the Scripture: Ps. 49:12, 20; Jud. 1:10; & "These, as natural brute beasts, made to be taken and destroyed, speak evil of the things that they understand not; and shall utterly perish in their own corruption," 2 Pet. 2:12.—H&F.

those that are above him, and how to affront those that are below him; and a thousand other ways murmurers have to expend that precious time that some would redeem with a world; as Queen Elizabeth on her deathbed cried out, "Time, time, a world of wealth for an inch of time."[1] The murmurer lavishly and profusely trifles away that precious time, that is his greatest interest in this world to redeem, Eph. 5:16.[2] Every day, every hour in the day, is a talent[3] of time and God expects the improvement of it and will charge the non-improvement of it upon you at last, Mat. 25:14-30 and 1 Pet. 4:1-3.[4] Caesar observing some ladies in Rome that spent much of their time in making much of little dogs and monkeys, asked them, whether the women in that country had no children to make much of?[5] Ah, murmurers, murmurers, you who by your murmuring trifle away so many godly hours and seasons of mercy. Have you no God to honor? Have you no Christ to believe in? Have you no hearts to change, no sins to be pardoned, no souls to save, no hell to escape, no heaven to seek after? Oh, if you have, why do you spend so much of your precious time in murmuring against God, against men, against this or that thing? Eternity rides upon the back of time. *Hoc est momentum*, "This is the moment": if it be well improved, you are made safe forever; if not, you are undone forever. *Aut malè, aut nihil, aut aliud agendo.*

I have read of Archias a Lacedaemonian, that while he

---

1. *Sumptus preciosissimus tempus:* "Time is of precious cost," says Theophrastus.
2. "See then that ye walk circumspectly, not as fools, but as wise, Redeeming the time, because the days are evil. Wherefore be ye not unwise, but understanding what the will of the Lord is," Eph. 5:15-17.—H&F.
3. A weight or a coin.—H&F.
4. Also: "Meditate upon these things; give thyself wholly to them; that thy profiting may appear to all, etc." 1 Tim. 4:13-16; "Take heed, brethren, lest there be in any of you an evil heart of unbelief, in departing from the living God. But exhort one another daily, while it is called Today; lest any of you be hardened through the deceitfulness of sin," Heb. 3:12-13.—H&F.
5. Plutarch in the life of *Pericles.*

was rioting and quaffing in the midst of his banqueting, one delivers him a letter, purposely to signify that there were some that lay in wait to take away his life, and withal desires him to read it instantly, because it was a serious business and matter of great concern to him. "Oh," said he, *"seria cras,"* "I will think of serious things tomorrow," but that night he was slain.[1] Ah, murmurer, cease from murmuring today, or else you may be forever undone by murmuring tomorrow. The old saying, *Nunc aut nunquam,* "Now or never," so say I, "Now or never, now or never give over murmuring," and let it swallow up no more of your precious time. What would not many a murmurer give for one of those days, yea, for one of those hours which he has trifled away in murmuring, when it is a day too late![2]

The Rabbins[3] glory in this conceit, that a man has so many bones as there be letters in the decalogue, and just so many joints and members as there be days in the year; to shew that all our strength and time should be expended in God's service. Ah, murmurers! You will gain more by one day's faithful serving of God, than ever you have gained by murmuring against God. But,

Of all men, Christians have least cause to be murmuring under any dispensation.

Consider this, Christians, *that of all men in the world, you have least cause, yea, no cause, to be murmuring and muttering under any dispensation that you meet with in this world.* Is not God your portion? Chrysostom propounds this question,

---

1. Plutarch.
2. "Today if ye will hear his voice, harden not your hearts, as in the provocation. For some, when they had heard, did provoke: howbeit not all that came out of Egypt by Moses. But with whom was he grieved forty years? Was it not with them that had sinned, whose carcases fell in the wilderness? And to whom sware he that they should not enter into his rest, but to them that believed not? So we see that they could not enter in because of unbelief," Heb. 3:15-19.—H&F.
3. Obsolete: Rabbis or Rabbinate.—H&F.

"Was Job miserable when he had lost all that God had given him?" And he gives this answer, "No, he had still that God that gave him all."[1] Is not Christ your treasurer? Is not heaven your inheritance? And will you murmur? Have you not much in hand and more in hope? Have you not much in possession, but much more in reversion;[2] and will you murmur? Has not God given you a changed heart, a renewed nature, and a sanctified soul; and will you murmur? Has he not given you himself to satisfy you,[3] his Son to save you, his Spirit to lead you, his grace to adorn you, his covenant to assure you, his mercy to pardon you, his righteousness to clothe you; and will you murmur?[4] Has he not made you a friend, a son, a brother, a bride, an heir; and will you murmur? Has not God often turned your water into wine, your brass into silver, and your silver into gold; and will you murmur? When you were dead, did he not quicken you; and when you were lost, did he not seek you; and when you were wounded, did he not heal you; and when you were falling, did he not support you; and when you were down, did he not raise you; and when you were staggering, did he not establish you; and when you were erring, did he not reduce[5] you; and when you were tempted, did he not succor you; and when you were in danger, did he

---

1. Lam. 3:24; Eph. 3:8; & 1 Pet. 3:4. Chrysostom, hom. 4, *de Patientia Jobi*.

2. In law, the returning of an estate to the heir.—H&F.

3. *Omne bonum in summo bono*, "God is all in all, and all without all."

4. "That we are in darkness and do not ourselves know what would be best for us; that God has made no earthly comforts full and lasting on purpose that Christians, seeing the vanity of all worldly enjoyments, may not desire to set up their rest here, but be obliged to think of another life where all tears will be wiped away; that God often punishes us in this world that he may not be obliged to punish us hereafter. It is thus a Christian may be taught to submit to God's dispensations and to make an advantage of what the world calls misfortunes, afflictions, calamities, judgements. And that instead of being impatient, fretful or dejected, he should rather rejoice in tribulation, in wrongs, in losses, in sufferings, and be glad that he has a proper occasion of offering his will as a sacrifice to the will of God, which is a most acceptable oblation." Thomas Wilson, Instructions for Ministers, *To Persons in Affliction*, 1708.—H&F.

5. Archaic, literally 'to bring back,' from Latin *re* and *ducere*, to lead again or lead back.—H&F.

not deliver you; and will you murmur? What! You that are so highly advanced and exalted above many thousands in the world? Murmuring is a black garment and it suits none so ill as saints.

Murmuring makes the life of man miserable.

Lastly, consider *that murmuring makes the life of man imperceptibly miserable.* Every murmurer is his own executioner. Murmuring vexes the heart; it wears and tears the heart, it enrages and inflames the heart, it wounds and stabs the heart. Every murmurer is his own martyr, every murmurer is a murderer; he kills many at once, viz., his joy, his comfort, his peace, his rest, his soul. No man is so inwardly miserable as the murmurer; no man has such inward gripes and griefs as he, such inward bitterness and heaviness as he, such inward contentions and combustions as he. Every murmurer is his own tormentor. Murmuring is a fire within that will burn up all, it is an earthquake within that will overturn all, it is a disease within that will infect all, it is a poison within that will prey upon all.

And thus I have finished with those motives that may persuade us not to murmur nor mutter, but to be mute and silent under the greatest afflictions, the saddest providences, and the sharpest trials that we meet with in this world.

❧ THE OBJECTIONS ❧

I shall now address myself to answer those objections and to remove those impediments which hinder poor souls from being silent and mute under the afflicting hand of God.

Objection 1.
"If I knew that I was afflicted in love, I would hold my peace under my affliction."

"Sir, did I but know that I was afflicted in love, I would hold my peace under my affliction, I would sit mute before the Lord; but oh, how shall I come to understand that these strokes are the strokes of love, that these wounds are the wounds of a friend?"

I answer:

If your heart be drawn out to the Lord by afflictions, then the afflictions are in love.

If your heart be more drawn out to the Lord by your afflictions, then the afflictions are in love. If they are so sanctified as that they draw out your soul to love the Lord more and to fear the Lord more, and to please the Lord more, and to cleave to the Lord more, and to wait on the Lord more, and to walk with the Lord more, then they are in love.[1] Oh, then

---

1. "Whatever be the ground of one's distress, it should drive him to, not from God." John Flavel, Keeping the Heart.—H&F.

they are the wounds of a friend indeed.[1] It is reported of the lioness, that she leaves her young whelps until they have almost killed themselves with roaring and yelling, and then at the last gasp, when they have almost spent themselves, she relieves them, and by this means they become more courageous; and so if the afflictions that are upon us do increase our courage, strengthen our patience, raise our faith, inflame our love, and enliven our hopes, certainly they are in love, and all our wounds are the wounds of a friend. But,

> *If you are more careful to glorify God & be kept from sinning under the affliction, than how to get out of it, then your affliction is in love.*

If you are more careful and studious how to glorify God in the affliction, and how to be kept from sinning under the affliction, than how to get out of the affliction, then certainly your affliction is in love, Dan. 3 and Heb. 11. Where God smites in love, there the soul makes it his study how to glorify God, and how to lift up God, and how to be a name and an honor to God. The daily language of such a soul under the rod is this: Lord, stand by me that I sin not, uphold me that I sin not, strengthen me that I sin not.[2] He that will not sin to repair and make up his losses, though he knew assuredly that the committing of such a sin would make up all again,[3] he may conclude that his affliction is in love.

---

1. Ps. 18:1-7, 116:1-8, 119:67-69; & Isa. 38:1, *seq.*
2. "Lord, I cry unto thee: make haste unto me; give ear unto my voice, when I cry unto thee. Let my prayer be set forth before thee as incense; and the lifting up of my hands as the evening sacrifice. Set a watch, Oh Lord, before my mouth; keep the door of my lips. Incline not my heart to any evil thing, to practise wicked works with men that work iniquity: and let me not eat of their dainties," Ps. 141:1-4.—H&F.
3. Ps. 15, 69:4-5, and "For this is thankworthy, if a man for conscience toward God endure grief, suffering wrongfully. For what glory is it, if, when ye be buffeted for your faults, ye shall take it patiently? But if, when ye do well, and suffer for it, ye take it patiently, this is acceptable with God," 1 Pet. 2:19-20.—H&F.

He that will not break the hedge of a fair command to avoid the foul way of some heavy affliction, may well conclude that his affliction is in love. Christians! What say you, when you are in the mount; do you thus address the Lord? "Lord, take care of your glory, and let me sink in my affliction rather than sin under my affliction." If this is the bent and frame of your heart, it is certain that the affliction that is upon you is in love. The primitive times afforded many such brave spirits, though this age affords but few.

If you enjoy the special presence of God with your spirit in your affliction, then your affliction is in love.

If you enjoy the special presence of God with your spirit in your affliction, then your affliction is in love, Ps. 23:4-6.[1] "When thou passest through the waters, I will be with thee; and through the rivers, they shall not overflow thee: when thou walkest through the fire, thou shalt not be burnt, neither shall the flames kindle upon thee," Isa. 43:2. Have you a special presence of God with your spirit, strengthening of that, quieting of that, stilling of that, satisfying of that, cheering and comforting of that? "In the multitude of my thoughts"—that is, of my troubled, intricate, ensnared, intertwined, and perplexed thoughts, as the branches of a tree by some strong wind are twisted one within another, as the Hebrew word properly signifies—"thy comforts delight my soul," Ps. 94:19. Here is a presence of God with his soul, here is comforts and delights that reach the soul, here is a cordial to strengthen the spirit. When all things went cross with Andronicus, the old emperor of Constantinople,[2] he took a Psalter into his hand and opening the same, he

---

1. "Yea, though I walk through the valley of the shadow of death, I will fear no evil: for thou art with me; thy rod and thy staff they comfort me. Thou preparest a table before me in the presence of mine enemies: thou anointest my head with oil; my cup runneth over. Surely goodness and mercy shall follow me all the days of my life: and I will dwell in the house of the Lord for ever," Ps. 23:4-6.—H&F.

2. [Richard] Knowlles' Turk. Hist. [1610.—G.]

lighted upon Ps. 68:14, "When the Almighty scattered kings, they shall be white as snow in Salmon"; which Scripture was a mighty comfort and refreshment to his spirit. Now you are to remember that Salmon signifies shady and dark; so was this mount, by the reason of many lofty fair-spread trees that were near it, but made lightsome[1] by snow that covered it. So that to be white as snow in Salmon, is to have joy in affliction, light in darkness, mercy in misery, etc. And thus God was to the Psalmist as snow in Salmon in the midst of his greatest afflictions. When Paul would wish his dear son Timothy the best mercy in all the world, the greatest mercy in all the world, the most comprehensive mercy in all the world, a mercy that carries the virtue, value, and sweetness of all mercies in it, he wishes the presence of God with his spirit: "The Lord Jesus Christ be with thy spirit," 2 Tim. 4:22, in point of honor, in point of profit and pleasure, in point of safety and security, and in point of comfort and joy; it is the greatest blessing and happiness in this world to have the presence of God with our spirits, especially in times of trials: "For which cause we faint not; but though our outward man perish, yet the inward man is renewed day by day," 2 Cor. 4:16. By the "outward man," you are to understand not merely our bodies, but our persons, estates, and outward condition in this world; and by the "inward man," you are to understand our souls, our persons considered according to our spiritual estate. Now, when the inward man gains new strength by every new trouble, when as troubles, pressures, afflictions, and tribulations are increased, a Christian's inward strength is increased also, then his afflictions are in love. When the presence of God is with our inward man, cheering, comforting, encouraging, strengthening, and renewing of that, we may safely conclude that all these trials, though they are never so sharp and smart, yet they are in love.

---

1. Luminous.—H&F.

I have read of a company of poor Christians that were banished into some remote parts, and one standing by, seeing them pass along, said that it was a very sad condition those poor people were in, to be thus hurried from the society of men and to be made companions with the beasts of the field. True, said another, it was a sad condition indeed if they were carried to a place where they should not find their God; but let them be of good cheer, God goes along with them and will exhibit the comforts of his presence wherever they go. The presence of God with the spirits of his people is a well of comfort that can never be drawn dry; an everlasting spring that will never fail, Heb. 13:5-6. Well, Christian, you are under many great troubles, many sore trials: but tell me, does God give unto your soul such cordials, such supports, such comforts, and such refreshments, that the world knows not of? Oh, then, certainly your affliction is in love.

If by your affliction you are made more conformable
to Christ, then your afflictions are in love.

If by your affliction you are made more conformable to Christ in his virtues, then certainly your afflictions are in love. Many are conformable to Christ in their sufferings, that are not made conformable to Christ in his virtues by their sufferings;[1] many are in poverty, neglect, shame, contempt, reproach, etc., like to Christ, who yet by these are not made more like to Christ in his meekness, humbleness, heavenliness, holiness, righteousness, faithfulness, fruitfulness, goodness, contentedness, patience, submission, subjection.[2] Oh, but if in these things you are made more like to Christ, without all peradventure your afflictions are in love. If by afflictions the soul be led to show forth or to preach the virtues of

---

1. "And though I bestow all my goods to feed the poor, and though I give my body to be burned, and have not charity, it profiteth me nothing," 1 Cor. 13:3.—H&F.
2. Witness Judas, Demas, and those in the sixth chapter of John, and many Quakers and other deluded people amongst us at this day.

Christ, as the word imports in 1 Pet. 2:9,[1] then certainly those afflictions are in love; for they never have such an operation but where they are set on by a hand of love. When God strikes as an enemy, then all those strokes do but make a man more an enemy to God, as you see in Pharaoh and others; but when the strokes of God are the strokes of love, oh, then they do but bring the soul nearer to Christ and transform the soul more and more into the likeness of Christ, Isa. 26:8-10. If by your afflictions you are made more holy, humble, heavenly, etc., they are in love. Every afflicted Christian should strive to be honored with that eulogy of Salvian, *Singularis domini praeclarus imitator,* "An excellent disciple of a singular master." But,

If by outward afflictions your soul is brought
more under the inward teachings of God,
doubtless your afflictions are in love.

If by outward afflictions your soul is brought more under the inward teachings of God, doubtless your afflictions are in love: "The blueness of a wound cleanseth away evil: so do stripes the inward parts of the belly," Pro. 20:30. "Blessed is the man whom thou chastenest, Oh Lord, and teachest him out of thy law," Ps. 94:12.[2] All the chastening in the world, without divine teaching, will never make a man blessed; that man that finds correction attended with instruction and lashing with lessoning, is a happy man. "Before I was afflicted I went astray: but now have I kept thy Word," Ps. 119:67. If God, by the affliction that is upon you, shall teach you how to loathe sin more, how to trample upon the world more, and how to walk with God more, your afflictions are in love. If God shall teach you by afflictions how to die to sin more, and how to die to your relations more, and how to die to your self-interest more, your afflictions are in love. If God shall teach you by afflictions how to live to

---

1. *Exangeilete,* publicly to set forth.
2. Also 2 Sam. 24, Ps. 19 and 51.—H&F.

Christ more, how to lift up Christ more, and how to long for Christ more, your afflictions are in love. If God shall teach you by afflictions to get assurance of a better life, and to be still in a gracious readiness and preparedness for the day of your death, your afflictions are in love. If God shall teach you by afflictions how to mind heaven more, how to live in heaven more, and how to be fitted for heaven more, your afflictions are in love. If God by afflictions shall teach your proud heart how to lie more low, and your hard heart how to grow more humble, and your censorious heart how to grow more charitable, and your carnal heart how to grow more spiritual, and your froward heart how to grow more quiet, etc., your afflictions are in love. When God teaches your reins as well as your brains, your heart as well as your head, these lessons, or any of these lessons, your afflictions are in love. Pambo, an illiterate dunce, as the historian terms him, was learning that one lesson, "I said I will take heed to my ways that I sin not with my tongue," and yet, after nineteen years had not learned it.[1] Ah, it is to be feared that there are many who have been in the school of affliction more than nineteen years and yet have not learned any saving lesson all this while. Surely their afflictions are not in love but in wrath. Where God loves, he afflicts in love, and wherever God afflicts in love, there he will, first or last, teach such souls such lessons as shall do them good to all eternity. But,

If God suit your burdens to your backs,
your afflictions are in love.

If God suit your burdens to your backs, your trials to your strength, according to that golden promise, your afflictions are in love: "There hath no temptation taken you, but such as is common to man: but God is faithful, who will not suffer you to be tempted above what ye are able; but will with the temptation also make a way to escape, that ye may be

---

1.　Socrates, l. ii. c. 18.

able to bear it," 1 Cor. 10:13. When God's strokes and a Christian's strength are suited one to another, all is in love. "I will correct thee in measure, and will not leave thee altogether unpunished, etc." Jer. 30:11 and 46:28. Let the load be never so heavy that God lays on, if he put under[1] his everlasting arms, all is in love, Gen. 49:23-24. As Egypt had many venomous creatures, so it had many antidotes against them. When God shall lay antidotes into the soul against all the afflictions that befall a Christian, then they are all in love. It is no matter how heavy the burden is, if God gives a shoulder to bear it: all is in love; it is no matter how bitter the cup is, if God give courage to drink it; it is no matter how hot the furnace is, if God gives power to walk in the midst of it: all is in love.

If you are willing to remain in the furnace until your dross is consumed & the cure is wrought, all is in love.

If you are willing to remain in the furnace until your dross is consumed; if you are willing that the plaster should remain on, though it smarts, until the cure is wrought; if you are willing that the physic should work, though it makes you sick, until the humors be driven out; all is in love: "But he knoweth the way that I take: when he hath tried me, I shall come forth as gold," Job 23:10. "I will bear the indignation of the Lord, because I have sinned against him, until he plead my cause, and execute judgment for me: he will bring me forth to the light, and I shall behold his righteousness," Mic. 7:9. Cain and Saul, and Pharaoh, were all for the removing of the stroke, the affliction, but they do not cry out, "Our sins are greater than we are able to bear"; but they cry out, "Our punishment is greater than we are able to bear"; they cry not out, "Lord, take away our sins," but "Lord, remove the

---

1. Lend strength from; as in the verse sited: "the arms of his hands were made strong by the hands of the mighty God of Jacob," Gen. 49:24.—H&F.

stroke of your hand."[1] Oh, but when an affliction comes in love upon a soul, the language of that soul is this: "Lord, remove the cause rather than the effect, the sin rather than the punishment, my corruption rather than my affliction. Lord, what will it avail me to have the sore healed over if corruption still remain within? There is no evil, Lord, to the evil of sin; and therefore deliver me rather from the evil of sin than the evil of suffering. I know, Lord, that affliction cannot be so displeasing to me as sin is dishonorable and displeasing to you; and therefore, Lord, let me see an end of my sin, though in this world I should never see an end of my sorrows; oh, let me see an end of my corruptions, though I should never see an end of my corrections; Lord, I had rather have a cure for my heart than a cure for my head, I had rather be made whole and sound within than without, I had rather have a healthy soul than a healthy body, a pure inside than a beautiful outside." If this be the settled frame and temper of your spirit, certainly your afflictions are in love.

There was one who, being under exceeding great pains and torments in his body, occasioned by many sore diseases that were upon him, cried out, "Had I all the world I would give it for ease, and yet for all the world I would not have ease until the cure is wrought." Surely his afflictions were in love. The first request, the great request, and the last request of a soul afflicted in love, is, "A cure, Lord! A cure, Lord! A cure, Lord, of this wretched heart and this sinful life and all will be well, all will be well."

If you live a life of faith in afflictions,
then your afflictions are in love.

Lastly, *if you live a life of faith in your afflictions, then your afflictions are in love.* Now, what is it to live by faith in

---

1. "And Cain said unto the Lord, My punishment is greater than I can bear," Gen. 4:13. 1 Sam. 15:24-26; Exo. 7-10; also Heb. 12:15-17 and Act. 8:18-24.

affliction, but to live in the exercising of faith upon those precious promises that are made respecting an afflicted condition?[1] God has promised to be with his people in their afflictions, "When thou passest through the waters, I will be with thee; and through the rivers, they shall not overflow thee, etc." Isa. 43:2-3. He has promised to support them under their affliction, "Fear thou not; for I am with thee: be not dismayed; for I am thy God: I will strengthen thee; yea, I will help thee; yea, I will uphold thee with the right hand of my righteousness," Isa. 41:10. He has promised to deliver his people out of their afflictions, "Offer unto God thanksgiving; and pay thy vows unto the most High: And call upon me in the day of trouble: I will deliver thee, and thou shalt glorify me," Ps. 50:15. He has promised to purge away his people's sins by affliction, "And I will turn my hand upon thee, and purely purge away thy dross, and take away all thy tin," Isa. 1:25. He has promised to make his people more partakers of his holiness by affliction, "They verily for a few days chastened us after their own pleasure; but he for our profit, that we might be partakers of his holiness," Heb. 12:10. He has promised to make affliction an inlet to a more full and sweet enjoyment of himself, "I will have mercy upon her that had not obtained mercy; and I will say to them which were not my people, Thou art my people; and they shall say, Thou art my God, etc." Hos. 2:14-23. He has promised that he will never leave nor forsake his people in their afflictions, Heb. 13:5-6; he has promised that all their afflictions shall work for their good, Zec. 13:9 and Rom. 8:28.[2] Now if your faith is enlarged to feed upon

---

1. These following promises have been choice cordials to many Christians under sore distresses: "Thou wilt keep him in perfect peace, whose mind is stayed on thee: because he trusteth in thee." Isa. 26:3 "For thus saith the high and lofty One that inhabiteth eternity, whose name is Holy; I dwell in the high and holy place, with him also that is of a contrite and humble spirit, to revive the spirit of the humble, and to revive the heart of the contrite ones." Isa. 57:15. Also: 1 Tim. 1:15; Joh. 10:27-29; Mat. 11:28-30; & 1 Joh. 3:14.

2. "We know that all things work together for good to them that love God, to them who are the called according to his purpose." Rom. 8:28.

these promises, if these are heavenly manna to your faith and your soul lives upon them and draws strength and sweetness from them, under all the trials and troubles that are upon you, your afflictions are in love.

If your faith can extract comfort and sweetness out of these precious promises in your saddest distresses, and gather one contrary out of another, "honey out of the rock, and oil out of the flinty rock," Deu. 32:13, your afflictions are in love. The promises are abundant and God delights that faith should draw upon them; they are *pabulum fidei, et anima fidei,* "the food of faith, and the very soul of faith"; they are an everlasting spring that can never be drawn dry; they are an inexhaustible treasure that can never be exhausted; they are a garden of paradise, and full of such choice flowers that will never fade but always be fresh, sweet, green, and flourishing; and if, in the day of affliction, they prove thus to your soul, your afflictions are in love. Sertorius[1] paid what he promised with fair words, but God does not. Men many times disown their words, but God will never disown his; for all his promises in Christ are "yea and in him Amen," 2 Cor. 1:20. Has he spoken it, and shall it not come to pass? If in all your troubles your heart be drawn out to act in faith upon the promises, your troubles are from love.

Objection 2.
"But the Lord has smitten me in my dearest comforts, and how then can I hold my peace?"

"Oh, but, sir! The Lord has smitten me in my nearest and dearest comforts and contentments, and how then can I hold my peace? God has taken away a husband, a wife, a child, an only child, a bosom-friend, and how then can I be silent?"

To this I answer:

---

1. Plutarch, *Sertorius.*—G.

*If God did not strike you in that which was
dear to you, it would not be an affliction.*

*If God did not strike you in that mercy which was near and
dear unto you, it would not amount to an affliction.* That is
not worthy of the name of an affliction that does not strike
at some bosom mercy; that trouble is no trouble that does
not touch some choice contentment; that storm is no storm
that only blows off the leaves, but never hurts the fruit;
that thrust of a weapon is no thrust that only touches the
clothes, but never strikes the skin; that cut is no cut that
only cuts the cap, but never touches the head; neither is
that affliction any affliction that only reaches some remote
enjoyment, but never reaches a Joseph, a Benjamin, etc.

The best mercy is not too good for God.

The best mercy is not too good for the great God. The best of
the best is not good enough for him who is goodness itself;
the best child, the best yoke-fellow, the best friend, the best
jewel in all your crown must be readily resigned to your
God. There is no mercy, no enjoyment, no contentment
worthy of God, but the best. The milk of mercy is for
others, the cream of mercy is due to God. The choicest, the
fairest, and the sweetest flowers are fittest for the bosom of
God; if he will take the best flower in all the garden and
plant it in a better soil have you any cause to murmur? Will
you not hold your peace?

*Your nearest & dearest mercies were the
Lord's before they were yours.*

*Your nearest and dearest mercies were the Lord's first before they
were yours, and they are always the Lord's more than they were
yours.* When God bestows a mercy, he does not relinquish
his own right in that mercy: "All things come of thee, and of
thine own have we given thee," 1 Chr. 29:14. The sweetness
of the mercy is yours, but the sovereign right to dispose of

your mercies is the Lord's. *Quicquid es, debes creanti; quicquid potes, debes redimenti,*[1] "Whatsoever you are, you owe to him that made you; and whatsoever you have, you owe to him that redeemed you." You say it is but just and reasonable that men should do with their own as they please, and is it not just and reasonable that God, who is the highest Lord, should do with his own as he pleases? Do you believe that the great God may do in heaven what he pleases? And on the seas what he pleases? And in the nations and kingdoms of the world what he pleases? And in your heart what he pleases? And do you not believe that God may do in your house what he pleases, and do with your mercies what he pleases? "Behold, he taketh away"—he snatches away, it may be a husband, a wife, a child, an estate—"who can hinder him? Who will say unto him, what doest thou?"[2] Job 9:12. Who dares cavil against God? Who dares question that God that is unquestionable, that chief Lord that is uncontrollable, and who may do with his own what he pleases? "And all the inhabitants of the earth are reputed as nothing: and he doeth according to his will in the army of heaven, and among the inhabitants of the earth; and none can stay his hand, or say unto him, What doest thou?" Dan. 4:35.[3] Where is the prince, the peasant, the master, the servant, the husband, the wife, the father, the child, that dares say to God, "What doest thou?" Isa. 45:9.[4] In matters of arithmetical accounts, set one against ten, ten against a hundred, a hundred against a thousand, a thousand against

---

1. Bernard.

2. Job plainly alludes to God's taking away his children, servants, and cattle.

3. These are the words spoken by Nebuchadnezzar after that time during which he was driven from his kingdom, when his reason had again returned to him. He lifted up his eyes and "blessed the most High" and honored him "whose dominion is everlasting," for at that moment he came to know "that the most High ruleth in the kingdom of men, and giveth it to whomsoever he will," Dan. 4.—H&F.

4. "Woe unto him that striveth with his Maker! Let the potsherd strive with the potsherds of the earth. Shall the clay say to him that fashioneth it, What makest thou? Or thy work, He hath no hands?" Isa. 45:9.

ten thousand, although there be great odds, yet there is some comparison; but if a man could set down an infinite number, then there could be no comparison at all because the one is infinite, the other finite; so set all the princes and powers of the earth in opposition to God, but they shall never be able to withstand him. It was once the saying of Pompey that with one stamp of his foot he could raise all Italy in arms;[1] but let the great God but stamp with his foot and he can raise all the world in arms to own him, to contend for him, or to revenge any affronts that are put by any upon him. Therefore who shall say unto him, "What doest thou?" Water is stronger than earth, fire stronger than water, angels stronger than men, and God stronger than them all; and therefore who shall say unto God, "What doest thou?" when he takes their nearest and their dearest mercies from them? But,

It may be you have not made an improvement
of your nearest & dearest mercies.

It may be you have not made a happy improvement of your nearest and dearest mercies while you enjoyed them. You have been taken with your mercies, but your heart has not been taken up in the improvement of them. There are many who are very much taken with their mercies, who make no conscience of improving their mercies. Have your nearest and dearest mercies been a star to lead you to Christ? Have they been a cloud by day and a pillar of light by night to lead you towards the heavenly Canaan? Have they been a Jacob's ladder to your soul? Have you been provoked by them to give up yourself to God as "a living sacrifice?" Rom. 12:1. Have you improved your nearest and dearest mercies to the inflaming of your love to God, to the strengthening of your confidence in God, to the raising of your communion with God, and to the engaging of your heart to a more close and circumspect walking before God,

---

1. Plutarch *in vita Pompeii.*

etc.? If you have not thus improved them, you have even more cause to be mute than to murmur; to be silent than to be impatient, to fall out with yourself rather than to fall out with your God. Children and fools are taken with many things, but improve nothing. Such children and fools are most men; they are much taken with their mercies, but they make no improvement of their mercies, and therefore no wonder if God strip them of their mercies. The candle of mercy is not set up to play by but to work by.

Pliny speaks of one Cressinus,[1] who improved a little piece of ground to a far greater advantage than his neighbors could a greater quantity of land. Thereupon he was accused of witchcraft; but he, to defend himself, brought into the court his servants and their working tools and said, *Veneficia mea, Quirites, haec sunt,* "These are my witchcrafts," "Oh you Romans; these servants, and these working tools are all the witchcraft that I know of." When the people heard this plea, with one consent they acquitted him and declared him not guilty; and so his little piece of ground was secured to him. There is no way to secure your mercies but by the improving of them; there is nothing that provokes God to strip you of your mercies like the non-improvement of them: "Take therefore the talent from him, and give it unto him which hath ten talents, etc." Mat. 25:28-29. By some stroke or other God will take away the mercy that is not improved. If your slothfulness has put God upon passing a sentence of death upon your dearest mercy, thank yourself and hold your peace.

> *If God had made you a precedent to others, you must hold your peace; how much more when God has made others a precedent to you!*

If, in this case, God had made you a precedent to others, you would have to have held your peace; how much more then should

---

1. C. Furius Chresimus, Pliny, Lib. xviii. c. 8.

you be mute when God has made many others a precedent to you!
Did not God smite Aaron in his dear and near enjoyments,
Lev. 10:1-2, and does he not hold his peace? Did not God
smite David in his Absalom, and Abraham in his Sarah, and
Job in his sons, daughters, estate, and body, and Jonah in his
gourd? Are you more beloved than these? No. Have you
more grace than these? No. Have you done more for divine
glory than these? No. Are you richer in spiritual experiences
than these? No. Have you attained to higher enjoyments
than these? No. Have you been more serviceable in your
generation than these? No. Have you been more exemplary
in your life and conversation than these, etc.? No. Then why
should you murmur and fret at that which has been the
common lot of the dearest saints?

Though God has smitten you in this or that near and dear
enjoyment, it is your wisdom to hold your peace, for that
God that has taken away one, might have taken away all.
Justice writes a sentence of death upon all Job's mercies at
once, and yet he holds his peace, Job 1; and will you not
hold yours, though God has cropped the fairest flower in all
your garden?

Anytus, a young spark of Athens,[1] came revelling into
Alcibiades' house; and as he sat at supper with some
strangers, he arose suddenly and took away one half of
his place.[2] Thereupon the guests stormed. He bade them
be quiet and told them that he had dealt kindly with him,
since he had left the one half, whereas he might have taken
all. So when our hearts begin to storm and take on when
God smites us in this nearest mercy and in that dearest
enjoyment, oh let us lay the law of silence upon our hearts!
Let us charge our souls to be quiet! For that God that has
taken away one, might have taken away all; and he that has

---

1. The foremost of the accusers of Socrates, and the infamous friend of
Alcibiades. Cf. Plato and Plutarch, *sub nomine*.—G.
2. 'Plate'—Ed.

taken away one friend, might have taken away every friend; and he that has taken away a part of your estate, might have taken away your whole estate. Therefore hold your peace; let others murmur, but you be mute.

> *It may be that your sins have been much about*
> *your nearest & dearest enjoyments.*

It may be that your sins have been much about your nearest and dearest enjoyments. It may be that you have over-loved them, and over-prized them, and over-much delighted yourself in them; it may be that they have often had your heart when they should have had but your hand; it may be that care, that fear, that confidence, that joy that should have been expended upon more noble objects, has been expended upon them. Your heart, oh Christian, is Christ's, and it may be that you have embraced your mercies as more dear to you and Christ has been put out; you have had room for them, when you have had none for him; they have had the best, when the worst have been counted good enough for Christ. Ah! How often has one creature comfort and sometimes another come between Christ and your souls! How often have your dearest enjoyments displaced Christ! May it not be said of your nearest and dearest mercies, that they have taken Christ's place in your hearts; that place wherein Christ delights to rest and repose himself. Now, if a husband, a child, a friend shall take up that room in your soul that is proper and peculiar to God, God will either embitter it, remove it, or be the death of it. If once the love of a wife runs out more to a servant than to her husband, the master will turn him out of doors, though otherwise he is a servant worth gold. The sweetest comforts of this life are like treasures of snow: do but take a handful of snow in your hands and it will soon melt away, but if you let it abide in its proper place, it will continue for some time. And so it is with the contentments of this world; if you grasp them in your hands and lay them too near your hearts, they will quickly melt and vanish away; but if you will not hold them too fast in your hands, nor lay them too close to your hearts, they will abide longer with you. There are those that love their mercies into their graves, that hug their mercies to death, that kiss them until they kill them. Many a man has slain his mercies, by setting too great a value upon them; many a man has sunk his ship of mercy, by taking up in it; over-loved mercies are seldom long lived: "Thus saith the Lord God; Behold, I will profane my sanctuary, the excellency of your strength, the desire of your eyes, and that which your soul pitieth, etc. When I take from them the joy of their glory, the desire of their eyes, and that whereupon they set their minds," Eze. 24:21, 25. The way to lose your mercies is to indulge them; the way to destroy them is to fix your minds and hearts upon them. You may write bitterness and death upon that mercy first that has first taken away your heart from God. Now, if God has stripped you of that very mercy with which you have often committed spiritual adultery and idolatry, have you any cause to murmur? Have you not cause rather to hold your peace and to be mute before the Lord? Christians, your hearts are Christ's royal throne and on this throne Christ will be chief and he will endure no competitor. If you shall attempt to enthrone the creature, be it never so near and dear unto you, Christ will dethrone it, he will destroy its comeliness; he will quickly lay them in a bed of dust who shall aspire to his royal throne. But,

> *You have no cause to murmur because of*
> *the loss of such enjoyments, considering the*
> *spiritual mercies that you still enjoy.*

You have no cause to murmur because of the loss of such near and dear enjoyments, considering those more noble and spiritual mercies and favors that you still enjoy. Grant that Joseph is not, and Benjamin is not, Gen. 42:36, yet Jesus is; he is "the same yesterday, and today, and the same forever," Heb. 13:8; your union and communion with Christ remains and the immortal seed abides in you still, "Everyone who has been begotten of God does not sin, because His seed abides in him, and he is not able to sin, because he has been born of God," 1 Joh. 3:9; the Sun of righteousness shines upon you still; you are in favor with God still, and you are under the anointing of the Spirit still, and under the influences of heaven still, etc.; and why then should you mutter and not rather hold your peace? I have read of one Didymus, a godly preacher, who was blind; Alexander, a godly man, once asked him, whether he was not sore troubled and afflicted for want of his sight? "Oh yes!" said Didymus, "it is a great affliction and grief unto me." Then Alexander chided him, saying, "Has God given you the excellency of an angel, of an Apostle, and are you troubled for that which rats and mice and brute beasts have?"[1] So say I. Ah, Christians, has God blessed you with "all spiritual blessings in heavenly places," Eph.1:3-4? Has the Lord given you himself for a portion? Has he given you his Son for your redemption and his Spirit for your instruction; and will you murmur? Has he given his grace to adorn you, his promises to comfort you, his ordinances to better you, and the hopes of heaven to encourage you; and will you mutter? Paulinus Nolanus,[2] when his city was taken from him, prayed thus: "Lord!" said he, "let me not be troubled at the loss of my gold, silver, honor, etc., for you are all, and much more than all these to me." In the want of all your sweetest enjoyments, Christ will be all in all unto you. "My jewels are my husband," said Phocion's wife;[3] my ornaments are my two sons, said the mother of the Gracchi; my treasures are my friends, said Constantius; and so may a Christian under his greatest losses say, Christ is my richest jewels, my chiefest treasures, my best ornaments, my sweetest delights. Look what all these things are to a carnal heart, a worldly heart, that and more is Christ to me.

---

1. Jerome.
2. Paulinus of Nola.—G.
3. Plutarch *in vita* Phocion.

> *If, by smiting you in your dearest enjoyments,*
> *God shall put you to mortifying your dearest*
> *sins, you have no cause to murmur.*

If God, by smiting you in your nearest and dearest enjoyments,
shall put you to a more thorough smiting and mortifying of your
dearest sins, you have no cause to murmur. God cures David of
adultery by taking his beloved child. There is some Delilah,
some darling, some beloved sin or other, that a Christian's
calling, condition, constitution, or temptations leads him
to entertain withal and to embrace in his own bosom,
rather than some other. As in a piece of ground that lies
untilled, among the great variety of weeds found growing
there, there is usually some master-weed that is more
rife and more rank than all the rest; and so it is in a man,
that although in some degree or other, more or less, there
is a mixture of elements and not any is wholly wanting,
yet there is some one that is predominant and gives the
denomination to the man's constitution. In this regard,
some are said to be of a sanguine, some of a phlegmatic,[1]
some of a choleric,[2] and some of a melancholy constitution.
So it is also in the souls of men: though there be a general
mixture and medley of all evil and corrupt qualities, yet
there is usually some one that is paramount, which, like the
prince of devils, is most powerful and prevalent, that sways
and shows forth itself more eminently and evidently than
any other of them do. And as in every man's body there is a
seed and principle of death, yet in some there is a proneness
to one kind of disease more than another that may hasten
death. So, though the root of sin and bitterness has spread
itself over all, yet every man has his inclination to one kind
of sin over another, and this may be called a man's particular
sin, his bosom-sin, his darling sin. Now, it is one of the
hardest works in this world to subdue and bring under this
bosom-sin. Oh, the prayers, the tears, the sighs, the sobs,

---

1. Dull; not easily excited.—H&F.
2. Easily irritated and excited.—H&F.

the groans, the gripes that it will cost a Christian before he brings under this darling sin!

So it is in the mortifying, in the crucifying of sin; a man may easily subdue and mortify such and such sins, but when it comes to the head-sin, to the master-sin, to the bosom-sin, oh, what tugging and pulling is there, what striving and struggling is there to be rid of that sin, to put down that sin! Now, if the Lord, by smiting you in some near and dear enjoyment, shall bring your heart to the smiting of your master-sin, and shall so sanctify the affliction as to make it a channel to the mortification of your bosom corruption, what eminent cause will you have rather to bless him, than to sit down and murmur against him! And doubtless if you are dear to God, God will, by striking your dearest mercy, put you upon striking at your darling sin. Therefore hold your peace, even when God touches the apple of your eye.

The Lord has many ways to make up the
loss of a near & dear mercy to you.

Consider *that the Lord has many ways to make up the loss of a near and dear mercy to you;* he can make up your loss in something else that may be better for you, and he will certainly make up your loss, either in kind or in worth: "Everyone that hath forsaken houses, or brethren, or sisters, or father, or mother, or wife, or children, or lands, for my name's sake, shall receive an hundredfold, and shall inherit everlasting life," Mat. 19:29. He took from David an Absalom and he gave him a Solomon; he took from him a Michal and gave him a wise Abigail; he took from Job seven sons and three daughters and afterwards he gives him seven sons and three daughters; he took from Job a fair estate and at last doubled it to him; he removed the bodily presence of Christ from his disciples, but gave them more abundantly of his spiritual presence, which was by far the greater and the sweeter mercy: "It is expedient for you that I go away: for if I go not away, the Comforter will not come unto you; but if I depart, I will send him unto you, etc." Joh. 16:7-11. If Moses is taken away, Joshua shall be raised in his place;[1] if David be gathered to his fathers, a Solomon shall succeed him in his throne; if John be cast into prison, rather than the pulpit standing empty, a greater than John, even Christ himself, will begin to preach. In the loss of creature comforts, he that lives upon God shall find all made up in the God of comforts; he shall be able to say, "Though my child is not, my friend is not, my yoke-fellow is not, yet my God liveth," and "blessed be my rock; and let the God of my salvation be exalted," Ps. 18:46. Though this mercy is not, and that mercy is not, yet covenant-mercies, yet "the sure mercies of David" continue, Isa. 59:3;[2] these bed and board with me, these will go to the grave and to glory with me. I have read of a godly man, who, living near a philosopher, did often attempt to persuade him to become a Christian. "Oh! But," said the philosopher, "I must, or may, lose all for Christ," to which the good man replied, "If you lose anything for Christ, he will be sure to repay it a hundredfold." "Yes, but," said the philosopher, "will you be bound for Christ, that if he does not pay me, you will?" "Yes, that I will," said the good man. So the philosopher became a Christian and the good man entered into bond for performance of the covenants. Some time after it happened that the philosopher fell sick on his deathbed and, holding the bond in his hand, sent for the party engaged, to whom he gave up the bond and said, "Christ has paid all, there is nothing for you to pay, take your bond and cancel it." Christ will suffer none of his children to go by[3] the loss; he has all and he will make up all to them. In the end, Christ will pay

---

1. "And the Lord said unto Moses, Take thee Joshua the son of Nun, a man in whom is the spirit, and lay thine hand upon him; And set him before Eleazar the priest, and before all the congregation; and give him a charge in their sight," Num. 27:18-23.—H&F.

2. "Incline your ear, and come unto me: hear, and your soul shall live; and I will make an everlasting covenant with you, even the sure mercies of David," Isa. 55:3.—H&F.

3. To incur.—H&F.

the reckoning. No man shall ever have cause to say that he has been a loser by Christ. And, therefore, you have much cause to be mute, you have no cause to murmur, though God has snatched the fairest and the sweetest flower out of your bosom.

How can you tell if that which you call a dear mercy, might have proved the greatest cross?

How can you tell if that which you call a near and dear mercy, if it had been allowed to continue longer, might have proved to you the greatest cross, the greatest calamity and misery that you ever met with in this world?[1] Our mercies, like choice wines, many times turn into vinegar; our fairest hopes are often blasted; and that very mercy which we sometimes have said should be a staff to support us, has proved a sword to pierce us. How often have our most flourishing mercies withered in our hands, and our bosom contentments been turned into gall and wormwood! Many parents who have sought the lives of their children with tears, have lived afterwards to see them take such courses and come to such dismal ends as have brought their grey head with sorrow to their graves.[2] Well, Christian, it may be the Lord has taken from you such a hopeful son or such a dear daughter and you say, "How can I hold my peace?" But harken, Christian, harken, can you tell me how long you might have travailed in birth with them again before they had been twice born? Would not every sin that they had committed against your gracious God caused a new throe in your soul? Would not every temptation that they had fallen before been as a dagger at your heart? What are those pains, and pangs, and throes of childbirth to those after-pains, pangs, and throes that might have been brought upon you by the sins and sufferings of

---

1. The Lamentations of Jeremiah are a full proof of this.
2. This age affords many sad instances of this nature. Who can think of Tyburn and question it; and of killing and drowning, and say, "How can this be?"

your children? Well, Christians, hold your peace, for you do not know what thorns in your eyes, what goads in your sides, nor what spears in your hearts, such near and dear mercies might have proved had they been longer continued.

You cannot tell how bad your heart might have proved under the enjoyment of those dear mercies that you have lost.

You cannot tell how bad your heart might have proved under the enjoyment of those nearest and dearest mercies that now you have lost.[1] Israel was very bad while they were in the wilderness, but they were much worse when they came to possess Canaan, that land of desires. Man's blood is apt to rise with the outward good.[2] In the winter, men gird their clothes close about them, but in the summer they let them hang loose. In the winter of adversity, many a Christian girds his heart close to God, to Christ, to the Gospel, to godliness, to ordinances, to duties, etc., who, in the summer of mercy, hangs loose from all.

Ah, how bad, how rotten, how base would many have proved had God not touched their health, wealth, friendship, etc.! Near and dear relations—they stick close to us—and if God did not pull off this layer, how apt would we be to corrupt ourselves; therefore God is fain[3] to remove these from us and strip us of our dearest enjoyments and sweetest contentments that our souls might better prosper

---

1. Deu. 32:5, to the end. "Thy children have forsaken me, and sworn by them that are no gods: when I had fed them to the full, they then committed adultery, and assembled themselves by troops in the harlots' houses. They were as fed horses in the morning: every one neighed after his neighbour's wife, etc." Jer. 5:7-9. "As they were increased, so they sinned against me: therefore will I change their glory into shame, etc." Hos. 4:7-14. Also Jer. 2:21-31 & 22:21.

2. "Their houses are safe from fear, neither is the rod of God upon them, etc. They spend their days in wealth, and in a moment go down to the grave. Therefore they say unto God, Depart from us; for we desire not the knowledge of thy ways. What is the Almighty, that we should serve him? And what profit should we have, if we pray unto him?" Job 21:7-15.—H&F.

3. Is pleased to do a necessary thing: glad to evade the evil and secure the good.—H&F.

and thrive. Who can seriously consider this and not hold his peace, even when God takes a jewel out of his bosom? Heap all the sweetest contentments and most desirable enjoyments of this world upon a man, but they will not make him a Christian; heap them upon a Christian, but they will not make him a better Christian. Many a Christian has been made worse by the good things of this world;[1] but where is the Christian that has been bettered by them?[2] Therefore, be quiet when God deprives you of them.

Let your heart be more affected with spiritual losses &
your soul will be less afflicted with temporal losses.

Lastly, *let your heart be more affected with spiritual losses, and then your soul will be less afflicted with those temporal losses that you mourn under.*[3] Have you lost nothing of that presence of God that you once had with your spirit? Have you lost none of those warnings, meltings, quickenings, and cheerings that you once had? Have you lost nothing of your communion with God, nor of the joys of the Spirit, nor of that peace of conscience that you once enjoyed? Have you lost none of that ground that you once gained against sin, Satan, and the world? Have you lost nothing of that holy vigor and heavenly heat that you once had in your heart? If you have not, which would be a miracle and a wonder, why do you complain of this or that temporal loss? For what is this but to complain of the loss of your purse when your God is safe? If you are a loser in spiritual things, why do you not

---

1. "What is a man profited, if he shall gain the whole world, and lose his own soul? Or what shall a man give in exchange for his soul?" Mat. 16:26.— H&F.

2. "Godliness with contentment is great gain. For we brought nothing into this world, and it is certain we can carry nothing out. And having food and raiment let us be therewith content. But they that will be rich fall into temptation and a snare, and into many foolish and hurtful lusts, which drown men in destruction and perdition, etc." 1 Tim. 6:6-12. Also, Mar. 4:18-19.—H&F.

3. *Qui te non habet, Domine Deus, totum perditit.* Bernard. ["Whoever of you has not the Lord God, has lost all."—H&F.]

rather complain that you have lost your God than that you have lost your gold; and that you have lost your Christ than that you have lost your husband; and that you are damnified in spiritual things than that you art damnified in temporal things? Do you mourn over the body that the soul has left? Mourn rather over the soul that God has forsaken, as Samuel did for Saul, says one, 1 Sam. 15:35.

I have read of Honorius, a Roman emperor, who was simple and childish; when one told him Rome was lost, he was exceedingly grieved, and cried out, "Alas! Alas!" For he supposed that it was his hen that was called Rome, which hen he exceedingly loved; but when it was told him that it was his imperial city of Rome, that was besieged by Alaricus and taken, and all the citizens rifled and made a prey to the rudeness of enraged soldiers, then his spirits were revived that his loss was not so great as he imagined.[1] Now, what is the loss of a husband, a wife, a child, a friend, to the loss of God, Christ, the Spirit, or the least measure of grace or communion with God? And yet so simple and childish are many Christians that they are more affected and afflicted with the loss of this and that poor temporal enjoyment than they are with the loss of their most spiritual attainments. Ah, Christians, be but more affected with spiritual losses and you will be more quiet and silent under temporal losses.

---

1. Grotesque as this anecdote sounds, it is historical. When Rome was plundered by Alaric, a eunuch who had the care of the royal poultry, announced to Honorius that "Rome was destroyed." "And yet," was the reply, "she just ate out of my hands," referring to a favorite hen of great size which he called Rome. "I mean," said the eunuch, "that the city of Rome has been destroyed by Alaric." "But I," said the emperor, "thought that my hen 'Rome' was dead." So stupid, adds Procopius, do they say this emperor was.—G.

Objection 3.
"But my afflictions have been long upon me, how then can I hold my peace?"

"Oh, but my afflictions, my troubles have been long upon me, how then can I hold my peace?" Were they but of yesterday, I would be quiet; but they are of a long continuance; and therefore how can I be silent, etc.?

To this I answer:

You cannot date your affliction from the first day of your pollution.

You cannot date your affliction from the first day of your pollution. You have been polluted from the womb, but you have not been afflicted from the womb: "I was shapen in iniquity; and in sin did my mother conceive me," Ps. 51:5. Many have been the days and the years since you were born in sin; few have been the days and the years that you have experienced sorrow. You cannot easily number the days of your sinning, you can easily number the days of your sufferings; you cannot number your days of mercy, you can easily number your days of calamity; you cannot number your days of health, but you can easily tell over[1] your days of sickness.

Your afflictions are not so long in duration as the afflictions of some other saints.

Your afflictions are not so long in duration as the afflictions of some other saints. Compare your winter nights and the winter nights of other saints; your storms and troubles and other saints' storms and troubles; your losses and other saints' losses; your miseries and other saints' miseries;

---

1. Narrate.—H&F.

witness the proofs in the margin.[1] Your afflictions are but as a moment, they are but as yesterday compared with the afflictions of other saints, whose whole lives have been made up of sorrows and sufferings, as the life of Christ was. Many a man's life has been nothing but a lingering death: "And another dieth in the bitterness of his soul, and never eateth with pleasure," Job 21:25. There are those that have never a good day all their days, who have not a day of rest among all their days of trouble, nor a day of health among all their days of sickness, nor a day of gladness among all their days of sadness, nor a day of strength among all their days of weakness, nor a day of honor among all their days of reproach; whose whole life is one continued winter's night, who every day drink gall and wormwood, who lie down sighing, who rise groaning, and who spend their days in complaining, "No sorrow to our sorrows, no sufferings to our sufferings!" Some there are who have always tears in their eyes, sorrows in their hearts, rods on their backs, and crosses in their hands: but it is not so with you;[2] therefore be silent.

---

1. "Thou holdest mine eyes waking: I am so troubled that I cannot speak, etc." Ps. 77. "Thou hast laid me in the lowest pit, in darkness, in the deeps. Thy wrath lieth hard upon me, and thou hast afflicted me with all thy waves, etc." Ps. 88. "A deep sleep fell upon Abram; and, lo, an horror of great darkness fell upon him. And he said unto Abram, Know of a surety that thy seed shall be a stranger in a land that is not theirs, and shall serve them; and they shall afflict them four hundred years," Gen. 15:12-13; also Exo. 12:40-42, Jer. 25:11-12, & 38:4-13.

2. While this is true of some and in some respects, yet, surely there are as many today that experience the same throughout their entire lives; and to such is that word of exhortation spoken, as well as to all others, namely, to suffer with patience and to endure to the end (Jam. 5:10-11), to walk by faith and not by sight, to faint not, knowing that all things work together for good to as many as believe (Rom. 8:28); for, "though our outward man perish, yet the inward man is renewed day by day. For our light affliction, which is but for a moment, worketh for us a far more exceeding and eternal weight of glory" (2 Cor. 4:16-17).—H&F.

The longer your affliction has continued,
the sweeter heaven will be to you.

The longer your affliction has continued, the sweeter heaven will be to you at last; the longer the Israelites had been in the wilderness, the sweeter was Canaan to them at last; the longer the storm, the sweeter the calm; the longer the winter nights, the sweeter the summer days.[1] Long afflictions will much set off the glory of heaven.[2] The harbor is most sweet and desirable to them that have been long tossed upon the seas; so will heaven be to those who have been long in a sea of trouble. The new wine of Christ's kingdom is most sweet to those that have long been drinking gall and vinegar. The crown of glory will be most delightful to them who have been long in combating with the world, the flesh, and the devil: "Blessed are those servants, whom the lord when he cometh shall find watching: verily I say unto you, that he shall gird himself, and make them to sit down to meat, and will come forth and serve them," Luk. 12:37. The longer our journey is the sweeter will be our end, and the longer our passage is the sweeter will our haven be. The higher the mountain, the gladder we shall be when we have gotten to the top of it. The longer the heir is kept from his inheritance, the more delight he will have when he comes to possess it.

---

1. "When the Lord turned again the captivity of Zion, we were like them that dream. Then was our mouth filled with laughter, and our tongue with singing: then said they among the heathen, The Lord hath done great things for them. The Lord hath done great things for us; whereof we are glad. Turn again our captivity, Oh Lord, as the streams in the south. They that sow in tears shall reap in joy. He that goeth forth and weepeth, bearing precious seed, shall doubtless come again with rejoicing, bringing his sheaves with him," Ps. 126:1-6.—H&F.

2. Consider the example of Lazarus; "Remember that thou in thy lifetime receivedst thy good things, and likewise Lazarus evil things: but now he is comforted, and thou art tormented, etc." Luk. 16:19-26.—H&F.

*Afflictions are not long, but short, if compared to
the eternity of glory reserved for the saints.*

*Our afflictions are not long, but short, if compared to that
eternity of glory that is reserved for the saints:* "For which
cause we faint not; but though our outward man perish,
yet the inward man is renewed day by day. For our light
affliction, which is but for a moment, worketh for us a
far more exceeding and eternal weight of glory, etc." 2
Cor. 4:16-18. In these words, you shall find for affliction,
glory; for light afflictions, a weight of glory; and for short
momentary afflictions, eternal glory. There will quickly be
an end of your sadness, but there will never be an end of
your happiness;[1] there will soon be an end of your calamity
and misery, there will never be an end of your felicity and
glory.[2] The kingdoms of this world are not lasting, much
less are they everlasting; they all have their climacteric[3]
years, but the kingdom of heaven is an everlasting kingdom
of which there is no end. There are seven sorts of crowns
that were in use among the Roman victors, but they were
all fading and perishing; but the crown of glory that God
will at last set upon the heads of his saints shall continue
as long as God himself continues.[4] Who can look upon
those eternal mansions that are above, and those everlasting
pleasures that are at God's right hand and say that his
affliction is long? "Let not your heart be troubled: ye believe
in God, believe also in me. In my Father's house are many
mansions, etc. I go to prepare a place for you. And if I go
and prepare a place for you, I will come again, and receive
you unto myself; that where I am, there ye may be also." Joh.

---

1.   "Thou wilt shew me the path of life: in thy presence is fulness of joy; at
thy right hand there are pleasures for evermore, etc." Ps. 16:9-11.—H&F.
2.   "An inheritance incorruptible, and undefiled, and that fadeth not away,
reserved in heaven for you," 1 Pet. 1:3-7.—H&F.
3.   Finite.—H&F.
4.   "Be thou faithful unto death, and I will give thee a crown of life," Rev.
2:11. Also: "There is laid up for me a crown of righteousness, etc. and not to
me only, but unto all them also that love his appearing," 2 Tim. 4:8.—H&F.

14:1-3. Well, Christian, let your affliction be ever so long, yet one hour in the bosom of Christ will make you forget both the length and strength of all your afflictions.

The longer you have been afflicted, the more you have been enriched in spiritual experiences.

The longer you have been afflicted, the more you have been enriched in spiritual experiences: "For as the sufferings of Christ abound in us, so our consolation also aboundeth by Christ," 2 Cor. 1:5. The lower the ebb the higher the tide, the more pain the more gain, the more afflicted the more comforted, the lower we are cast the higher we shall be raised. Of all Christians, there are none so rich in spiritual experiences, as those that have been long in the school of affliction.[1] Oh, the blessed stories that such can tell of the power of God supporting them, of the wisdom of God directing them, of the favor of God comforting them,[2] of the presence of God assisting them. Oh, the tokens of love that they are able to produce since they have been in the furnace of affliction. Oh, the sin that long afflictions have discovered and mortified. Oh, the temptations that long afflictions have prevented and vanquished. You shall as soon number the stars of heaven and the sands of the sea, as you shall number up the heavenly experiences of such Christians that have been long under afflictions. The afflicted Christian's heart is fullest in spiritual treasure.[3] Though he may be poor in the world, yet he is rich in faith and holy experiences, Jam. 2:5; and what are all the riches of this world to spiritual experiences? One spiritual

---

1. "For they verily for a few days chastened us after their own pleasure; but he for our profit, that we might be partakers of his holiness. No chastening for the present seemeth to be joyous, but grievous: nevertheless afterward it yieldeth the peaceable fruit of righteousness unto them which are exercised thereby," Heb. 12:11-13.

2. "As the sufferings of Christ abound in us, so our consolation also aboundeth by Christ," 2 Cor. 1:5.—H&F.

3. "Tribulation worketh patience; and patience, experience; and experience, hope: and hope maketh not ashamed, etc." Rom. 5:3-5.

experience is of more worth than a world, and upon a dying bed and before a judgment seat, every man will be of this opinion. The men of this world will with much quietness and calmness of spirit bear much and suffer much and suffer long when they find that their sufferings add to their revenues; and shall nature do more than grace? It is the common voice of nature; how shall we come to be great and high, and rich in the world? "The hand of the diligent maketh rich," Pro. 10:4. We care not what we suffer, nor how long we suffer, so that we may but add "house to house,"[1] heap to heap, bag to bag, and land to land. Oh, how much more then should Christians be quiet and calm under all their afflictions, though they are ever so long, considering that they do but add jewels to a Christian's crown; they do but add to his spiritual experiences. The long afflicted Christian has the fullest and the greatest trade; and in the day of account, will be found the richest man.[2]

> *Long afflictions are sometimes but a*
> *preparation to long-lived mercies.*

Long afflictions are sometimes but a preparation to long-lived mercies. Joseph's thirteen years imprisonment was but a preparative to fourscore years reigning like a king; David's seven years banishment was but a preparation to forty years reigning in much honor and glory; Job's long afflictions were but preparatives to more long-lived mercies, as you may see in that last chapter of Job; and those sad and sore trials that the Jews have been under for over sixteen hundred years are to prepare them for those matchless mercies and those endless glories, in some sense, that God in the latter days will crown them with: "Oh thou afflicted,

---

1. A reference to Isa. 5:8.
2. "Every man's work shall be made manifest: for the day shall declare it, because it shall be revealed by fire; and the fire shall try every man's work of what sort it is. If any man's work abide which he hath built thereupon, he shall receive a reward. If any man's work shall be burned, he shall suffer loss: but he himself shall be saved; yet so as by fire," 1 Cor. 3:13-15.—H&F.

tossed with tempests, and not comforted, behold, I will lay thy stones with fair colors, and lay thy foundation with sapphires. And I will make thy windows of agates, and thy gates of carbuncles, and all thy borders of pleasant stones. And all thy children shall be taught of the Lord, and great shall be the peace of thy children. In righteousness shalt thou be established: thou shalt be far from oppression, for thou shalt not fear; and from terror, for it shall not come near thee," Isa. 54:11-14. Though they have been long afflicted and tossed, yet they shall at last be established upon glorious foundations; God will not only raise them out of their distressed estate wherein now they are, but he will advance them to a most eminent and glorious condition in this world; they shall be very glorious and outshine all the world in spiritual excellencies and outward dignities:[1] "The sons also of them that afflicted thee shall come bending unto thee, and all they that despised thee shall bow themselves down at the soles of thy feet: and they shall call thee, the city of the Lord, the Zion of the Holy One of Israel. Whereas thou hast been forsaken and hated,

---

1. Our author shifts this blessing to the future, which blessing was fulfilled in Jesus Christ in the day of salvation, when the foundation was established in Jesus Christ, that immovable cornerstone, and upon the Apostles (Rev. 21:14); to this was Israel after the flesh destined and through it was Jerusalem, which is the mother of us all (Gal. 4:26), enriched by the glory of the nations (Rev. 21:24-26) and become an eternal excellency; the children all being taught of God ("It is written in the prophets, 'And they shall be all taught of God.' Every man therefore that hath heard, and hath learned of the Father, cometh unto me," Joh. 6:45); righteousness having been established by faith in Jesus Christ (Rom. 3:22), and salvation being proclaimed through repentance and the grace of the Gospel. All the promises to the people and nation of Israel were fulfilled through the Gospel, which came first to the Jews and through the Jews, "for salvation is of the Jews," (Joh. 4:22), to all men, for God made both one ("he is our peace, who hath made both one, and hath broken down the middle wall of partition between us," Eph. 2:14). God, says Peter, "put no difference between us and them, purifying their hearts by faith," Act. 15:9. The interpretation regarding the physical nation of Israel has become very popular today. Its real origin, however, is in a peculiar line of interpretation proposed first by Irenaeus and Hippolytus. Generally ignored for its unscriptural basis and conclusions, it was revived and popularized primarily through Counter-Reformation eschatology; the same being assimilated by Scofield into his system of interpretation and through that, disseminated widely in modern times.—H&F.

so that no man went through thee, I will make thee an eternal excellency, a joy of many generations," Isa. 60:14-15.

Ah, Christians, do not mutter nor murmur under your long afflictions, for you do not know but that by these long afflictions God may prepare and fit you for such favors and blessings that may never have end. By long afflictions God many times prepares his people for temporal, spiritual, and eternal mercies.[1] If God by long afflictions makes more room in your soul for himself, his Son, his Spirit, his Word; if by long afflictions he shall crucify your heart more to the world and to your relations, and frame and fashion your soul more for celestial enjoyments; have you any cause to murmur? Surely no. But,

> *The longer a saint is afflicted on earth, the*
> *more glorious he shall shine in heaven.*

The longer a saint is afflicted on earth, the more glorious he shall shine in heaven; the more affliction here, the more glory hereafter.[2] This truth may be made out thus:

First. *The more gracious souls are afflicted, the more their graces are exercised and increased.* Now, the more grace here, the more glory hereafter; the higher in grace, the higher in glory. Grace differs nothing from glory but in name: grace is glory in the bud, and glory is grace at the full. Glory is nothing but the perfection of grace; happiness is nothing but the perfection of holiness. Grace is glory in the seed, and glory is grace in the flower; grace is glory militant, and glory is grace triumphant. Grace and glory differ *non specie sed gradu,* "in degree, not kind," as the learned speak. Now, it is most certain that the more gracious souls are afflicted, the more their graces are exercised; and the more grace is

---

1. "Rejoice, and be exceeding glad: for great is your reward in heaven: for so persecuted they the prophets which were before you." Mat. 5:10-12.—H&F.
2. 2 Cor. 4:16-18.

exercised, the more it is increased, Rom. 5:3-5, as I have sufficiently demonstrated in this treatise already. But,

Second. *The longer a gracious soul is afflicted, the more his religious duties will be multiplied.*[1] "For my love they are my adversaries; but I give myself unto prayer," or as the Hebrew reads, "but I am prayer," or "a man of prayer," Ps. 109:4. In times of afflictions a Christian is all prayer; he is never so much a man of prayer, a man given up to prayer, as in times of affliction.[2] A Christian is never so frequent, so fervent, so abundant in the work of the Lord, as when he is afflicted: "Lord! In trouble have they visited thee, they poured out a prayer when thy chastening was upon them," Isa. 26:16. Now, they do not only pray, but they pour out a prayer; they were freely, largely, and abundantly in prayer when the rod was upon them. Look as men plentifully pour out water for the quenching of a fire, so did they plentifully pour out their prayers before the Lord; and as affliction puts a man to being much in prayer, so it puts him upon other duties of religion answerably. Now, this is most certain, that though God will reward no man *for* his works,[3] yet he will reward every man *according to* his works: "Therefore, my beloved brethren, be ye stedfast, unmoveable, always abounding in the work of the Lord; forasmuch as ye know that your labor is not in vain in the Lord," 1 Cor. 15:58. "But this I say, he which soweth sparingly shall reap sparingly; and he which soweth bountifully shall reap bountifully," or he which soweth in benedictions[4] or blessings shall reap in benedictions, as it runs in the original, 2 Cor. 9:6.

---

1. "Rejoicing in hope; patient in tribulation; continuing instant in prayer," Rom. 12:12. Also 2 Cor. 11 & 1 Cor. 4:11-13.—H&F.

2. Ps. 42, 63, 116:1-4.

3. Salvation is not of debt according to our works, but of grace according to faith, Rom. 4:3-8, Gal. 2:16, "For by grace are ye saved through faith; and that not of yourselves: it is the gift of God: Not of works, lest any man should boast," Eph. 2:8-9. Heavenly rewards, however, are granted of God: Mat.5:12, 6:1-6, Luk. 6:23, Mar. 9:41, 12:41-44, & 1 Cor. 3:8-14.—H&F.

4. The Vulgate has: 'Qui seminat in benedictionibus de benedictionibus et metet.'—H&F.

It is an excellent observation of Calvin upon God's rewarding the Rechabites' obedience, Jer. 35:19, "God," says he, "often recompenses the shadows and seeming-appearance of virtue, to show what complacency[1] he takes in the ample rewards he has reserved for true and sincere piety." Now, if the longer a Christian is afflicted, the more his religious services will be multiplied and the more they are multiplied, the more his glory at last will be increased, then the longer a saint is afflicted on earth, the more glory he shall have when he comes to heaven. But,

Third. *The longer any saint is afflicted, the more he will be transformed into the image and likeness of Christ.*[2] It is one of God's great designs and ends in afflicting of his people, to make them more conformable to his Son; and God will not lose his end. Men often lose theirs, but God never has nor will lose his; and experience tells us that God does every day, by afflictions, accomplish his end upon his people. The longer they are afflicted, the more they are made conformable to Christ in meekness, lowliness, spiritualness, heavenliness, in faith, love, self-denial, pity, compassion, etc. Now certainly, the more like to Christ, the more beloved of Christ. The more a Christian is like to Christ, the more he is the delight of Christ; and the more like to Christ on earth, the nearer the soul shall sit to Christ in heaven. Nothing makes a man more conformable to Christ than afflictions. Justin Martyr, in his second Apology for the Christians, has observed that there is scarce any prediction or prophecy concerning our Savior, Christ the Son of God, to be made man, but the heathen writers, who were all after Moses, did from that time invent some fable and feign it to have been acted by some one or other of Jupiter's sons; only the prophecies about the cross of Christ they have

---

1. Pleasure; satisfaction.—H&F.
2. "For whom he did foreknow, he also did predestinate to be conformed to the image of his Son, that he might be the firstborn among many brethren." Rom. 8:29; also Phi. 3:10-11.

taken for the ground of no fable. They have not, among all their fictions, told us of any one of Jupiter's sons that was crucified, that acted his part upon the cross.[1] Many would wear the crown with Christ, that do not care for bearing the cross with Christ. But,

Impatience will but lengthen the day of your sorrows.

The longer your afflictions have been, the greater cause you have to be silent and patient, for impatience will but lengthen the day of your sorrows. Every impatient act adds one link more to the chain; every act of frowardness adds one lash more to those that have already been laid out; every act of muttering will but add stroke to stroke, and sting to sting; every act of murmuring will but add burden to burden, and storm to storm. The most compendious way to lengthen out your long afflictions is to fret, and vex, and murmur under them. As you would see a speedy end of your long afflictions, sit mute and silent under them.

God's time is the best time.

God's time is the best time; mercy is never nearer. Salvation is at hand, deliverance is at the door, when a man's heart is brought into such a frame as to be freely willing that God should time his mercy and time his deliverance for him, Act. 27. The physician's time is the best time for the patient to have ease. The impatient patient cries out to his physician, "Oh, sir, a little ease, a little refreshment! Oh the pains, the tortures, that I am under! Oh, sir, I think every hour two, and every two ten, until comfort comes, until refreshment comes!" But the prudent physician has turned the hourglass, and is resolved that this physic shall work so long, though his patient frets, flings, roars, tears. So, when we are under afflictions, we are apt to cry out, "How

---

1. Gale's 'Court of the Gentiles' is an elaborate demonstration of this remark of Brooks. For the non-imitation of the crucifixion, see Justin Martyr: Apol. §72.—G.

long, Lord, shall it be before ease comes, before deliverance comes? Oh the tortures, oh the torments, that we are under! Lord, a little refreshment! Oh how long are these nights! Oh how tedious are these days!" But God has turned our glass and he will not hearken to our cry until our glass be out. After all our fretting and flinging, we must stay his time, who knows best when to deliver us and how to deliver us out of all our troubles, and who will not stay a moment when the glass is out that he has turned.[1] But,

Your afflictions shall last no longer than there is need.

Lastly, *your afflictions shall last no longer than there is need and then they shall work for your good.* It is with souls as it is with bodies; some bodies are more easily and more suddenly cured than others are, and so are some souls. God will not suffer the plaster[2] to lie one day, no, not one hour, no, not a moment, longer than there is need. Some flesh heals quickly; proud flesh is long at healing. By affliction God quickly heals some, but others are long at healing: "If need be, ye are in heaviness, through manifold temptations, etc." 1 Pet. 1:6-7, or through various afflictions. The burden shall lie no longer upon you than it necessarily must; your pain shall endure no longer than it necessarily must; your physic shall make you sick no longer than it necessarily must, etc. Your heavenly Father is a physician as wise as he is loving. When your heart begins to grow high, he sees there is need of some heavy affliction to bring it low; when your heart grows cold, he sees there is need of some fiery affliction to heat it and warm it; when your heart grows dull and dead, he sees there is need of some sharp affliction to enliven and quicken it. And as your afflictions shall continue no longer than there is need, so they shall last no longer than

---

1. "Have mercy upon me, Oh Lord; for I am weak: Oh Lord, heal me; for my bones are vexed. My soul is also sore vexed: but thou, Oh Lord, how long? etc." Ps. 6:1-6. Also Ps. 13:1-2, 94:10-13, & Rev. 6:9-11.

2. An external application of some medicinal treatment that is of a harder consistency than an ointment.—H&F.

they shall work for your good.[1] If all along they shall work for your good, you have no cause to complain that your afflictions are long. That they shall thus work for your good, I have fully showed in the former part of this book.

Objection 4.
"I would be mute and silent under my afflictions, but my afflictions multiply & increase."

"I would be mute and silent under my afflictions, but my afflictions daily multiply and increase upon me, like the waves of the sea, they come rolling over the neck of one another, etc., and how then can I hold my peace? How can I lay my hand upon my mouth, when the sorrows of my heart are daily increased?"

I answer thus:

Your afflictions are not so many as your sins.

Your afflictions are not so many as your sins: "Mine iniquities have taken hold upon me, etc., they are more than the hairs of mine head," Ps. 40:12. Your sins are as the stars of heaven and as the sand upon the sea, that cannot be numbered. There are three things that no Christian can number: his sins; divine favors; the joys and pleasures that are at Christ's right hand; but there is no Christian so poor an accountant, but that he may quickly sum up the number of his troubles and afflictions in this world. Your sins, oh Christian, are like the Syrians that filled the country, but your afflictions are

---

1. "Our faithful and good Shepherd affords to us," says John Newton, "strength according to our day. He knows our frame, and will lay no more on us than he will enable us to bear; yea, I trust, no more than he will cause to work for our good." "Our comforts," he says, "come free and undeserved. But, when we are afflicted, it is because there is a need for it. He does it not willingly. Our trials are either salutary medicines, or honorable appointments, to put us in such circumstances as may best qualify us to show forth his praise." John Newton, Letter I, Works.—H&F.

like the two little flocks of kids that pitched before them, 1 Kin. 20:27; therefore hold your peace.

If they should not be mute whose afflictions increase,
then none will be found silent under afflictions.

If they should not be mute and silent under their afflictions, whose afflictions are increased and multiplied upon them, then there are none in the world who will be found mute and silent under their afflictions: for certainly there are none who do not find the waters of affliction to grow daily upon them. If this is not so, what means the bleating of the sheep and the lowing of the oxen? 1 Sam. 15:14. What means the daily sighs, groans, and complaints of Christians, if their troubles are not still increasing upon them? Every day brings us tidings of new straits, new troubles, new crosses, new losses, new trials, etc.

Your afflictions are not as many as they might have been.

Your afflictions are not so many as God might have exercised you with. God could as easily exercise you with ten as with two, and with a hundred as with ten, and with a thousand as with a hundred. Let your afflictions be never so many, yet, they are not so many as they might have been, had God either consulted with your sins, with your deserts, or with his own sense of justice. There is no comparison between those afflictions that God has inflicted upon you and those that he might have inflicted. "If thou, Lord, shouldest mark iniquities, Oh Lord, who shall stand? But there is forgiveness with thee, that thou mayest be feared," Ps. 130:3-4. You have not one burden of a thousand that God could have laid on, but he would not; therefore hold your peace.

Your afflictions are not so many as your mercies.

Your afflictions are not so many as your mercies, no, they are not even to be named in the day wherein your mercies are spoken of.

What are your crosses to your comforts, your miseries to your mercies, your days of sickness to your days of health, your days of weakness to your days of strength, your days of scarcity to your days of plenty? And this is that which the wise man would have us seriously to consider: "In the day of adversity consider"—but what must we consider?—"that God hath set the one over against the other," Ecc. 7:14. As God has set winter and summer, night and day, fair weather and foul, one over against another,[1] so let us set our present mercies over against our present troubles and we shall presently find that our mercies exceed our troubles, that they mightily over-balance[2] our present afflictions; therefore let us be silent, let us lay our hands upon our mouths.

In a just account, your afflictions are not
as many as that of other saints.

If you take a just and righteous account, you will find that your afflictions are not as many as the afflictions that have befallen other saints. Have you reckoned up the affliction that befell Abraham, Jacob, Joseph, Job, the prophets and Apostles?[3] If you have, you will say that your afflictions are no afflictions to those that have befallen them; their lives were filled up with sorrows and sufferings, but are yours so? Therefore embrace the rod[4] and be silent. It may be, if you look upon your relations, your friends, your neighbors, you may find

---

1. One as well as the other.—H&F.

2. Outweigh.—H&F.

3. Read but of the ten persecutions, and you will be full of this opinion. [Read of John Huss, William Tyndale, Anne Askew, and of so many multitudes of others recorded in the Acts and Monuments (Foxes' Book of Martyrs), the Martyr's Mirror (T. J. Van Braght), Israel of the Alps (A. Muston), History of the Waldenses (Jean Paul Perrin), A Defence of the Vaudois (J. R. Peyran), and so many more who fulfilled the exhortation, "be thou faithful unto death, and I will give thee a crown of life, etc." Rev. 2:10-11.—H&F.]

4. Receive the affliction and bear all with patience inasmuch as it is meant for good and works greater godliness, purity, and righteousness within; see Heb. 12:5-11, especially verse 9: "we have had fathers of our flesh which corrected us, and we gave them reverence: shall we not much rather be in subjection unto the Father of spirits, and live?"—H&F.

many whose afflictions, in number and weight, do much outweigh yours; therefore be silent, murmur not, hold your peace.

In a just account, you will find that your afflictions are not so many as attended our Lord Jesus.

If you take a just and righteous account, you will find that your afflictions are not so many as attended our Lord Jesus, whose whole life, from the cradle to the cross, was nothing but a life of sufferings.[1] Osorius, writing of the sufferings of Christ, says, that the crown of thorns bored his head with seventy-two wounds. Many seventy-two afflictions did Christ meet with while he was in this world. None can be ignorant of this who have but read the New Testament. He is called "a man of sorrows," Isa. 53:3; his whole life was filled up with sorrows. When he was but a little past thirty years of age, sorrows, pains, troubles, oppositions, persecutions, had so worn him, that the Jews judged him towards fifty, Joh. 8:57. A man may as well compare the number of his bosom friends with the stars of heaven, as compare his afflictions and the afflictions of Christ together. "For thy sake I have borne reproach; shame hath covered my face. I am become a stranger unto my brethren, and an alien unto my mother's children. For the zeal of thine house hath eaten me up; and the reproaches of them that reproached thee are fallen upon me, etc. Reproach hath broken my heart; and I am full of heaviness: and I looked for some to take pity, but there was none; and for comforters, but I found none." Ps. 69:1-21.

Muttering & murmuring will but add to the number.

Muttering and murmuring will but add to the number of your afflictions. When the child is under the rod, his crying and fretting does but add to his punishment and correction.

---

1. "He was oppressed, and he was afflicted, yet he opened not his mouth: he is brought as a lamb to the slaughter, and as a sheep before her shearers is dumb, so he openeth not his mouth, etc." Isa. 53; read the whole chapter.

"A wise son heareth his father's instruction: but a scorner heareth not rebuke." Pro. 13:1; but of this enough has already been said.

Though your afflictions are many, yet they are not
so many as the joys at Christ's right hand.

Lastly, *though your afflictions are many, yet they are not so many as the joys, the pleasures, and the delights that are at Christ's right hand.* As the pleasures of heaven are matchless and endless, so they are numberless.[1] Augustine, says, concerning what we know of heaven, that it is but a little drop of the sea and a little spark of the great furnace;[2] those good things of eternal life are so many that they exceed number; so great that they exceed measure; so precious that they are above all estimation. *Nec Christus, nec coelum patitur hyperbolem,* "neither Christ nor heaven can be hyperbolized"; for every affliction many thousands of joys and delights will attend the saints in a glorified estate. What will that life be, or rather, what will not that life be, says one, speaking of heaven, since all good either is not at all or is in such a life; light which place cannot comprehend; voices and music which time cannot ravish away; scents which are never dissipated; a feast which is never consumed; a blessing which eternity bestows, but eternity shall never see at an end.

Objection 5.
"My afflictions are very great, how then can I hold my peace?"

"My afflictions are very great, how then can I hold my peace? Though they were many, yet if they were not great, I

---

1. "Thou wilt shew me the path of life: in thy presence is fulness of joy; at thy right hand there are pleasures for evermore," Ps. 16:11; Isa. 64:4; & "Eye hath not seen, nor ear heard, neither have entered into the heart of man, the things which God hath prepared for them that love him," 1 Cor. 2:9.

2. Aug. *de Triplici habitu,* c. iv.

would be mute, but alas! They are very great. Oh! How can I be silent under them? How can I now lay my hand upon my mouth?"

To this I answer,

Though afflictions are great, they are not so great as your sins:

Though your afflictions are great, yet they are not so great as your sins, you yourself being judge; therefore hold your peace:[1] "And after all that is come upon us for our evil deeds, and for our great trespasses, seeing that thou our God hast punished us less than our iniquities deserve," Ezr. 9:13. They that were under the sense and guilt of great sins, have cause to be silent under their greatest sufferings. Never complain that your afflictions are great, until you can say that your sins are not great. It is but justice that great afflictions should attend great sins; therefore be quiet. Your sins are like great rocks and mighty mountains, but your afflictions are not so; therefore lay your hand upon your mouth. The remembrance of great sins should cool and calm a man's spirit under his greatest troubles; and if the sense of your great sins will not stop your mouth and silence your heart, I do not know what will.

It may be that your afflictions are not great, if you look at them through the Scripture.

It may be that your afflictions are not great, if you look upon them through the spectacles of Scripture, 1 Pet. 5:10.[2] Flesh and blood many times looks upon molehills as mountains, and scratches upon the hand as stabs at the heart; and of the miniscule we frame a Goliath. Carnal reason often looks upon troubles through false glasses. As there are

---

1. Read Ps. 106 & Neh. 9.
2. "But the God of all grace, who hath called us unto his eternal glory by Christ Jesus, after that ye have suffered a while, make you perfect, stablish, strengthen, settle you," 1 Pet. 5:10.—H&F.

some glasses that make great things seem little, so there are others that make little things seem great, and it may be that you look upon your afflictions through one of them. Look upon your afflictions in the glass of the Word; look upon them in a Scriptural garb and then they will be found to be but little. He that shall look at afflictions through a Gospel glass, shall be able to say that heavy afflictions are light, long afflictions are short, bitter afflictions are sweet, and great afflictions are little, 2 Cor. 4:16-18.[1] It is good to make a judgment of your afflictions by a Gospel light and by a Gospel rule.

Artemon, an engineer, was afraid of his own shadow.[2] Men that look not upon their afflictions in a Scriptural garb, will be afraid even of the shadow of trouble, they will cry out, "There is no affliction like our affliction, no burden like our burden, no cross like our cross, no loss like our loss"; but one look through a Gospel glass would make them change their tone. The lion is not always so great nor so terrible as he is painted; neither are our troubles always so great as we fancy them to be. When Hagar's bottle of water was spent, she sat down and fell to weeping, as if she had been utterly undone, Gen. 21:17-19; her provision and her patience, her bottle and her hope were both out together; but her affliction was not so great as she imagined, for there was a well of water near, though for a time she saw it not. So also many Christians, they eye the empty bottle, the cross, the burden that is at present upon them and then they fall to weeping, to whining, to complaining, to repining, to murmuring, as if they were utterly undone; and yet, a well of water, a well of comfort, a well of refreshment, a well of deliverance is near, and their case is in no way so sad nor so

---

1. "For which cause we faint not; but though our outward man perish, yet the inward man is renewed day by day. For our light affliction, which is but for a moment, worketh for us a far more exceeding and eternal weight of glory," 2 Cor. 4:16-17.—H&F.
2. Plutarch, *Pericles*, 27; Diod. xii. 28.—G.

bad as they imagine it to be. "For a small moment have I forsaken thee; but with great mercies will I gather thee. In a little wrath I hid my face from thee for a moment; but with everlasting kindness will I have mercy on thee, saith the Lord thy Redeemer," Isa. 54:7-8.

The greater your afflictions, the nearer is deliverance.

The greater your afflictions are, the nearer deliverance is to you. When these waters rise high, then salvation comes upon the wings; when your troubles are very great, then mercy will ride post[1] to deliver you:[2] "For the Lord shall judge his people, and repent himself for his servants, when he seeth that their power (or hand) is gone," Deu. 32:36. Israel of old, and England of late years, has often experienced this truth. Wine was nearest, when the water-pots were filled with water up to the brim, Joh. 2:7; so oftentimes mercy is nearest, deliverance is nearest, when our afflictions are at the highest.[3] When a Christian is brim-full of troubles, then the wine of consolation is at hand; therefore hold your peace, murmur not, but sit silent before the Lord.

Your afflictions are not great if compared
to the glory that shall be revealed.

Your afflictions are not great if compared to the glory that shall be revealed: "For our light affliction, which is but

---

1. Swiftly or expeditiously.—H&F.
2. Scripture and history speaks fully to this head.
3. As the deliverance wrought by God for Israel at the very moment they were trapped against the sea by the Egyptians, "And Moses said unto the people, Fear ye not, stand still, and see the salvation of the Lord, which he will shew to you to day: for the Egyptians whom ye have seen to day, ye shall see them again no more for ever. The Lord shall fight for you, and ye shall hold your peace," Exo. 14:13-14. As Jonah in the belly of the whale when he cried out in his affliction, "and he heard me; out of the belly of hell cried I, and thou heardest my voice," Jon. 2. As the Apostles, when "there came down a storm of wind on the lake; and they were filled with water, and were in jeopardy," awoke Jesus saying, "master, we perish. Then he arose, and rebuked the wind and the raging of the water: and they ceased, and there was a calm. And he said unto them, Where is your faith?" Luk. 8:22-25.—H&F.

for a moment, worketh for us a far more exceeding and eternal weight of glory," 2 Cor. 4:17. "For I reckon, that the sufferings of this present time are not worthy to be compared with the glory that shall be revealed in us," or "upon us," Rom. 8:18. The Apostle, upon reckoning up his accounts, concludes that all the pains, chains, troubles, trials, and torments that he met with in this world was not to be put in the balance with the glory of heaven. As the globe of the earth, which after the mathematicians' account is many thousands of miles in compass, yet being compared unto the greatness of the starry sky's circumference, is but a little point; so the troubles, afflictions, and sorrows of this life, in respect of eternal happiness and blessedness, are to be reputed as nothing; they are but as the prick of a pin to the starry heavens. They that have heard most of the glory of heaven, have not heard one quarter of that which the saints shall find there; that glory is unconceivable and inexpressible. Augustine in one of his epistles relates that the very same day wherein Jerome died, he was in his study and had gotten pen, ink, and paper to write something of the glory of heaven to Jerome, and suddenly he saw a light breaking into his study, and a sweet smell that came unto him, and this voice he thought he heard: "Oh Augustine! What are you doing? Do you think to put the sea into a little vessel? When the heavens shall cease from their continual motion, then shall you be able to understand what the glory of heaven is and not before, except you come to feel it as I do now."[1] Such is the splendor, the brightness, the glory, the happiness, and blessedness that is reserved for the saints in heaven that, had I all the tongues of men on earth and all the excellencies of the angels in heaven, yet I would not be able to conceive nor to express that vision of

---

1. One of the commonplaces in the biographies of Augustine and Jerome. See Ep. of the former.—G.

glory to you.[1] It is best to hasten to that end, that we may feel and enjoy that which we shall never be able to declare.

*Your afflictions are not great if compared
with the torments of the damned.*

Your afflictions are not great if compared with the afflictions and torments of such of the damned, who when they were in this world, never sinned at so high a rate as you have done. Doubtless there are many now in hell, who never sinned against such clear light as you have done, nor against such special love as you have done, nor against such choice means as you have done, nor against such precious mercies as you have done, nor against such singular remedies as you have done. Certainly there are many now roaring in everlasting burnings, who never sinned against such deep convictions of conscience as you have done, nor against such close and strong reasonings of the Spirit as you have done, nor against such free offers of mercy and rich tenders[2] of grace as you have done, nor against such sweet wooings and multiplied entreaties of our Savior as you have done; therefore hold your peace. What are your afflictions and your torments compared to the torments of the damned, whose torments are numberless, without ease, without remedy, and endless; whose pains are without intermission or mitigation; who have weeping served up for the first course and gnashing of teeth for the second and the gnawing worm for the third and intolerable pain for the fourth—yet the pain of the body is but the body of pain, the very soul of sorrow and pain is the soul's sorrow and pain—and an everlasting alienation and separation from God for the fifth? Ah, Christian, how can you seriously think on these things and

1. If we should wonder at the little that is spoken of the joys and comforts of heaven, we need only consider the slowness of the fleshly man to believe and to comprehend spiritual truths, and then remember the saying of Jesus: "If I have told you earthly things, and ye believe not, how shall ye believe, if I tell you of heavenly things?" Joh. 3:12.—H&F.
2. Offers, that is, to pay a debt.—H&F.

not lay your hand upon your mouth when you are under the greatest sufferings? Your sins have been far greater than many of those who are now damned, and your great afflictions are but a mosquito bite to theirs; therefore be silent before the Lord.

*If your afflictions are so great, what folly would
it be for you to increase them by murmuring!*

Lastly, *if your afflictions are so great, then what madness and folly would it be for you to make them greater by murmuring!* Every act of murmuring will but add load unto load, and burden to burden. The Israelites under great afflictions fell to murmuring and their murmuring proved their utter ruin, as you may see in that Num. 14, "And all the children of Israel murmured, etc." Murmuring will but put God upon heating the furnace hotter; therefore hold your peace, "Neither murmur ye, as some of them also murmured, and were destroyed of the destroyer. Now all these things happened unto them for ensamples: and they are written for our admonition," 1 Cor. 10:10-11. But of this I have spoken sufficiently already.

Objection 6.
"My afflictions are greater than other men's afflictions, and how then can I be silent."

"Oh, but my afflictions are greater than other men's afflictions, and how then can I be silent? Oh, there is no affliction to my affliction, how can I hold my peace?"

I answer:

It may be that your sins are greater than other men's sins.

It may be that your sins are greater than other men's sins. If you have sinned against more light, more love, more mercies, more experiences, more promises than others, no wonder if your afflictions are greater than others.[1] If this is your case, you have more cause to be mute than to murmur; and certainly, if you do but seriously look into the black book of your conscience, you will find greater sins there than any you can charge upon any person or persons on earth. If you will not, I think you will justly incur the censure which that sour philosopher passed upon grammarians, viz., that they were better acquainted with the evils of Ulysses than with their own.[2] Never complain that your afflictions are greater than others, except you can evidence that your sins are lesser than others.

*It may be that you are under some present
indisposition that deprives you of right judgment.*

*It may be you are under some present indisposition that deprives
you of making a right judgment of the different dealings of
God with yourself and others.*[3] When the mind is disquieted, and the brain troubled, many things seem to be that are not; and then little things seem very great. Oh, the strange passions, the strange imaginations, the strange conclusions, that attend a disordered judgment. "Do ye imagine to reprove words, and the speeches of one that is desperate," or "despondent," says Job, "which are as wind?" Job 6:26. When the mind is disturbed, many times men do not know what they say and do not know what they do. "Jesus taketh with him Peter, and James, and John, and leadeth them up into an high mountain, etc. And there appeared unto them Elias with Moses: and they were talking with Jesus. And Peter answered and said to Jesus, Master, it is good for us to be here: and let us make three tabernacles; one for thee,

---

1. Consider the judgement against David in the case of Bathsheba, 2 Sam. 12, because, in his own judgement, "he did the thing, and he had no pity;" consider also his prayer, Ps. 51, amidst this judgement and in which he prays, "Restore unto me the joy of thy salvation; and uphold me with thy free spirit. Then will I teach transgressors thy ways; and sinners shall be converted unto thee," Ps. 51:12-13.—H&F.

2. Diogenes *apud Laertium*.

3. Deu. 28:28. Good men are sometimes strangely besotted and infatuated.

and one for Moses, and one for Elias. For he wist not what to say; for they were sore afraid. And there was a cloud that overshadowed them, etc." Mar. 9:2-6. It may be, when these clouds are blown over and your mind cleared and your judgment settled, you will be of another opinion. It is good to appeal from a disordered mind to a clear composed mind, for that is the way to make a righteous judgment of all the righteous dispensations of God, both towards ourselves and towards others.

It may be that it is very necessary that your afflictions are greater than others.

It may be that the Lord sees that it is very needful that your afflictions should be greater than others.[1] It may be that your heart is harder than other men's hearts, and prouder and stouter than other men's hearts; it may be that your heart is more impure than others, and more carnal than others, or else more passionate and more worldly than others, or else more deceitful and more hypocritical than others, or else more cold and careless than others, or else more secure than others, or more formal and lukewarm than others. Now, if this is your case, certainly God sees it very necessary for the breaking of your hard heart and the humbling of your proud heart, and the cleansing of your foul heart, and the spiritualizing[2] of your carnal heart, etc., that your afflictions should be greater than others; and therefore hold your peace. Where the disease is strong, the physic must be strong, else the cure will never be wrought. God is a wise physician and he would never give strong physic if weaker could effect the cure, "For I have wounded thee with the wound of an enemy, with the chastisement of a cruel one,

---

1. Nothing but strong medicines will cure some.
2. "For ye are yet carnal: for whereas there is among you envying, and strife, and divisions, are ye not carnal, and walk as men?" 1 Cor. 3:3, "For they that are after the flesh do mind the things of the flesh; but they that are after the Spirit the things of the Spirit. For to be carnally minded is death; but to be spiritually minded is life and peace," Rom. 8:5-6.—H&F.

for the multitude of thine iniquity; because thy sins were increased, etc., I will heal thee of thy wounds, saith the Lord," Jer. 30:14-17, and "I will not make a full end of thee, but correct thee in measure; yet will I not leave thee wholly unpunished," Jer. 46:28.[1] The more rusty the iron is, the more often we put it into the fire to purify it; and the more crooked it is, the more blows and the harder the blows we give to straighten it. You have been long gathering rust, and therefore, if God deals with you thus, you have no cause to complain.

> *Though your afflictions are greater than some, yet there are many whose are greater than yours.*

Though your afflictions are greater than this and that particular man's afflictions, yet doubtless there are many thousands in the world whose afflictions are greater than yours. Can you seriously consider the sore calamities and miseries that the devouring sword has brought upon many thousands of Christians in foreign places, and say that your afflictions are greater than theirs? Surely not. Consider the dismal effects of war:[2] the sword knows no difference between Catholics and Lutherans, as once the Duke of Medina Sidonia said, between the innocent and the guilty, between young and old, between bond and free, between male and female, between the precious and the vile, the godly and the profane, between the prince and the subject, between the nobleman and the beggar. The sword eats the flesh and drinks the blood of all sorts and of both sexes without putting any difference between one or the other. The poor Protestants under the Duke of Savoy, and those in Poland, Denmark, Germany, and several other places have found it so; many of their wounds are not healed to this day. Who

---

1. Consider the prayer of Solomon when he stood before the people, 1 Kin. 8:22, 30-51, which is an acknowledgement of sin, "for there is no man who does not sin," (ver. 46) and of punishment, and of repentance and turning toward God.—H&F.

2. Read the History of the Bohemian Persecution.

can retain in his fresh and bleeding memory the dreadful work that the sword of war has made in this nation and not say, "Surely many thousands have been greater sufferers than I have; they have resisted unto blood, but I have not," Heb. 12:4. But,

As your afflictions are greater, it may be that your mercies are greater, and if so, hold your peace.

As your afflictions are greater than other men's, so it may be that your mercies are greater than other men's mercies; and if so, your have no cause to do other than to hold your peace. As Job's afflictions were greater than other men's, so his mercies were greater than other men's, and Job wisely sets one against the other, and then lays his hand upon his mouth: "Naked came I out of my mother's womb, and naked shall I return thither: the Lord gave, and the Lord hath taken away; blessed be the name of the Lord. In all this Job sinned not, nor charged God foolishly," Job 1:21-22. It may be that you have had more health than others, and more strength than others, and more prosperity than others, and more smiling providences than others, and more good days than others, and more sweet and comfortable relations than others; and if this is your case, you have much cause to be mute, you have no cause to murmur. If now your winter nights be longer than others, remember your summer days have formerly been longer than others; and therefore hold your peace. But,

By great afflictions the Lord may increase your graces.

Lastly, *by great afflictions the Lord may increase your graces and greaten your name and fame in the world:* "Take, my brethren, the prophets, who have spoken in the name of the Lord, for an example of suffering affliction, and of patience. Behold, we count them happy which endure. Ye have heard of the patience of Job, and have seen the end of the Lord; that the Lord is very pitiful, and of tender mercy," Jam.

5:10-11. By Job's great afflictions, God increased his faith and increased his patience, and increased his integrity, and increased his wisdom and knowledge, and increased his experience, and increased his name and fame in the world, as you all know who have but read that book. Bonds and afflictions waited on Paul in every city, Act. 20:23,[1] and "Are they ministers of Christ? (I speak as a fool) I am more; in labours more abundant, in stripes above measure, in prisons more frequent, in deaths oft. Of the Jews five times received I forty stripes save one. Thrice was I beaten with rods, once was I stoned, etc." 2 Cor. 11:23-28; his afflictions and sufferings were very great, but by them the Lord increased his spirit, his zeal, his courage, his confidence, his resolution, and his name and fame, both among sinners and saints. Certainly, if you are dear to Christ, he will increase you in spirituals,[2] by all the great afflictions that are upon you; he will raise your faith, and inflame your love, and quicken your hope, and brighten your zeal, and perfect your patience, and perfume your name, and make it like a precious ointment, "like a precious ointment," Ecc. 7:1 and Pro. 22:1; so that good men shall say, and bad men shall say, "Lo, here is a Christian indeed, here is a man more worth than the gold of Ophir"; therefore, hold your peace, though your afflictions are greater than others.

Objection 7.
"I would be silent, but my outward affliction is attended with sore temptations."

"I would be silent, but my outward affliction is attended with sore temptations; God has not only outwardly afflicted

---

1. "And now, behold, I go bound in the spirit unto Jerusalem, not knowing the things that shall befall me there: Save that the Holy Spirit witnesseth in every city, saying that bonds and afflictions abide me. But none of these things move me, neither count I my life dear unto myself, so that I might finish my course with joy," Act. 20:22-24.—H&F.
2. Those things that pertain to the spirit: faith, purity, holiness, etc.—H&F.

me, but Satan is let loose to buffet me, and therefore how can I be silent? How can I hold my peace, now that I have fallen under manifold temptations?"

To this I answer:

Those that God loves best are usually tempted most.

No man is the less beloved because he is tempted; nay, those that God loves best are usually tempted most: "For we wrestle not against flesh and blood, but against principalities, against powers, against the rulers of the darkness of this world, against spiritual wickedness in high places," Eph. 6:12. Witness David, Job, Joshua, Peter, Paul, yea, Christ himself—"Jesus led up of the Spirit into the wilderness to be tempted of the devil," Mat. 4:1—who, as he was beloved above all others, so he was tempted above all others: he was tempted to question his Sonship; he was tempted to the worst idolatry, even to worship the devil himself; to the greatest infidelity, to distrust his Father's providence, and to use unlawful means for necessary supplies; and to test God, "Cast thyself down," etc. Those that were once glorious on earth, and are now triumphing in heaven, have been sorely tempted and assaulted. It is as natural and common for the choicest saints to be tempted, as it is for the sun to shine, the birds to fly, the fire to burn. The eagle complains not of her wings, nor the peacock of his train, nor the nightingale of her voice, because these are natural to them; no more should saints complain of their temptations, because they are natural to them: "Think it not strange concerning the fiery trial which is to try you, as though some strange thing happened unto you: But rejoice, inasmuch as ye are partakers of Christ's sufferings; that, when his glory shall be revealed, ye may be glad also with exceeding joy," 1 Pet. 4:12-13. Our whole life, says Augustine, is nothing but a tentation.[1] The best men have been worst tempted; therefore, hold your peace.[2]

Temptation resisted & bewailed will
never hurt you nor harm you.

Temptation that is resisted and bewailed will never hurt you nor harm you. Distasteful temptations seldom or never prevail. So long as the soul finds them distasteful and the will remains firmly averse to them, they can do no hurt; so long as the language of the soul is, "Get thee behind me, Satan," Mat. 16:23, the soul is safe. It is not Satan tempting, but my assenting; it is not his enticing, but my yielding, that mischiefs[3] me. Temptations may be troubles to my mind, but they are not sins upon my soul while I am in arms against them. If your heart trembles and your flesh quakes when Satan tempts, your condition is good enough; if Satan's temptations are your greatest afflictions, his temptations shall never worst[4] you nor harm you; and therefore, if this be your case, hold your peace.

Temptations are evidences that you are dear to
God & that it shall go well with you forever.

Temptations are rather hopeful evidences that your estate is good, that you are dear to God, and that it shall go well with you forever. God had but one Son without corruption, but he had none without temptation, "In all things it behoved him to be made like unto his brethren, that he might be a merciful and faithful high priest, etc. For in that he himself hath suffered being tempted, he is able to succour them that are tempted," Heb. 2:17-18. Pirates make the fiercest assaults upon those vessels that are most richly laden; so

---

1. Archaic, temptation, from *tentatio*, to test or try.—H&F.
2. "I am without, set upon by all the world, and within by the devil and all his angels," said Luther.
3. Hurts, harms and injures.—H&F.
4. Get the advantage over.—H&F.

does Satan upon those souls that are most richly laden with the treasures of grace, with the riches of glory. Pirates let empty vessels pass and pass again without assaulting them; so Satan allows souls that are empty of God, of Christ, of the Spirit and of grace, pass and pass again without tempting or assaulting them. When nothing will satisfy the soul but a full departure out of Egypt—from the bondage and slavery of sin—and that soul is firmly resolved upon a march out of Egypt,[1] then Satan, Pharaoh-like, will furiously pursue after that soul with horses and chariots, that is, with a whole army of temptations.[2] Well, when it is worst with a tempted soul, that soul may safely argue: "If God were not my friend, Satan would not be so much my enemy; if there were not something of God within me, Satan would never make such attempts to storm me; if the love of God were not set upon me, Satan would never shoot so many fiery darts to wound me; if the heart of God were not towards me, the hand of Satan would not be so strong against me." When Beza was tempted, he made this answer, "Whatsoever I was, Satan, I am now 'in Christ a new creature,' and it is that which troubles you; I might have so continued long enough before you would have vexed at it, but now I see you envy me the grace of my Savior." Satan's malice to tempt is no sufficient ground for a Christian to dispute God's love; if it were, there is no saint on earth that should quietly possess divine favor for a week, a day, or an hour. The jailor is quiet when his prisoner is in bolts, but if he has escaped, then he pursues him with hue[3] and cry. The wolf flies not upon a painted sheep any more than Satan does upon those he has in chains. Therefore hold

---

1. "They that say such things declare plainly that they seek a country, etc. They desire a better country, that is, an heavenly: wherefore God is not ashamed to be called their God: for he hath prepared for them a city." Heb. 11:14-16.—H&F.

2. Israel going into Egypt had no opposition, but travelling into the Promise Land, they were never free it.

3. In law, a hue and cry is the pursuit of a felon or offender, with loud outcries or clamor to give an alarm.—H&F.

your peace, though you are inwardly tempted, as well as outwardly afflicted.

Christ is interceding for you.

While Satan is tempting you, Christ in the court of glory is interceding for you:[1] "And the Lord said, Simon, Simon, behold, Satan hath desired to have you, that he may sift you as wheat: but I have prayed for thee, that thy faith fail not," Luk. 22:31-32. Satan would fain have been shaking him as wheat is shaken in a fan; but Christ's intercession frustrates the temptations that Satan has designed. Whenever Satan stands at our elbow to tempt us, Christ stands at his Father's to intercede for us: "He ever lives to make intercession," Heb. 7:25. Some of the learned think that Christ intercedes only by virtue of his merits, others think that it is done only by speaking on our behalf; it is probable that it is done in both ways: it is unlikely that the mouth which pleaded so much for us on earth, Joh. 17, should be altogether silent for us in heaven? Christ is a person of highest honor, he is greatest in the court of heaven and he always stands between us and danger. If there is any evil plotted or designed against us by Satan, the great accuser of the brethren, he foresees it and by his intercession prevents it. When Satan puts in his pleas and commences suit upon suit against us, Christ still undertakes our cause; he answers all his pleas and non-suits[2] Satan at every turn and in despite of hell he

---

1. "It is Christ that died, yea rather, that is risen again, who is even at the right hand of God, who also maketh intercession for us," Rom. 8:34. "If any man sin, we have an advocate with the Father, Jesus Christ the righteous," 1 Joh. 2:1. See also Zec. 3:1-4.

2. Causes failure of the suit (against those that belong to Christ). It should be noted here however, that Satan, who previously had free access to come and go in heaven itself and before God, and accused the righteous before God, (Job 1:6) was, at the time of Jesus' death, cast out of heaven: "Now is the judgment of this world: now shall the prince of this world be cast out," Joh. 12:31, "Now is come salvation, and strength, and the kingdom of our God, and the power of his Christ: for the accuser of our brethren is cast down, which accused them before our God day and night," Rev. 12:10.

keeps us in divine favor. When Satan pleads, "Lord! Here are such and such sins that your children have committed! And here are such and such duties that they have omitted! And here are such and such mercies that they have not improved! And here are such and such ordinances that they have slighted! And here are such and such motions of the Spirit which they have quenched!" Divine justice answers, "All this is true, but Christ has appeared on their behalf; he has pleaded their cause; he has fully and fairly answered whatever has been objected and given complete satisfaction to the utmost farthing; so that here is no accusation nor condemnation that can stand in force against them." Upon this account the Apostle triumphs in that Rom. 8:34, "Who is he that condemneth? It is Christ that died, yea rather, that is risen again, who is even at the right hand of God, who also maketh intercession for us." Christ's intercession should be the soul's anchor-hold in time of temptation. In the day of your temptation you need not be disturbed nor disquieted, but in peace and patience possess your own soul,[1] considering what a friend you have in the court of glory and how he is most active for you when Satan is most busy tempting you.

All temptations shall work for the good & gain of the saints.

Lastly, *all temptations that the saints meet with shall work much for their good and shall be much for their gain.* The profit and the advantage that will redound to tempted souls by all their temptations is very great, "All things work together for good to them that love God, to them who are the called according to his purpose. For whom he did foreknow, he

---

Nevertheless, the pleadings of Satan against us, as our author relates, are made by assault upon the conscience, and Christ, who "is able to succour them that are tempted," intercedes: "Rejoice not against me, Oh mine enemy: when I fall, I shall arise, etc." Mic. 7:8-9, and "There is therefore now no condemnation to them which are in Christ Jesus, who walk not after the flesh, but after the Spirit, etc." Rom. 8:1-2.—H&F.

1. "In your patience possess ye your souls," Luk. 21:19.—H&F.

also did predestinate to be conformed to the image of his Son, that he might be the firstborn among many brethren," Rom. 8:28-29. Now this will appear to be a most certain truth by an introduction of the particulars:

By temptations, God multiplies and increases his children's spiritual experiences, the increase of which is better than the increase of gold.[1] In the school of temptation, God gives his children the greatest experience of his power in supporting them, of his Word in comforting them, of his mercy in warming them, of his wisdom in counselling them, of his faithfulness in the joy within them, and of his grace in strengthening them: "My grace shall be sufficient for thee," 2 Cor. 12:9. Paul never experienced so deeply what almighty power was, what the everlasting arms of mercy were, and what infinite grace and goodness was, as when he was buffeted by Satan.

All their temptations shall be curative, and their temptations shall be happy preventions of great abominations: "Lest I should be exalted above measure through the abundance of the revelations, there was given to me a thorn in the flesh, the messenger of Satan to buffet me, lest I should be exalted above measure," 2 Cor. 12:7. It is twice in that one verse: he begins with this thought and he ends with it. If he had not been buffeted he might have been more highly exalted in his own conceit than he was before "the abundance of the revelations," 2 Cor. 2:7. Ah, tempted souls! You say you are naught, very naught,[2] but had it not been for the school of temptation, you might have been brought to nothing before this. You say you are sick, you are even sick to death. But, your sickness might, before this time, have killed you had temptations not been a curative to you. Are you bad under

---

1. "We glory in tribulations also: knowing that tribulation worketh patience; And patience, experience; and experience, hope," Rom. 5:3-4, Frequent engagements add to the soldier's skill, and much increase his experiences.
2. Brought to nothing.—H&F.

temptations? Doubtless you would have been much worse had not God made temptation a diet-drink[1] to you.

Temptation shall much promote the exercise of grace. As the spring in the watch sets all the wheels turning, so temptation sets faith to work, and love to work, and repentance to work, and hope to work, and holy fear to work, and godly sorrow to work. As the wind sets the mill to work, so the wind of temptations sets the graces of the saints in motion. Now faith runs to Christ, now it embraces a promise, now it pleads the blood of Christ, now it looks to the recompense of the reward, now it takes the sword of the Spirit, etc.; now love cleaves to Christ, now love hangs upon Christ, now love will fight to the death for Christ; now hope flies to the horns of the sanctuary, now hope puts on her helmet, now hope casts her anchor upon that within the veil,[2] etc. Grace is never more employed than when a Christian is most tempted. Satan made a bow of Job's wife, of his rib, as Chrysostom speaks, and shot a temptation by her at Job, thinking to have shot him through the heart: "Curse God, and die," she said, but the activity of Job's graces was a breastplate that made him temptation-proof.

By temptations, the Lord will make you more serviceable and useful to others.[3] There is none so fit and able to relieve tempted souls, to sympathise with tempted souls, to succor tempted souls, to counsel tempted souls, to pity tempted souls, to support tempted souls, to bear with tempted souls, and to comfort tempted souls, than those who have been in the school of temptations: "Blessed be God, even the Father of our Lord Jesus Christ, the Father of mercies, and the God of all comfort; who comforteth us in all our

---

1. A drink prepared with medicinal ingredients.—H&F.
2. "Which hope we have as an anchor of the soul, both sure and stedfast, and which entereth into that within the veil," Heb. 6:19.
3. The most skillful commanders and leaders are of the greatest service and use to the soldiers.

tribulation, that we may be able to comfort them which are in any trouble, by the comfort wherewith we ourselves are comforted of God," 2 Cor. 1:3-4. By temptations God trains up his servants, and fits and capacitates them to succor and shelter their fellow-brethren.[1] "One tempted Christian," says Luther, "is more profitable and useful to other Christians than a hundred," I may add, than a thousand, that have not known the depths of Satan, that have not been in the school of temptation.[2] He that is master of arts in the school of temptation has learned an art to comfort, to succor, and gently to handle tempted and distressed souls, infinitely beyond what all human arts can reach unto. There is no doctor to him that has been in the school of temptation; all other doctors are but illiterate to him.

It is an honor to the saints to be tempted, and consequently to have an honorable conquest over the tempter. It was a great honor to David that he should be put to fight hand to hand with Goliath and in the end, to overcome him, 1 Sam. 17; but it was a far greater honor for Job and Paul, that they should be put to combat in the open field with Satan himself and in the end to gain a famous conquest over him: Job 1 and 2 Cor. 12:7-10. It was a very great honor to David's three mighty men that in jeopardy of their lives they broke through the host of the Philistines to bring water to David out of the well of Bethlehem, and did accomplish it in spite of all the strength and power of their enemies, though it was at the most extreme hazard of their blood and lives, 2 Sam. 23:13-18. But it is a far greater honor to the saints to be furnished with a spirit of strength, courage, and valor to break through an army of temptations

---

1. "In all things it behoved him to be made like unto his brethren, that he might be a merciful and faithful high priest, etc. For in that he himself hath suffered being tempted, he is able to succour them that are tempted," Heb. 2:17-18.—H&F.

2. Luther on Gen. 27 & Rev. 2:24.

and in the end to triumph over them, Rom. 8:15-28, and yet, all the saints have this honor: "But God is faithful, who will not suffer you to be tempted above that ye are able ; but will with the temptation also make a way to escape, that ye may be able to bear it," 1 Cor. 10:13; "And the God of peace shall tread Satan under your feet shortly," Rom. 16:20; "I write unto you, fathers, because ye have known him that is from the beginning. I write unto you, young men, because ye have overcome the wicked one. I write unto you, children, because ye have known the Father. I have written unto you, fathers, because ye have known him that is from the beginning. I have written unto you, young men, because ye are strong, and the Word of God abideth in you, and ye have overcome the wicked one," 1 Joh. 2:13-14. "We know that whosoever is born of God sinneth not," 1 Joh. 5:18, that is, "that sin that is unto death," ver. 16; neither does he sin as other men do: delightfully, greedily, customarily, resolvedly, impenitently, etc. "But he that is begotten of God keepeth himself, and that wicked one toucheth him not." The glorious victory that the people of God had over Pharaoh and his great host, Exo. 14, was a figure of the glorious victory that the saints shall obtain over Satan and his instruments. This is clear from Rev. 15:3, where we have the song of Moses and of the Lamb. But why the song of Moses and of the Lamb, except to hint this to us, that the overthrow of Pharaoh was a figure of the overthrow of Satan? And the triumphal song of Moses was a figure of that song which the saints shall sing for their overthrow of Satan. As certainly as Israel overcame Pharaoh, so certainly shall every true Israelite overcome Satan. The Romans were worsted[1] in many fights, but never were they overcome in a given war; in the long run they overcame all their enemies. Though a Christian may be worsted by Satan in some particular skirmishes, yet in the long run he is sure of an honorable conquest. God puts a great deal of honor upon a

---

1. Defeated.—H&F.

poor soul when he brings him into the open field to fight it out with Satan.[1] By fighting, he overcomes and he gains the victory, he triumphs over Satan and leads captivity captive. It is the glory of a Christian to be made strong to resist, and to have his resistance crowned with a happy conquest.

By temptations, the Lord will make his people more frequent and more abundant in the work of prayer. Every temptation proves a strong alarm to prayer. When Paul was in the school of temptation, he prayed three times, that is, often, 2 Cor. 12:8-9. Days of temptation are days of great supplication: Christians usually pray most when they are tempted most. They are most busy with God when Satan is most busy with them. A Christian is most upon his knees when Satan stands most at his elbow.

Augustine was a man much tempted and a man much in prayer. "Holy prayer," says he, "is a shelter to the soul, a sacrifice to God, and a scourge to the devil."

Luther was a man under manifold temptations and a man much in prayer. He is said to have spent three hours every day in prayer. He used to say that prayer was the best book in his study.

Chrysostom was much in the school of temptation and delighted much in prayer. "Oh!" says he, "it is more bitter than death to be spoiled of prayer," and hereupon, as he observes, Daniel chose rather to run the hazard of his life than to lose his prayer. But,

By temptations, the Lord will make his people more and more conformable to the image of his Son. Christ was much tempted, he was often in the school of temptation; and

---

1. "When they had called the apostles, and beaten them, they commanded that they should not speak in the name of Jesus, and let them go. And they departed from the presence of the council, rejoicing that they were counted worthy to suffer shame for his name," Act. 5:40-41.—H&F.

the more often a Christian is tempted and resists the enticement, the more into the likeness of Christ he will be transformed: "For whom he did foreknow, he also did predestinate to be conformed to the image of his Son, that he might be the firstborn among many brethren," Rom. 8:29. Of all men in the world, tempted souls do most resemble Christ to the very life—in meekness, in lowliness, in holiness, in heavenliness, etc. The image of Christ is most fairly stamped upon tempted souls. Tempted souls are much in looking upward to Jesus, and every gracious look upon Christ changes the soul more and more into the image of Christ. Tempted souls experience much of the succoring of Christ, and the more they experience the sweetness of the succoring of Christ, the more they grow up into the likeness of Christ. Temptations are the tools by which the Father of spirits does more and more carve, form, and fashion his precious saints into the similitude and likeness of his dearest Son.

Lastly, taking many things in one: *God, by temptations, makes sin more hateful, and the world less delightful, and relations less hurtful.* By temptations, God discovers to us our own weakness and the creature's insufficiency in the hour of temptation to help us or succor us. By temptations, God will brighten our Christian armor and make us stand more upon our Christian watchfulness, and keep us closer to a succoring Christ. By temptations, the Lord will make his ordinances to be more highly prized and heaven to be more earnestly desired. Now seeing that temptations shall work so eminently for the saints' good, why should not Christians be mute and silent? Why should they not hold their peace and lay their hands upon their mouths, though their afflictions are attended with great temptations?

Objection 8.
"God has forsaken me, & how then can I be silent?"

"Oh, but God has deserted me! He has forsaken me, and he that should comfort my soul stands afar off! How can I be silent? The Lord has hid his face from me; clouds are gathered about me; God has turned his back upon me; how can I hold my peace?"

Supposing that the desertion is real and not in appearance only, as sometimes it falls out?

I answer:

It has been the common lot of the choicest saints to be deserted & forsaken by God.

It has been the common lot, portion, and condition of the choicest saints in this world to be deserted and forsaken by God: "Thou didst hide thy face, and I was troubled. I cried to thee, Oh Lord, etc." Ps. 30:6-7; "Will the Lord cast off for ever? and will he be favourable no more? Is his mercy clean gone for ever?" Ps. 77:7-10; "Thy wrath lieth hard upon me, and thou hast afflicted me with all thy waves, etc." Ps. 88:3-9; "He hideth himself on the right hand, that I cannot see him, etc." Job 23:8-12; "I will wait upon the Lord, that hideth his face from the house of Jacob, and I will look for him. Behold, I and the children whom the Lord hath given me are for signs and for wonders, etc." Isa. 8:17-18, and "I will bear the indignation of the Lord, because I have sinned against him, until he plead my cause, etc." Mic. 7:9. If God deals no worse with you than he has dealt with his most bosom friends, with his choicest jewels, you have no reason to complain.[1] But,

---

1. Christians, especially those who preach or are inclined to follow that teaching that would have the victory here in this life, according to the wealth and well-being of this age, should call to mind the Scriptures that prove otherwise, that have this the battleground (Mat. 10:16-39, Eph. 6:13-17); this the testing ground (Jam. 1:2-4, 1 Pet. 1:6-9); this the place of

God's forsaking of you is not total.

God's forsaking of you is only partial, it is not total: "Thou hast maintained my right and my cause," Ps. 9:4 and "The arms of his hands were made strong by the hands of the mighty God," Gen. 49:23-24. God may forsake his people in part, but he never wholly forsakes them; he may forsake them in respect of his quickening presence, and in respect of his comforting presence, but he never forsakes them in respect of his supporting presence; "My grace is sufficient for thee; for my strength is made perfect in weakness," 2 Cor. 12:9; "The steps of a good man are ordered by the Lord; and he delighteth in his way. Though he fall, he shall not be utterly cast down: for the Lord upholdeth him with his hand," Ps. 37:23-24. God's supporting hand of grace is still under his people: "My soul followeth hard after thee: thy right hand upholdeth me," Ps. 63:8. Christ has always one hand to uphold his people: "My sheep hear my voice, and I know them, and they follow me: And I give unto them eternal life; and they shall never perish, neither shall any man pluck them out of my hand. My Father, which gave them me, is greater than all; and no man is able to pluck them out of my Father's hand," Joh. 10:27-28. The everlasting arms of God are always upholding his people, Deu. 33:27. And this the

---

Satan's dominion (Col. 1:13, 1 Joh. 2:15-17, 2 Cor. 4:3-4) where the saints themselves are his prey, "And he opened his mouth in blasphemy against God, to blaspheme his name, and his tabernacle, and them that dwell in heaven. And it was given unto him to make war with the saints, and to overcome them," Rev. 13:6-7, although he cannot overcome even the least of them, "he that is begotten of God keepeth himself, and that wicked one toucheth him not. And we know that we are of God, and the whole world lieth in wickedness," 1 Joh. 5:18-19, "Ye are of God, little children, and have overcome them: because greater is he that is in you, than he that is in the world," 1 Joh. 4:4. The victory is spiritual. "We have this treasure in earthen vessels, that the excellency of the power may be of God, and not of us. We are troubled on every side, yet not distressed; we are perplexed, but not in despair; persecuted, but not forsaken; cast down, but not destroyed; always bearing about in the body the dying of the Lord Jesus, that the life also of Jesus might be made manifest in our body," 2 Cor. 4:7-10.—H&F.

saints have always found; witness Noah, Moses, Abraham, David, Job, etc.

Geographers write of a place that is so curiously situated that the sun is never out of sight. Though the children of God sometimes are under some clouds of afflictions, yet the Sun of mercy, the Sun of righteousness, is never quite out of sight. But,

God's love abides & is an everlasting love.

Though God has forsaken you,[1] *yet his love abides and continues constant toward you:* he loves you "with an everlasting love," Jer. 31:3. Where he loves, "he loves them to the end," Joh. 13:1. "But Zion said, The Lord hath forsaken me, and my Lord hath forgotten me." But was not Zion mistaken? Yes, "Can a woman forget her sucking child, that she should not have compassion on the son of her womb? Yea, they may forget, yet I will not forget thee. Behold, I have engraven thee upon the palms of my hands; thy walls are continually before me," Isa. 49:14-16.[2] Look! As persons engrave the mark, name, or picture of those whom they dearly love and entirely affect,[3] upon some stone that they wear at their breasts, or upon some ring that they wear on their finger, so has God imprinted Zion upon the palms of his hands; she was still in his eye, and always dear to his heart, though she thought not so. As Joseph's heart was full of love to his brethren, Gen. 42:24 and 43:30, even then when he spoke roughly to them and withdrew himself from them, for he was fain to go aside and ease his heart by weeping; so the

---

1. "If his children forsake my law, and walk not in my judgments; If they break my statutes, and keep not my commandments; Then will I visit their transgression with the rod, and their iniquity with stripes. Nevertheless my lovingkindness will I not utterly take from him, nor suffer my faithfulness to fail. My covenant will I not break, nor alter the thing that is gone out of my lips," Ps. 89:30-34.—H&F.

2. The very heathen has observed that God does not love his children with a weak affection, but with a strong masculine love. Seneca.

3. Regard with fondness.—H&F.

heart of God is full of love to his people, even then when he seems to be most displeased with them, and to turn his back upon them. Though God's dispensations may be changeable towards his people, yet his gracious disposition is unchangeable towards them: "For I am the Lord, I change not; therefore ye sons of Jacob are not consumed," Mal. 3:6. When God puts the blackest veil of all over his face, yet then his heart is full of love to his people, then his bowels are yearning towards them: "Is Ephraim my dear son? Is he a pleasant child? For since I spake against him, I do earnestly remember him still; therefore my bowels are troubled for him: I will surely have mercy upon him, saith the Lord," Jer. 31:20. The mother's bowels cannot more yearn after the tender babe than God does after his distressed ones. When God turns aside from his people, he cannot but cast an eye of love towards them: "How shall I give thee up, Oh Ephraim, etc!" Hos. 11:8. There are four divers 'hows' in the text, the like of which are not to be found in the whole book of God. I am even at a stand still, justice calls for vengeance, but mercy interposes; my bowels yearn, my heart melts, "Oh, how shall I give you up! Oh, I cannot give you up! I will not give you up!" God's love is always like himself, unchangeable; his love is everlasting; it is a love that never decays nor grows cold.

Though the Lord has hid his face, yet
you have his presence with you.

Though the Lord has hid his face from you, yet certainly you have his secret presence with you. God is present when he is seemingly absent: "The Lord was in this place, and I knew it not," says Jacob, Gen. 28:16. The sun may shine when we do not see it.[1] God is in your house, he is in your heart, though you see him not, you feel him not, though you hear

---

1. "Are sense and feelings suitable to judge of the dispensations and designs of God? Can their testimony be safely relied upon? Is it safe to argue thus: 'If God had any love for my soul, I should feel it now, as well as in former times;

him not: "I will never leave thee, nor forsake thee," Heb.
13:5. Are you not now induced to prize God and Christ,
and his love above all the world? Yes. Are you not now
induced to give the Lord many a secret visit, in a corner,
behind the door, in some place where none can see you nor
hear you but the Lord? Ps. 42:1-3, 63:1-3. Yes. Are there
not strong sighings, pantings, and longings after a clearer
vision of God, and after a fuller fruition of God? Yes. Are
you not more affected and afflicted with the withdrawing
of Christ than you are with the greatest afflictions that
ever befell you? Augustine, contemplating the answer of
God to Moses, "Thou canst not see my face and live," Exo.
33:20, makes this quick and sweet reply, "Then, Lord! Let
me die, that I may see thy face." Do you not often tell
God that there is no punishment to the punishment of
loss, and no hell to that of being forsaken of God? Do you
not find a secret power in your soul, drawing you forth to
struggle with God, to lay hold on God, and patiently to
wait on God, until he shall return unto you and lift up the
light of his countenance upon you? Well, then, you may be
confident that you have the secret and blessed presence of
God with you, though God, in regard of his comfortable
presence, may be departed from you. Nothing less than the
secret presence of God with a man's spirit will keep him
waiting and working until the "Sun of righteousness" shines
upon him, Mal. 4:2.[1] If any vain persons should put that
deriding question to you saying, "Where is your God?" You
may safely and boldly answer them, "My God is here; he is
near to me, he is round about me, yea, he is in the midst of

but I cannot feel it, therefore it is gone'? May you not as well conclude, when
the sun is invisible to you, that it has ceased to exist?" John Flavel, Keeping
the Heart.—H&F.

1.   Also: "I will look unto the Lord; I will wait for the God of my salvation:
my God will hear me. Rejoice not against me, Oh mine enemy: when I fall,
I shall arise; when I sit in darkness, the Lord shall be a light unto me. I will
bear the indignation of the Lord, because I have sinned against him, until he
plead my cause, and execute judgment for me: he will bring me forth to the
light, and I shall behold his righteousness," Mic. 7:7-9.—H&F.

me." "The Lord thy God in the midst of thee is mighty, he will save, he will rejoice over thee with joy, he will rest in his love, he will joy over thee with singing," Zep. 3:17. The bush was not consumed all the while it burned with fire, because God was in the midst of it. It is no argument that Christ is not in the ship because tempests and storms arise.

God will return again.

Though God be gone, yet he will return again. Though your sun be now set in a cloud, yet it will rise again; though sorrow may abide for a night, "yet joy comes in the morning," Ps. 30:5.[1] A Christian's mourning shall last but until morning: "He will turn again, he will have compassion upon us," Mic. 7:19; "In the multitude of my thoughts within me, thy comforts delight my soul," Ps. 94:19; "For a moment have I forsaken thee, but with great mercies will I gather thee. In a little wrath I hid my face from thee for a moment, but with everlasting kindness will I have mercy on thee, saith the Lord thy Redeemer; for the mountains shall depart, and the hills be removed, but my kindness shall not depart from thee; neither shall the covenant of my peace be removed, saith the Lord, that hath mercy on thee," Isa. 54:7-10. God will not suffer his whole displeasure to rise upon his people, neither will he forsake them totally or finally. "I visit their transgression with the rod, and their iniquity with stripes. Nevertheless my lovingkindness will I not utterly take from him, nor suffer my faithfulness to fail," Isa. 89:32-33. The saints shall taste but some sips of the cup of God's wrath, their storm shall end in a calm, and their winter night shall

---

1. "I waited patiently for the Lord; and he inclined unto me, and heard my cry. He brought me up also out of an horrible pit, out of the miry clay, and set my feet upon a rock," Ps. 40:1-2, & 42:5, 8-9, 11. [Also: "Who is among you that feareth the Lord, that obeyeth the voice of his servant, that walketh in darkness, and hath no light? Let him trust in the name of the Lord, and stay upon his God," Isa. 50:10.—H&F.]

be turned into a summer day, but sinners shall drink the dregs.[1] But,

God's deserting & forsaking of his people
shall work for their good.

Lastly, *God's deserting and God's forsaking of his people shall in many ways work for their good.* As,

God, by withdrawing from his people, will prepare and fit them for greater refreshings, manifestations, and consolations: "They that lay wait for my soul take counsel together, saying, God hath forsaken him: persecute and take him; for there is none to deliver him," Ps. 71:10-11. But shall this forlorn condition work for his good? Yes, ver. 20-21, "Thou, which hast shewed me great and sore troubles, shall quicken me again, and shalt bring me up again from the depths of the earth. Thou shalt increase my greatness, and comfort me on every side." When Joseph's brethren were in their greatest distress, then Joseph made himself known most fully to them, Gen. 45:1-4; so does Christ, our spiritual Joseph, to his people. Hudson the martyr, deserted at the stake, escaped from under his chain, but having prayed earnestly, was comforted immediately and suffered valiantly.[2]

By God's withdrawing from his people, he prevents his people's withdrawing from him; and so by an affliction, he prevents sin. For God to withdraw from me is but my affliction, but for me to withdraw from God, that is my sin: "Beware that thou forget not the Lord thy God," Deu. 8:11. Therefore it would be better for me that God should withdraw a thousand times from me, than that I should once withdraw from God. God therefore forsakes us that we may not

---

1. "For the time is come that judgment must begin at the house of God: and if it first begin at us, what shall the end be of them that obey not the Gospel of God? And if the righteous scarcely be saved, where shall the ungodly and the sinner appear?" 1 Pet. 4:17-18.—H&F.

2. Clark's 'Martyrologie,'—G.

forsake our God. God sometimes hides himself from us that we may cleave more closely to him and hold fast upon him. God sometimes hid himself from David: "Thou didst hide thy face, and I was troubled," Ps. 30:7, or, I was alarmed, I trembled. And is that all? No. "I cried to thee, Oh Lord, and unto the Lord I made my supplication," ver. 8. Now he cries louder and cleaves closer to God than before. So in Ps. 63:1-2, "Oh God, thou art my God; early will I seek thee: my soul thirsteth for thee, my flesh longeth for thee in a dry and thirsty land, where no water is; to see thy power and thy glory, so as I have seen thee in thy sanctuary." How do those withdrawings of God work? This you see in ver. 8, "My soul followeth hard after thee," or, as the Hebrew has it, "My soul cleaveth after thee." The Psalmist now follows God even hard at the heels, as we say. But,

The Lord, by withdrawing from his people, will enhance and increase the value and commend the worth, the excellence, the sweetness, and the usefulness of several precious promises, which otherwise would be to the soul as fountains and as weapons that have never been used: "Whereby are given unto us exceeding great and precious promises: that by these ye might be partakers of the divine nature, having escaped the corruption that is in the world through lust," 2 Pet. 1:4. As in Mic. 7:18-19, "He will turn again, he will have compassion upon us etc."; and "With everlasting kindness will I have mercy on thee," Isa. 54:7-8, "I will never leave thee, nor forsake thee," Heb. 13:5-6, and "For thou, Lord, wilt bless the righteous; with favour thou wilt compass him," or crown him, "as with a shield," Ps. 5:12. The Lord will compass the righteous about with his favor, Ps. 112:4, "Unto the upright there ariseth light in darkness: he is gracious, and full of compassion, and righteous." And in Jer. 31:37, "Thus saith the Lord, If heaven above can be measured, and the foundations of the earth searched out beneath, I will also cast off all the seed of Israel, for all that they have done, saith the Lord."[1] As sure as heaven cannot be measured, nor the foundations of the earth searched by the skill or power of mortal man, so sure and certain it is that God will not utterly cast off his people, no, not for all the evil that they have done. Now how highly does a deserted soul value these precious promises? Well, says he, these promises are sweeter than honey; they are more precious than gold, than fine gold, than much gold, than all the gold in the world; I prefer them before my food, before my delightful food, yea, before my necessary food, before my appointed portion.[2] As Alexander laid up Homer's Illiad in a cabinet embroidered with gold and pearls; so deserted souls will lay up these precious promises in the cabinet of their hearts, as the choicest treasure the world affords. "The kingdom of heaven is like unto a merchant man, seeking goodly pearls: who, when he had found one pearl of great price, went and sold all that he had, and bought it," Mat. 13:45-46.

Dolphins, they say, love music, so do deserted souls the music of the promises. That promise, "This is a faithful saying, and worthy of all acceptation, that Christ Jesus came into the world to save sinners," 1 Tim. 1:15, was music to Bilney the martyr; and that promise, "My Father, which gave them me, is greater than all; and no man is able to pluck them out of my Father's hand," Joh. 10:29, was music to Ursinus; and that promise, "I dwell in the high and holy

---

1. Also, "He that loveth me shall be loved of my Father, and I will love him, and will manifest myself to him, etc." Joh. 14:21-23; "Ye have done all this wickedness: yet turn not aside from following the Lord, but serve the Lord with all your heart," 1 Sam. 12:20; & "Thy sun shall no more go down; neither shall thy moon withdraw itself: for the Lord shall be thine everlasting light, and the days of thy mourning shall be ended, etc." Isa. 60:19-22.

2. "It is good for me that I have been afflicted; that I might learn thy statutes. The law of thy mouth is better unto me than thousands of gold and silver," Ps. 119:72-72, "The statutes of the Lord are right, rejoicing the heart, etc. More to be desired are they than gold, yea, than much fine gold: sweeter also than honey and the honeycomb," 19:8-10; "Wisdom is better than rubies," Pro. 8:11; & "I have esteemed the words of his mouth more than my necessary food," Job 23:12.

place, with him also that is of a contrite and humble spirit, to revive the spirit of the humble, and to revive the heart of the contrite ones," Isa. 57:15, was music to another; and that promise, "Thou wilt keep him in perfect peace, whose mind is stayed on thee: because he trusteth in thee," Isa. 26:3, was music to another; and that to another, "Come unto me, all ye that labour and are heavy laden, and I will give you rest," Mat. 11:28. Promises that are suited to a deserted man's condition, make the sweetest music in his ear and are the most sovereign cordials that God can give to bear up the spirits; or that heaven afford or the soul desire: "He made him to ride on the high places of the earth, that he might eat the fruits of the field; and he made him to suck honey out of the rock, and oil out of the flinty rock," Deu. 32:13. Ah, the honey and the oil that deserted souls draw out of such promises that speak directly to their conditions!

By God's hiding his face and withdrawing himself from you, you will be enabled more feelingly and more experientially to sympathise with others and to have compassion on others that are or may be in the dark and forsaken by God, as you are now. A priest, therefore, was "ordained for men in things pertaining to God," that he could "have compassion on the ignorant, and on them that are out of the way; for that he himself also is compassed with infirmity," Heb. 5:1-2. So also we who partake of that heavenly calling: "Wherefore, holy brethren, partakers of the heavenly calling, consider the Apostle and High Priest of our profession, Christ Jesus; Who was faithful to him that appointed him," Heb. 3:1-2, "Remember them that are in bonds, as bound with them; and them which suffer adversity, as being yourselves also in the body," Heb. 13:3. In the natural body, if one member grieve and is in pain, all suffer with it. When a thorn has gotten into the foot, how does the back bend and the eyes pry,[1] and the hands go to pluck the thorn out! There

---

1. Look narrowly.—H&F.

is none so compassionate towards deserted souls as those who have been deserted and forsaken by God themselves. Oh, they know what an evil and a bitter thing it is to be left and forsaken by God, and therefore their bowels, their compassions run out much to others, yea, most to others. They know that there is no affliction, no misery, no hell, to that of being forsaken by God.

Anaxagoras, seeing himself old and forsaken by the world, laid himself down and covered his head, determining to starve himself to death with hunger.[1] But, alas! What is it to be forsaken by the world, compared to a man's being forsaken by God? Were there as many worlds as there are men in the world, it would be better that a man were forsaken by them all than to be forsaken by God with a *Non novi vos*, "I know you not," Mat. 7:23.The schools have long since concluded that *poena sensus*, "the pain of sense," is far greater than *poena damni*, "the pain of loss."[2] What a grief was it to Absalom to see the king's face clouded; and how sadly was Eli and his daughter-in-law affected with the loss of the ark, which was but a testimony of God's presence! But oh, how much more is a Christian affected and afflicted with the loss of the face and favor of God, the remembrance of which makes his heart to melt and his bowels to yearn towards those whose sun is set in a cloud?

Hereby the Lord will teach his people to set a higher value upon his face and favor when they come to enjoy it: David prayed, "Create in me a clean heart, Oh God; and renew a right spirit within me. Cast me not away from thy presence; and take not thy Holy Spirit from me. Restore unto me the joy of thy salvation; and uphold me with thy free spirit." Ps. 51:10-12. No man sets so high a value upon Christ, as he that has lost him and found him again, "For this my son was dead, and is alive again; he was lost, and is found. And

---

1. Plutarch.
2. Literally, *poena:* penalty or punishment.—H&F.

they began to be merry," Luk. 15:24. Jesus, in the Chinese tongue, signifies the rising sun, and so he is, "But unto you that fear my name shall the Sun of righteousness arise with healing in his wings; and ye shall go forth, and grow up as calves of the stall," Mal. 4:2, especially to souls that have been long clouded. The poor northern nations of Strabo, who lacked the light of the sun for some months, when the term of its return approaches, they climbed up to the highest mountains to see it, and he that spies it first was accounted the best and most beloved of God and usually they did choose him king; at such a rate did they prize the return of the sun. Ah, so it is with a poor soul, that for some months or years has been deserted; oh, how highly does he prize and value the Sun of righteousness returning to him and shining upon him! "Thy loving-kindness is better than life," Ps. 63:3, or, "better than lives," as the Hebrew has it, "chaiim." Divine favor is better than life; it is better than life with all its revenues, with all its appurtenances, as honors, riches, pleasures, applause, etc., yea, it is better than many lives put together. Now, you know at what a high rate men value their lives—they will bleed, sweat, part with an estate, yea, with a limb, yea, limbs, to preserve their lives. As he cried out, "Give me any deformity, any torment, any misery, but spare my life." Though life be so dear and precious to a man, yet a deserted soul prizes the returning of divine favor upon him above life, yea, above many lives. Many men have been weary of their lives, as is evident in Scripture and history, but no man was ever yet found that was weary of the love and favor of God. No man sets so high a price upon the sun as he that has laid long in a dark dungeon, etc. But,

Hereby the Lord will train up his servants in that precious life of faith, which is the most honorable and the most happy life in all the world: "For we walk by faith, and not by sight," 2 Cor. 5:7. The life of the senses and the life of human reason is a low[1] life and a mean[2] life; the life of faith is a noble life, a blessed life. When Elisha demanded of the Shunamite what he should do for her, whether he should speak for her to the king or the captain of the host, she answered, "I dwell among my people," 2 Kin. 4:13, that is, "I dwell nobly and happily among my people; I have no need to make any suit to king or captain." This she accounts her great happiness, and indeed it is the greatest happiness in this world to live much in the exercise of faith. No man lives so free a life, so holy a life, so heavenly a life, so happy a life, as he that lives a life of faith. In times of divine withdrawing, the soul is moved to hang upon God alone, Christ alone, a bare promise, Isa. 63:15-16. Now the soul is moved to the highest and the purest acts of faith, viz., to cleave to God, to hang upon God, and to carry itself sweetly and obediently towards God, though he frowns, though he chides, though he strikes, yea, though he kills, "Though he slay me, yet will I trust in him," Job 13:15. Those are the most excellent and heroic acts of faith that are most abstracted from the senses and human reason;[3] he that suffers his reason to usurp upon his faith, will never be an excellent Christian. He that goes to the school of his own reason has a fool for his schoolmaster; and he that suffers his faith to be overruled by his reason shall never lack woe. "Trust in the Lord with all thine heart; and lean not unto thine own understanding," Pro. 3:5. Where reason is strongest, faith usually is weakest. But now the Lord, by the forsaking of his people for a time,

---

1. Debased; less than intended and able to be.—H&F.

2. In this sense, spiritless.—H&F.

3. For example, it is said of Abraham, "who is the father of us all," Rom. 4:16, that "being not weak in faith, he considered not his own body now dead, when he was about an hundred years old, neither yet the deadness of Sara's womb: He staggered not at the promise of God through unbelief; but was strong in faith, giving glory to God; And being fully persuaded that, what he had promised, he was able also to perform," Rom. 4:19-21; and again, "By faith Abraham, when he was tried, offered up Isaac: and he that had received the promises offered up his only begotten son, Of whom it was said, That in Isaac shall thy seed be called: Accounting that God was able to raise him up, even from the dead," Heb. 11:17-19.—H&F.

makes them skilful in the life of faith, Jam. 1:2-4, which is the choicest and the sweetest life in this world. But,

By divine withdrawings, you are made more conformable to Christ your head, who was under spiritual desertion as well as you: "My God, my God, why hast thou forsaken me?" Mat. 27:46 and Ps. 22:1-2.[1] There is a hidden emphasis in the Hebrew word: *El* signifies a strong God; *Eli, Eli,* "My strong God, my strong God." The unity of Christ's person was never dissolved, nor were his graces ever diminished. In the midst of this terrible storm, his faith fortified and strengthened itself upon the strength of God, *"My* God, *my* God"; yet in respect of divine protection and divine solace, he was for a time forsaken by his Father.[2] And if this be your case, you are herein made conformable to your Lord and master; nay, you do but sip of that bitter cup of which Christ drank deep;[3] your cloud is no cloud to that which Christ was under. But,

Lastly, *by these transient and partial forsakings, the Lord will exceedingly sweeten the clear, full, constant, and uninterrupted enjoyment of himself in heaven to all his people:* "Thou, which hast shewed me great and sore troubles, shalt quicken me again, and shalt bring me up again from the depths of the earth," Ps. 71:20. Ah, how sweet and precious was the face

---

1. "My God, my God, why hast thou forsaken me? Why art thou so far from helping me, and from the words of my roaring? Oh my God, I cry in the daytime, but thou hearest not; and in the night season, and am not silent," Ps. 22:1-2.—H&F.

2. This is so on behalf of every man, as is evident from Ps. 22 where the reality is described in detail, and again in Hebrews, "We see Jesus, who was made a little lower than the angels for the suffering of death, crowned with glory and honour; that he by the grace of God should taste death for every man. For it became him, for whom are all things, and by whom are all things, in bringing many sons unto glory, to make the captain of their salvation perfect through sufferings," Heb. 2:9-10.—H&F.

3. "Remember the word that I said unto you, The servant is not greater than his lord. If they have persecuted me, they will also persecute you; if they have kept my saying, they will keep yours also. But all these things will they do unto you for my name's sake, because they know not him that sent me," Joh. 15:20-21.—H&F.

and favor of the father to the prodigal, "For this my son was dead, and is alive again; he was lost, and is found. And they began to be merry," Luk. 15:24! Onesimus departed from Philemon for a season, that he might receive him forever. "I say unto you, that likewise joy shall be in heaven over one sinner that repenteth," Luk. 15:7. So the Lord departs from his people for a time, that they may receive him forever; he hides himself for a season, that his constant presence amongst his children in glory may be the more sweet and delightful to them.

Objection 9.
"I am falsely accused & sadly reproached, and how then can I be silent?"

"Oh, but I am falsely accused and sadly reproached, and my good name, which should be as dear or dearer to me than my life, is defamed and things are laid to my charge that I never did, that I never knew, etc.; and how then can I be silent? How can I hold my peace? I cannot forget the proverb, *Oculus et fama non patiuntur jocos,* 'A man's eye and his good name can bear no jests'; and how then can I be mute to see men make jests upon my good name, and every day to see men lade it with all the scorn and contempt imaginable, that they may utterly blast it, etc.?"

To this I say:

Granted that a good name is one of the choicest jewels in a Christian's crown.

That it must be granted that a good name is one of the choicest jewels in a Christian's crown. Though a great name many times is little worth, yet a good name is rather to be chosen than great riches. It is better to have a good name abroad, than silver or gold laid up in a chest at home. "A good name is better than precious ointment," Ecc. 7:1. Precious ointments were greatly in use and highly esteemed amongst the Israelites; they were laid up amongst the most precious things even in the king's treasury, Isa. 39:2. Sweet ointments can affect the smell and comfort the brain, and delight the outward man; but they reach not the best part, the noble part, viz., the soul and the conscience of a Christian; but a good name does both. What is the perfume of the nostrils to the perfume of the heart?[1]

I have read that in some countries they have a certain art of drawing pigeons to their dove-houses by anointing the wings of one of them with sweet ointment, which pigeon, being sent abroad, does by the fragrance of that ointment, decoy, invite, and allure others to the house where it is a domestic. Such is the fragrance of a good name that it draws other men after the savor thereof. Among all sorts and ranks of men in the world, a good name has an attractive faculty: it is a precious ointment that draws hearers to attend good preachers, and patients to seek out physicians, clients to seek out lawyers, scholars to attend schoolmasters, and customers to frequent shopkeepers who have a good report of all good men. Let a man's good name be spoken and he will not lack anything that men or money can help him to.[2] A good name will bring a man into favor and keep a man in favor with all that are good; therefore, say the moralists:

> Omnia si perdas, famam servare memento,
> Qua semel amissa, postea nullus eris.

"Whatsoever commodity you lose, be sure yet to preserve that jewel of a good name." A Christian should be most chary[3] of his good name, for a good name answers to all things. *Ergo si bonam famam servasso, sat dives ero,* "If I may but keep a good name, I have wealth enough," said the

---

1. A good renown is better than a golden girdle. French Proverb.
2. Claudian, De Cons. Mall. Theod. v. 3.—G.
3. Careful.—H&F.

heathen Plautus. A Christian should rather forego gold than let go of a good name; and he that robs a Christian of his good name is a worse thief than he that robs him of his purse, and better deserves a hanging than he,[1] etc. But,

A good name once lost is very hardly recovered again.

It must be granted that a good name, once lost, is very hard to recover again. A man may more easily recover a lost friend or a lost estate than a lost name. A good name is like a princely structure, long in the rearing but quickly ruined. When once a good name leaves a man, it hardly returns to him again. A cracked[2] credit will hardly be soldered again. A man should stand upon nothing more than the credit of his conscience and the credit of his name.

Three things a Christian should stiffly labor to maintain: the honor of God; the honor of the Gospel; and the honor of his own name. If once a Christian's good name sets behind a cloud, it may be long before it rises again.

*It has been the portion of God's saints
to be slandered & vilified.*

Though all this be true, yet it has been the portion of God's dearest saints and servants to be slandered, reproached, vilified, and falsely accused:[3] "Let the lying lips be put to silence, which speak grievous things, proudly, and contemptuously against the righteous," Ps. 31:8. How sadly and falsely was

---

1. "A lying tongue hateth those that are afflicted by it," Pro. 26:28.—H&F.
2. Bad credit is hard to restore.—H&F.
3. "Blessed are they which are persecuted for righteousness' sake: for theirs is the kingdom of heaven. Blessed are ye, when men shall revile you, and persecute you, and shall say all manner of evil against you falsely, for my sake. Rejoice, and be exceeding glad: for great is your reward in heaven: for so persecuted they the prophets which were before you," Mat. 5:10-12; "If ye suffer for righteousness' sake, happy are ye: and be not afraid of their error, neither be troubled," 1 Pet. 3:14; "For thy sake I have borne reproach; shame hath covered my face," Ps. 69:7.

Joseph accused by his wanton mistress;[1] David by Doeg and Shimei;[2] Job of hypocrisy, impiety, inhumanity, cruelty, partiality, pride, and irreligion! Was not Naboth accused of speaking blasphemy against God and the king, 1 Kin. 21:12-13? Did not Haman present the Jews to the king as refractories and rebels, Est. 3? Was not Elijah accused of being the troubler of Israel,[3] and Jeremiah the trumpet of rebellion; the Baptist a stirrer up of sedition, and Paul a pestilent incendiary?[4] Were not the Apostles generally accounted deceivers and deluders of the people, and the offscouring of the world, etc.? Athanasius and Eustathius were each falsely accused of adultery.[5] Heresy and treason were charged upon Cranmer, parricide upon Philpot, sedition upon Latimer. As the primitive persecutors usually put Christians into bear skins and dog skins, and then baited them;[6] so they usually loaded their names and persons with all the reproach, scorn, contempt, and false reports imaginable, and then baited them, and then acted all their malice and cruelty upon them. I think there is no Christian who sooner or later, first or last, will not have cause to say with David, "False witnesses did rise up; they laid to my charge things that I knew not," Ps. 35:11; they charged me with such things whereof I was both innocent and ignorant. It was the saying of one Hippias that there was nothing so intolerable as accusation, because there was no punishment ordained by law for accusers as there was for thieves, although they stole friendship from men, which is

---

1. Gen. 39:13-20.

2. Ps. 52:1-2.

3. "And it came to pass, when Ahab saw Elijah, that Ahab said unto him, Art thou he that troubleth Israel? And he answered, I have not troubled Israel; but thou, and thy father's house, in that ye have forsaken the commandments of the Lord, and thou hast followed Baalim. 1 Kin. 18:17-18.—H&F.

4. Rom. 3:8; 1 Cor. 4:12-13.

5. Acts and Monuments by John Foxe.

6. As Tertullian, Minutius Felix, and others declare. [Cf. Clarke's 'Martyrologie,'—G.

the goodliest riches men can have. Well! Christians, seeing it has been the lot of the dearest saints to be falsely accused and to have their names and reputations in the world reproached, do you hold your peace, seeing that it is no worse with you than it was with them, "of whom this world was not worthy," Heb. 11:38. The Rabbins[1] say that the world cannot subsist without patient bearing of reproaches. But,

Our Lord Jesus Christ was sadly reproached & falsely accused.

Our Lord Jesus Christ was sadly reproached and falsely accused. His precious name, that deserves to be always written in characters of gold, as the Persians usually wrote their king's names, was often eclipsed. His sweet name, that was sweeter than all that is sweet, was often crucified before his body. Oh, the stones of reproach that were frequently cast upon that name by which we must be saved, if ever we are saved! Oh, the jeers, the scoffs, the scorns that were cast upon that name that alone can bless us! The name of Jesus, says Chrysostom, has a thousand treasures of joy and comfort in it. The name of a Savior, says Bernard, is honey in the mouth and music in the ear, and a jubilee in the heart; and yet, where is the heart that can conceive or the tongue that can express how much dung and filth has been cast upon Christ's name, and how many sharp arrows of reproach and scorn have been and daily, yea, hourly, are shot by the world at Christ's name and honor? Such ignominious reproaches were cast upon Christ and his name in the time of his life and at his death, that the sun did blush and masked itself with a cloud that he might no longer behold them. "The Son of man came eating and drinking, and they say, Behold a man gluttonous, and a winebibber, a friend of publicans and sinners," Mat. 11:19. But was he such a person? No, but "Wisdom is justified of her children." Wisdom's children will stand up and justify her before all the world. "Sir, we

---

1. Obsolete: Rabbinate; the Rabbis.—H&F.

remember that that deceiver said, while he was yet alive, After three days, I will rise again," Mat. 27:63. But was he a deceiver of the people?[1] No, he was "the faithful and true witness," Rev. 1:5 and chap. 3:14. "The people answered and said, Thou hast a devil: who goeth about to kill thee?" Joh. 7:20 and chap. 8:48, "Then answered the Jews, and said unto him, Say we not well, that thou art a Samaritan, and hast a devil?" And chap. 10:20, "And many of them said, He hath a devil, and is mad; why hear ye him?" It was a wonder of wonders that the earth did not open and swallow up these monsters, and that God did not rain fire out of heaven upon these horrid blasphemers; but their blasphemous assertions were denied and disproved by wisdom's children: ver. 21, "Others said, These are not the words of him that hath a devil: can a devil open the eyes of the blind?" The devil has no such power, nor any such goodness, as to create eyes in him that was born blind.

Will you yet see more scorn, dirt, and contempt cast upon the Lord of glory? Why, then, cast your eyes upon the following: "And the Pharisees also, who were covetous, heard all these things, and they derided him," Luk. 16:14, or as the Greek reads it, "They turned up their noses at him in scorn and derision." The Pharisees did not only laugh, fleer,[2] and jeer at Christ, but they also expressed external signs of scorn and derision in their countenance and gestures; they turned up their noses at him, they contemned him as a thing of nought. And in chap. 23:35, both people and rulers turned up their noses at him; for the original word is the same as that in the aforementioned chapter. He is accused for being an enemy to Caesar, Joh. 19:12. Now, who can seriously consider the scorn, reproach, and contempt that has been cast upon the name and honor of our Lord Jesus and not sit silent and mute under all the scorn and

---

1. The Greek word signifies one who professes an art of cozening people to their faces. ['Cozening,' that is, beguiling.—H&F.]
2. Sneer, make a wry face in contempt.—H&F.

contempt that has been cast upon his name or person in this world?

> *To be well spoken of & in favor with them that are out of favor with God is a reproach rather than an honor.*

To be well spoken of by them that are ill spoken of by God, to be in favor with them who are out of favor with God, is a reproach rather than an honor to a man. Our Savior himself testified that in the church and nation of the Jews, they that had the most general approbation and applause, they who were most admired and cried up, were the worst, not the best, men; they were the false, not the true, prophets: "Woe unto you when all men shall speak well of you, for so did their fathers to the false prophets," Luk. 6:26. "If the world hate you, ye know that it hated me before it hated you. If ye were of the world, the world would love his own: but because ye are not of the world, but I have chosen you out of the world, therefore the world hateth you," Joh. 15:18-19. Augustine feared the praises of good men and detested the praises of evil men. "I would not," says Luther, "have the glory and fame of Erasmus; my greatest fear is the praises of men." To be praised of evil men, said Bion, is to be praised for evil doing; for the better they speak of a man the worse he is, and the worse they speak of a man the better. The Lacedaemonians would not have a good saying sullied with a wicked mouth. A wicked tongue soils all the good that drops from it. It is a mercy to be delivered from the praises of wicked men; the applause of wicked men oftentimes become the saints' reproach. The heathen Socrates could say, *Quid mali feci?* "What evil have I done" that this bad man commends me. There is a truth in that saying of Seneca, *Recti argumentum est, pessimis displicere,* "The worst men are commonly most displeased with that which is best." Who can seriously dwell on these things and not be mute and silent under all the reproach and scorn that is cast upon his name and credit in this world?

*The Lord will wipe off the filth that wicked men
have cast upon the good names of his people.*

*There will come a day when the Lord will wipe off all the
dust and filth that wicked men have cast upon the good names
of his people.*[1] There shall be a resurrection of names as
well as of bodies; their names that are now buried in the
open sepulchres of evil throats shall surely rise again.[2]
Their innocency shall "shine forth as the light, and their
righteousness as the noonday," Ps. 37:6. Though the clouds
may for a time obscure the shining of the sun, yet the sun
will shine forth again as bright and glorious as ever: "The
righteous shall be had in everlasting remembrance," Ps.
112:6. Though the malicious slanders and false accusations
of wicked men may for a time cloud the names of the
saints, yet those clouds shall vanish and their names shall
appear transparent and glorious. God will take such care
of his people's good name that the infamy, calumnies, and
contumelies that are cast upon it shall not long stick. The
Jews rolled a stone upon Christ to keep him down that
he might not rise again, but an angel quickly rolled away
the stone and despite his keepers, he rose in a glorious
triumphant manner, Mat. 28:2. So, although the world may
roll this stone and that of reproach and contempt upon
the saints' good names, yet God will roll away all those
stones; and their names shall have a glorious resurrection
in despite[3] of men and devils. God always has one hand
to wipe away his children's tears from their eyes,[4] and God
always has another hand to wipe off the dust that lies upon

---

1. "Thou givest thy mouth to evil, and thy tongue frameth deceit. Thou
sittest and speakest against thy brother; thou slanderest thine own mother's
son. These things hast thou done, and I kept silence; thou thoughtest that I
was altogether such an one as thyself: but I will reprove thee, and set them in
order before thine eyes," Ps. 50:19-21.—H&F.

2. A reminiscence of Sibbes. Cf. Memoir.—G.

3. Defiance and contempt.—H&F.

4. "And God shall wipe away all tears from their eyes; and there shall be no
more death, neither sorrow, nor crying, neither shall there be any more pain:
for the former things are passed away," Rev. 21:4.—H&F.

his children's names. Wronged innocency shall not lie long under a cloud. Well, Christians, remember that the slanders and reproaches that are cast upon you are but badges of your innocency and glory: "If mine adversary should write a book against me: surely I would take it upon my shoulder, and bind it as a crown to me," Job 31:35-36. All reproaches are pearls added to a Christian's crown. Hence Augustine, *Quisquis volens detrahit famae meae, nolens addit mercedi meae,* "He that willingly takes from me my good name, unwillingly adds to my reward." This Moses knew well enough, which made him prefer Christ's reproach before Pharaoh's crown, Heb. 11:25-26. That God who knows all his children by name will not suffer their names to be long buried under the ashes of reproach and scorn; and therefore hold your peace. The more the foot of pride and scorn tramples upon your name for the present, the more splendent[1] and radiant it will be. Therefore lay your hand upon your mouth. But,

The Lord has been a swift witness against those who have falsely accused his children.

The Lord has been a swift and a terrible witness against such that have falsely accused his children and that have laded their names with scorn, reproach, and contempt: "Behold, the Lord cometh with ten thousands of his saints, To execute judgment upon all, and to convince all that are ungodly among them of all their ungodly deeds which they have ungodly committed," Jud. 14-15. Ahab and Jezebel, who suborned false witness against Naboth, had their blood licked up by dogs, 1 Kin. 21:20-24 and 2 Kin. 9:30-37. Amaziah, who falsely accused the prophet Amos to the king, met with this message from the Lord: "Thy wife shall be an harlot in the city, thy sons and daughters shall fall by the sword, and thy land shall be divided by line; thou shalt die in a polluted land," Amo. 7:17. Haman, who

---

1. Resplendent.—H&F.

falsely accused the Jews, was feasting one day with the king, and the next day made a feast for crows, Est. 7:5-10. The envious courtiers, who falsely accused Daniel, were devoured by lions, Dan. 6:24. Let me give you a taste of the judgments of God upon such persons out of histories.

Caiaphas the high-priest, who gathered the council and suborned false witnesses against the Lord Jesus, was shortly after put out of office, and one Jonathan substituted in his place, whereupon he killed himself.[1] John Cooper, a godly man, being falsely accused in Queen Mary's days by one Grimwood, shortly after the said Grimwood, being in perfect health, his bowels suddenly fell out of his body, and so he died miserably.[2]

Narcissus, a godly bishop of Jerusalem, was falsely accused by three men of many foul matters, who sealed their false testimonies with oaths and imprecations; but shortly after that, one of them, with his whole family and substance, was burnt with fire; another of them was stricken with a grievous disease, such as in his imprecation he had wished to himself; the third, terrified with the sight of God's judgment upon the former, became very penitent, and poured out the grief of his heart in such abundance of tears, that thereby he became blind.[3]

A wicked wretch, Nicephorus, under Commodus the emperor, accused Apollonius, a godly Christian, to the judges for certain grievous crimes, which, when he could

---

1. Josephus records that Vitellius the president of Syria, after he had come into Judea, released the garments of the high priests into the possession of the Jews again as a favor to them, and he deprived Joseph Caiaphas of the high priesthood and appointed Jonathan, son of Ananus, the former high priest, as his successor. Josephus, Antiquities of the Jews, Book 18, chap. 4. There does not seem to be grounds to believe that Caiaphas killed himself after being put out of that office.—H&F.

2. Acts and Monuments by John Foxe.

3. Eusebius relates this history.

not prove the same, he was adjudged to have his legs broken according to an ancient law of the Romans.

Gregory Bradway falsely accused one Brook; but shortly after, through terrors of conscience, he sought to cut his own throat, but being prevented, he fell mad.

I have read of Socrates' two false accusers, how that the one was trodden to death by the multitude and the other was forced to avoid the like by a voluntary banishment. I might produce a multitude of other instances, but let these suffice to evidence how swift and terrible a witness God has been against those that have been false accusers of his people and that have laded their precious names with scorn and reproach,[1] the serious consideration of which should make the accused and reproached Christian to sit dumb and silent before the Lord.

God himself is reproached daily.

Lastly, *God himself is reproached daily*. Men tremble not to cast scorn and contempt upon God himself. Sometimes they charge the Lord that his ways are not equal and that it is a wrong way that he goes in, "Ye say, The way of the Lord is not equal. Hear now, Oh house of Israel; Is not my way equal? Are not your ways unequal?" Eze. 18:25 and "What iniquity have your fathers found in me, that they are gone far from me, and have walked after vanity, and are become vain?" Jer. 2:5. Sometimes they charge God with cruelty, "My punishment is greater than I am able to bear," Gen. 4:13. Sometimes they charge God with partiality and respect of persons because here he strokes and there he strikes; here he lifts up, and there he casts down; here he smiles, and there he frowns; here he gives much, and there he gives nothing; here he loves, and there he hates; here he prospers one, and there he blasts another: "Where is the

---

1. For these references see Beard's Theatre of Judgment.

God of judgment?" Mal. 2:17, *i.e.* nowhere; either there is no God of judgment or at least not a God of exact, precise, and impartial judgment, etc. Sometimes they charge God with unbountifulness, saying that he is a God that will lay upon his people work that is too hard and too much, and will pay them no wages and give them no reward: "Ye have said, it is in vain to serve God, and what profit is it that we have kept his ordinances, and that we have walked mournfully before the Lord of hosts?" Mal. 3:14. Sometimes they charge God that he is a hard master and that he reaps where he has not sown and gathers where he has not strewed, Mat. 25:24, etc. Oh, the infinite reproach and scorn that is every day, that is every hour in the day cast upon the Lord, his name, his truth, his ways, his ordinances, and his glory! Alas, all the scorn and contempt that is cast upon all the saints all the world over is nothing to that which is cast upon the great God every hour; and yet he is patient.[1] Ah, how hardly[2] do most men think of God, and how hardly do they speak of God, and how unhandsomely[3] do they carry it towards God; and yet he bears. They that will not spare God himself, his name, his truth, his honor; shall we think it much that they spare not us or our names, etc.? Surely no.[4] Why should we expect that those should give us good words that cannot afford God a good word from one week's end to another? Yea, from one year's end to another? Why should we look that they should cry out "Hosanna, hosanna!" to us when every day they cry out of Christ, "Crucify him, crucify him!" "It is enough for the disciple that he be as his master, and the servant as his lord;

---

1. "But love ye your enemies, and do good, and lend, hoping for nothing again; and your reward shall be great, and ye shall be the children of the Highest: for he is kind unto the unthankful and to the evil. Be ye therefore merciful, as your Father also is merciful," Luk. 6:35-36; also Mat. 5:44-46.—H&F.

2. Severely and unfavorably.—H&F.

3. Rigorously; unfavorably; unfairly.—H&F.

4. "It were very strange that I should please a world of men, when God himself does not give every man content(ment)." Salvian.

if they have called the master of the house Beelzebub" (or a master-fly, or a dunghill god, or the chief devil)[1], "how much more shall they call them of his household!" Mat. 10:25. It is preferment enough for the servant to be as his Lord, and if the same persons do not hesitate to stain and blaspheme the name of the Lord, do not wonder that they taint your name. Let this suffice to quiet and silence your hearts, Christians, under all that scorn and contempt that is cast upon your names and reputations in this world.

Objection 10.
"I have sought the Lord for mercy & still God delays; how can I then hold my peace?"

The last objection is this: "In this my affliction I have sought the Lord for this and that mercy, and still God delays me and puts me off; I have several times thought that mercy had been near, that deliverance had been at the door, but now I see it is afar off; how can I then hold my peace? How can I be silent under such delays and disappointments?"

To this objection,
I give you these answers:

The Lord does not always time his answers to the swiftness of his people's expectations.

The Lord does not always time his answers to the swiftness of his people's expectations.[2] He that is the God of our mercies is the Lord of our times. God has delayed long his dearest saints and times belong to him, as well as issue:[3] "Oh Lord, how long shall I cry, and thou wilt not hear! Even cry out unto thee of violence, and thou wilt not help!" Hab. 1:2. "Behold, I cry out of wrong, but I have no answer; I cry, but

---

1. Literally, 'lord of the house,' referring to the prince of evil spirits. Thayer.—H&F.
2. Ps. 70:5, 94:3-4, 13:1-2; & Zec. 1:12.
3. The consequences or the end result.—H&F.

there is no judgment." Job 19:7. "I am weary of crying, my throat is dry, mine eyes fail while I wait for my God," Ps. 69:3. "Make no tarrying, Oh my God," Ps. 40:17. Though God had promised David a crown, a kingdom, yet he puts him off from day to day, and for all his haste he must stay[1] for it until the set time is come. Paul was delayed so long, until he even despaired of life, and had the sentence of death in himself, 2 Cor. 1:8-9. And Joseph was delayed so long, until the irons cut into his feet, Ps. 105:17-19.[2] So he delayed long the giving of comfort to Mr. Glover, though he had sought him frequently, earnestly, and denied himself to the death for Christ.[3] Augustine being under convictions, a shower of tears came from him, and casting himself on the ground under a fig tree, he cries out, "Oh Lord, how long?" How long shall I say, Tomorrow, tomorrow? Why not today, Lord, why not today? God does not always make haste to hear and save his dearest children. And therefore hold your peace. He deals no worse with you than he has done by his dearest jewels.

Though the Lord delays you for a time, yet he will come & deliverance shall come.

Though the Lord does defer and delay you for a time, yet he will come and mercy and deliverance shall certainly come.[4] He will not always forget the cry of the poor: "For yet a little while, and he that shall come will come, and will not tarry," Heb. 10:37.[5] "The vision is yet for an appointed time, but at the end it shall speak, and not lie: though it tarry, wait for it," Hab. 2:3. God will come, and mercy will come; though for the present your sun be set, and your God seems to

---

1. Wait.—H&F.
2. "He sent a man before them, even Joseph, who was sold for a servant: Whose feet they hurt with fetters: he was laid in iron: Until the time that his word came: the word of the Lord tried him," Ps. 105:17-19.
3. Clarke's 'Martyrologie.'—G.
4. Deu. 32:36; & Exo. 12:17, 41-42, 61.
5. *Mikron hoson hoson*, ['a little while'—H&F.] Heb. 10:37.

neglect you, yet your sun will rise again, and your God will answer all your prayers,[1] and supply all your necessities: "Thou which hast shewed me great and sore troubles, shalt quicken me again, and shalt bring me up again from the depths of the earth. Thou shalt increase my greatness, and comfort me on every side," Ps. 71:20-21. Three martyrs being brought to the stake all bound, one of them slipped from under his chain, to the admiration[2] of all, and falls down upon the ground and wrestled earnestly with God for a sense of his love, and God gave it to him then, and so he came and embraced the stake and died cheerfully a glorious martyr. God delays him until he was at the stake, and until he was bound, and then sweetly concedes himself to him.

Though God does delay you, yet he does not forget you.

Though God does delay you, yet he does not forget you. He remembers you still; you are still in his eye, "Behold, I have graven thee upon the palms of my hands," Isa. 49:14-16, and always upon his heart, "I do earnestly remember him still: therefore my bowels are troubled for him," Jer. 31:20. He can as soon forget himself, as forget his people. The bride shall sooner forget her ornaments, and the mother shall sooner forget her sucking child, Isa. 54:7-10,[3] and the

---

1. "And he spake a parable unto them to this end, that men ought always to pray, and not to faint; Saying, There was in a city a judge, which feared not God, neither regarded man: And there was a widow in that city; and she came unto him, saying, Avenge me of mine adversary. And he would not for a while: but afterward he said within himself, Though I fear not God, nor regard man; Yet because this widow troubleth me, I will avenge her, lest by her continual coming she weary me. And the Lord said, Hear what the unjust judge saith. And shall not God avenge his own elect, which cry day and night unto him, though he bear long with them? I tell you that he will avenge them speedily," Luk. 18:1-8.—H&F.

2. Wonder.—H&F.

3. "This is as the waters of Noah unto me: for as I have sworn that the waters of Noah should no more go over the earth; so have I sworn that I would not be wroth with thee, nor rebuke thee. For the mountains shall depart, and the hills be removed; but my kindness shall not depart from thee, neither shall the covenant of my peace be removed, saith the Lord that hath mercy on thee," Isa. 54:9-10.—H&F.

wife shall sooner forget her husband, "Thou shalt no more be termed Forsaken; neither shall thy land any more be termed Desolate: but thou shalt be called Hephzibah *(lit. 'my delight is in her')*, and thy land Beulah *(lit. 'married')*: for the Lord delighteth in thee, etc." Isa. 62:3-5, than the Lord shall forget his people. God always knows and remembers his people by name: "And the sheep hear his voice: and he calleth his own sheep by name, and leadeth them out," Joh. 10:3. Therefore be silent, hold your peace; your God has not forgotten you, though for the present he has delayed you.

> *God's time is always the best time: he*
> *chooses the best seasons to do us good.*

God's time is always the best time: God always takes[1] the best and fittest seasons to do us good. "Thus saith the Lord, In an acceptable time have I heard thee, and in a day of salvation have I helped thee," Isa. 49:8. I could have heard you before and have helped you before, but I have chosen the most acceptable time to do both. To fix for God his time[2] is to limit him: "Yea, they turned back and tempted God, and limited the Holy One of Israel," Ps. 78:41; it is to exalt ourselves above him, as if we were wiser than God. Though we are not wise enough to improve the times and seasons which God has set for us to serve and honor him in, yet we are apt to think that we are wise enough to set for God the time when he should hear and when he should save and when he should deliver. To circumscribe God to our time and to make ourselves lords of time, what is this but to divest God of his kingship and sovereignty of appointing the times? "It is not for you to know the times or the seasons, which the Father hath put in his own power," Act. 1:7 and "God that made the world and all things therein, seeing that he is Lord of heaven and earth," says Paul, "hath determined the times," Act. 17:24-26. It is only just and

---

1. Chooses or employs.—H&F.
2. To act.—H&F.

equal that God, who made time and has the sole power to appoint and dispose of time, should take his own time to do his people good. We are many times humorsome,[1] preposterous, and hasty; one moment we must have mercy or we die, we must have deliverance or we are undone; but our impatience will never help us to any mercy one hour or one moment before the time that God has set. "Be careful for nothing; but in every thing by prayer and supplication with thanksgiving let your requests be made known unto God. And the peace of God, which passeth all understanding, shall keep your hearts and minds through Christ Jesus," Phi. 4:6-7. The most good God will always take the best time to hand out mercies to his people. There is no mercy so fair, so ripe, so lovely, so beautiful, as that which God gives out in his own time. Therefore hold your peace; though God delays you, yet be silent, for there is no possibility of wringing a mercy out of God's hand until the mercy is ripe for us and we are ripe for the mercy: "I have seen the travail, which God hath given to the sons of men to be exercised in it. He hath made every thing beautiful in his time," Ecc. 3:10-11.

*The Lord will make his children amends for all
the delays that he exercises them with.*

The Lord in this life will certainly recompense and make his children amends for all the delays and put-offs[2] that he exercises them with in this world,[3] as he did Abraham in giving him such a son as Isaac was, and Hannah in giving her a Samuel. He delayed Joseph long, but at length he changes

---

1. Peevish; influenced by the humor of the moment.—H&F.
2. Deferring.—H&F.
3. "Return, Oh Lord, how long? And let it repent thee concerning thy servants. Oh satisfy us early with thy mercy; that we may rejoice and be glad all our days. Make us glad according to the days wherein thou hast afflicted us, and the years wherein we have seen evil," Ps. 90:13-15, and "Behold, we count them happy which endure. Ye have heard of the patience of Job, and have seen the end of the Lord; that the Lord is very pitiful, and of tender mercy," Jam. 5:11.—H&F.

his iron fetters into chains of gold, his rags into royal robes, his stocks into a chariot, his prison into a palace, his bed of affliction into a bed of down, his reproach into honor, and his thirty years of suffering into eighty years reigning in much grandeur and glory. So God delayed David long, but when his suffering hours were out,[1] he is anointed and the crown of Israel is set upon his head and he is made very victorious, very famous and glorious for forty years, 2 Sam. 1.[2] Well, Christians, God will certainly pay you interest upon interest for all the delays that you meet with; and therefore hold your peace. But,

*The Lord never delays mercy or deliverance
except upon great & weighty reasons.*

Lastly, *the Lord never delays the giving of this mercy or that deliverance or some other favor, except upon great and weighty reasons;* and therefore hold your peace.

But what are the reasons that God does so delay and put off his people from time to time, as we see he does?

First, *for the testing of his people, and for the differentiating and distinguishing of them from others.*[3] As the furnace tries

---

1. Completed in the dispensation of God.—H&F.
2. So the case with Elizabeth I, who, hope against hope, through perils and imprisonments, came at last to the throne of England in the cause of God and the truth of the Gospel; and who, last in line and least esteemed, upon the end of the reign of Mary Tudor, which closed the era of tyranny, burnings, and the suppression of the Bible, and upon the proclamation of her own succession to the throne, declared, "This is the Lord's doing and it is marvelous in our eyes!" Whereupon followed an illustrious reign of forty-three years in which the Gospel flourished, the Bible was freely printed, and England was a haven for the persecuted church.—H&F.
3. Take to heart the story of the woman of Canaan who cried to Jesus saying, "Have mercy on me, Oh Lord, thou Son of David; my daughter is grievously vexed with a devil. But he answered her not a word," even until the disciples asked him to send her away, even putting her off with, "I am not sent but unto the lost sheep of the house of Israel," and again with, "It is not meet to take the children's bread, and to cast it to dogs," but not only does she persist in faith through the delays and the 'put-offs', she answers—not rudely, not impatiently, not lacking heart, not doubting—but in faith,

gold, so delays will try what metal a Christian is made of. "I go forward, but he is not there; and backward, but I cannot perceive him: On the left hand, where he doth work, but I cannot behold him: he hideth himself on the right hand, that I cannot see him: but he knoweth the way that I take: when he hath tried me, I shall come forth as gold," Job. 23:8-10. Delays will try both the truth and the strength of a Christian's graces. Delays are a Christian touchstone, a *lapis Lydius,* that will try what metal men are made of, whether they be gold or dross, silver or tin, whether they be sincere or unsound, whether they be real or rotten. "Now for a season, if need be, ye are in heaviness through manifold temptations: that the trial of your faith, being much more precious than of gold that perisheth, though it be tried with fire, might be found unto praise and honour and glory at the appearing of Jesus Christ," 1 Pet. 1:6-7. As a father, by crossing and delaying his children, tries their dispositions and makes a full discovery of them, so that he can say that this child is of a muttering and grumbling disposition, and that is of an humorsome[1] and wayward disposition, but the rest are of a meek, sweet, humble, and gentle disposition: so the Lord, by the delaying and crossing of his children, discovers their different dispositions. The Lord by delays, which are stinging, tries his children; if they patiently, quietly, and sweetly can bear them, then the Lord will own them and make much of them, as those that are near and dear unto him; but if under delays they fall to crying, roaring, storming, vexing, and fretting, the Lord will not own them, but reckon them as "bastards, and not sons," Heb. 12:8. "And thou shalt remember all the way which the Lord thy God led thee these forty years in the wilderness, to humble thee, and to prove thee, to know what was in thine

---

comprehending the deeper things of God's promises and his covenant, saying, "yet the dogs eat of the crumbs which fall from their masters' table." Then only does Jesus heal her daughter, and not only that, he proclaims before all the greatness of her faith. Mat. 15:22-28.—H&F.

1. Peevish; influenced by the humor of the moment.—H&F.

heart, whether thou wouldest keep his commandments, or no. And he humbled thee, and suffered thee to hunger, and fed thee with manna, which thou knewest not, neither did thy fathers know; that he might make thee know that man doth not live by bread only, but by every word that proceedeth out of the mouth of the Lord doth man live," Deu. 8:2-3.

God delays that his children may experience his power, grace, love, & mercy.

God delays that his children may have the greater experience of his power, grace, love, and mercy in the end. Christ loved Martha and her sister and Lazarus, yet he defers his coming for several days. "This sickness is not unto death, but for the glory of God, that the Son of God might be glorified thereby," ver. 4. Lazarus must die, be put in the grave, and lie there until his body begins to decay. And why so, but that they might have the greater experience of his power, grace, and love towards them, Joh. 11:3-17.

God delays in order to sharpen his children's appetite & put an edge upon their desires.

God delays in order to sharpen his children's appetite, and to put a greater edge upon their desires; to make them cry out as a woman in travail or as a man that is in danger of drowning: "Oh Lord, have we waited for thee; the desire of our soul is to thy name, and to the remembrance of thee. With my soul have I desired thee in the night, etc." Isa. 26:8-9, 16. God delays, that his people may set upon him with greater strength and importunity; he puts them off that they may be moved with more life and vigor; God seems to be cold that he may make us the more hot; he seems to be slack that he may make us the more earnest; he seems to be backward that he may make us the more forward in pressing upon him. The father delays the child that he may make him the more eager, and so does God his children that he may make them the more divinely driven. When Balaam had once put off Balak, "he sent again," says the text, "certain princes more, and more honorable than they," Num. 22:15. Balaam's delays did but make Balak the more importunate, it did but increase and whet his desires. This is that which God aims at by all his putting off, to make his children more earnest, to provoke their spirits, and that they may send up more and yet more honorable prayers to him, that they may cry more earnestly, strive more mightily, and wrestle more importunately with God, and that they may take heaven with a more holy vehemence. Anglers draw back on the hook that the fish may be the more forward to bite; and God sometimes seems to draw back, but it is only that we may press on the more. And therefore, as anglers, when they have long waited and perceive that the fish do not so much as nibble at the bait, yet they do not impatiently throw away the rod or break the hook and line, but pull it up and look upon the bait and mend it, and so throw it in again: so also when a Christian prays and prays and yet nothing. "And he spake a parable unto them to this end, that men ought always to pray, and not to faint; saying, There was in a city a judge, which feared not God, neither regarded man: And there was a widow in that city; and she came unto him, saying, Avenge me of mine adversary. And he would not for a while: but afterward, etc." Luk. 18:1-4. God seems to be silent and heaven seems to be shut against him, yet let him not cast off prayer, but mend his prayer; pray with more believing, pray more affectionately, and pray more fervently, and then the fish will bite, then mercy will come and comfort will come and deliverance will come.[1] But,

---

1. Consider Jesus' prayer on the mount of Olives, "Father, if thou be willing, remove this cup from me: nevertheless not my will, but thine, be done, etc. And being in an agony he prayed more earnestly," Luk. 22:42-44. Consider the persistent earnestness of the prayer of the woman from Canaan, Mat. 15:22-28. And consider the end of our prayers, as Jesus prayed, "nevertheless not my will, but thine, be done," that this may temper our requests with an

God delays that he may make a fuller
discovery of his people to his people.

God delays and puts off his people many times that he may make
a fuller discovery of his people to themselves. Few Christians
see themselves and understand themselves. By delays God
discovers much of a man's sinful self to his religious self;
much of his worse part to his better part, of his ignoble part
to his most noble part. When the fire is put under the pot,
then the scum appears; so when God delays a poor soul,
oh, how does the scum of pride, the scum of murmuring,
the scum of quarrelling, the scum of distrust, the scum
of impatience, and the scum of despair discover itself in
the heart of a poor creature? I have read of a fool, who,
being left in a chamber and the door locked when he was
asleep, after he awoke and found the door fast and all the
people gone, cries out at the window, "Oh myself, myself,
Oh myself!" So when God shuts the door upon his people,
when he delays them and puts them off, ah, what cause have
they to cry out of themselves, to cry out of proud self, and
worldly self, and carnal self, and foolish self, and froward
self, etc.? We are very apt, says Seneca, *utimur perspicillis*
magis quam speculis, "to use spectacles to behold other men's
faults, rather than a looking-glass[1] to behold our own."
But now God's delays are as a looking-glass in which God
enables his people to see their own faults: "Truly God is
good to Israel, even to such as are of a clean heart. But
as for me, my feet were almost gone; my steps had well
nigh slipped. For I was envious at the foolish, when I saw
the prosperity of the wicked, etc. Until I went into the
sanctuary of God; then understood I their end. Surely thou
didst set them in slippery places: thou castedst them down
into destruction, etc. Thus my heart was grieved, and I was

---

acknowledgement of God's sovereignty: let our affections be set firmly upon
God's will, who "knoweth what things ye have need of, before ye ask him,"
Mat. 6:8.—H&F.
1. A mirror.—H&F.

pricked in my reins. So foolish was I, and ignorant: I was as a beast before thee." Ps. 73:1-21. Oh, that baseness, that vileness, that wretchedness, that sink of filthiness, that gulf of wickedness, that God by delays discovers[1] in the hearts of men! But,

God delays in order to enhance the
value of mercy & deliverance.

God delays and puts off his people in order to enhance the value and raise the price of mercy and the price of deliverance. We usually set the highest price, the greatest esteem upon such things that we obtain with greatest difficulty. What we purchase dearly, that we prize highly: "The kingdom of heaven is like unto a merchant man, seeking goodly pearls: Who, when he had found one pearl of great price, went and sold all that he had, and bought it," Mat. 13:45-46. The more sighs, tears, weeping, waiting, watching, striving, and earnest longing, this mercy and that deliverance, and some other favor costs us, the more highly we shall value them. When a delayed mercy comes, it tastes more like a mercy, it sticks more like a mercy, it warms more like a mercy, works more like a mercy, and it endears the heart to God more like a mercy than any other mercy that a man enjoys.

"This is the child," said Hannah—after God had long delayed her—"for which I prayed, and the Lord has given me my petition which I asked of him," 1 Sam. 1:27. Delayed mercy is the cream of mercy; there is no mercy so sweet, so dear, so precious to a man, as that which a man has gained after many delays. Mr. Glover, the martyr, sought the Lord earnestly and frequently for some special mercies, and the Lord delayed him long; but when he was even at the stake, then the Lord gave the mercies to him;

---

1. Discloses.—H&F.

and then, as a man overjoyed, he cries out to his friend, "He is come, he is come."[1] But,

> *The Lord delays his people that he may*
> *pay them in his own coin.*

The Lord delays his people that he may pay them in his own coin. God would sometimes retaliate upon the unjust to their destruction, "They would none of my counsel: they despised all my reproof. Therefore shall they eat of the fruit of their own way, and be filled with their own devices, etc," Pro. 1:23-33; but the children to their correction, "If his children forsake my law, and walk not in my judgments; If they break my statutes, and keep not my commandments; Then will I visit their transgression with the rod, and their iniquity with stripes. Nevertheless my lovingkindness will I not utterly take from him, nor suffer my faithfulness to fail." Ps. 89:30-33. The spouse puts off Christ: "I have put off my coat, how can I put it on, etc.?" Son. 5:3, and Christ puts her off, ver. 5-8. You have put off God from day to day, from month to month, yea, from year to year; and therefore, if God put you off from day to day, or from year to year, have you any cause to complain? Surely no. You have often and long put off the motions of his Spirit, the directions of his Word, the offers of his grace, the entreaties of his Son; and therefore, what can be more just than that God should delay you for a time, and put you off for a season, who have delayed him and put him off days without number? If God serves you as you have often served him, you have no reason to complain. But,

> *The Lord delays his people that heaven may*
> *be the more sweet to them at last.*

Lastly, *the Lord delays his people that heaven may be the more sweet to them at last.* Here they meet with many delays and

---

1. Clark's 'Martyrologie.'—G.

with much being put-off; but in heaven they shall never meet with once being put-off or with one delay. Here many times they call and cry and can get no answer; here they knock and bounce,[1] and yet the door of grace and mercy opens not to them; but in heaven they shall have mercy at the first word, at the first knock. There, whatever heart can wish shall without delay be enjoined. Here God seems to say sometimes that we have mistaken the way, that our requests are not upright, that we must not be first, that it is not the time; we are not altogether or wholly in his will. "For we know in part, and we prophesy in part. But when that which is perfect is come, then that which is in part shall be done away. When I was a child, I spake as a child, I understood as a child, I thought as a child: but when I became a man, I put away childish things. For now we see through a glass, darkly; but then face to face: now I know in part; but then shall I know even as also I am known," 1 Cor. 13:9-12. But in heaven, when we know even as we are known, all the sweetness and blessedness and happiness of that state shall present itself every hour to our souls. God has never, God will never, say to any of his saints in heaven, "tomorrow." Such language the saints sometimes hear here, but such language is not suitable to a glorified condition; and therefore, seeing that the Lord never delays his people, but upon great and weighty accounts, "now abideth faith, hope, charity," 1 Cor. 13:13, let his people be silent before him, let them not mutter nor murmur, but be mute. And so I have finished with the objections.

---

1. To send a heavy blow, as upon a closed door.—H&F.

❧ HELPS & DIRECTIONS ❧

to silence and still your soul under afflictions, trials, & sad providences.

I shall come now at the last to propound some helps and directions that may contribute to the silencing and stilling of your souls under the greatest afflictions, the sharpest trials, and the saddest providences that you meet with in this world; and so complete this discourse.

All the afflictions that come upon the saints are the fruits of divine love.

First, *all the afflictions that come upon the saints are the fruits of divine love*: "As many as I love, I rebuke and chasten: be zealous therefore, and repent," Rev. 3:19; "For whom the Lord loveth he chasteneth, and scourgeth every son whom he receiveth. If ye endure chastening, God dealeth with you as with sons; for what son is he whom the father chasteneth not?" Heb. 12:6-7; "Blessed is the man whom thou chastenest, Oh Lord, and teachest him out of thy law," Ps. 94:12. And in Job, "What is man, that thou shouldest magnify him? And that thou shouldest set thine heart upon him? And that thou shouldest visit him every morning, and try him every moment?" Job 7:17-18. "Behold, I have refined thee, but not with silver; I have chosen thee in the furnace of affliction," Isa. 48:10. When Munster lay sick, and his friends asked him how he did and how he felt, he pointed to his sores and ulcers, whereof he was full, and said, "These are God's gems and jewels wherewith he decks his best friends, and to me they are more precious than all the gold and silver in the world." A gentleman highly prizes his hawk, he feeds her with his own hand, he carries her upon his fist, he takes a great deal of delight and pleasure in her; and therefore he puts vervels[1] upon her legs, and a hood upon her head; he hoodwinks her, and fetters her, because he loves her, and takes delight in her; so the Lord by afflictions hoodwinks and fetters his children, but all is because he loves them, and takes delight and pleasure in them.[2] There cannot be a greater evidence of God's hatred and wrath, than his refusing to correct men for their sinful courses and vanities. "Why should you be smitten any more? You will revolt more and more: the whole head is sick, and the whole heart faint. From the sole of the foot even unto the head there is no soundness in it; but wounds, and bruises, and putrifying sores: they have not been closed, neither bound up, neither mollified with ointment," Isa. 1:5-6. Where God refuses to correct, there God resolves to destroy; there is no man so near the axe, so near the flames, so near hell, as he whom God will not so much as spend a rod upon. "But if ye be without chastisement, whereof all are partakers, then are ye bastards, and not sons," Heb. 12:8. God is most angry where he shews no anger. Jerome, writing to a sick friend, uses this expression: "I account it a part of unhappiness not to know adversity; I judge you to be miserable, because you have not been miserable." "Nothing," says Demetrius, "seems more unhappy to me, than he to whom no adversity has happened."[3] God afflicts you, oh Christian, in love, "For whom the Lord loveth he chasteneth, and scourgeth every son whom he receiveth," Heb. 12:6. And therefore Luther cries out, "Strike, Lord; strike, Lord, and spare not." Who can seriously muse upon

---

1. A silver ring with the owner's name engraved on it that is placed on the leg of a hawk.—H&F.
2. "Who is blind, but my servant? Or deaf, as my messenger that I sent? Who is blind as he that is perfect, and blind as the Lord's servant?" Isa. 42:19.—H&F.
3. *Nihil est infelicius eo cui nil unquam contigit adversi.* Seneca. [De Providentia.—G.]

this, and not hold his peace, and not be silent under the most smarting rod?

Consider that the miseries & losses of this world are all the hell you ever shall have.

Consider that the trials and troubles, the calamities and miseries, the crosses and losses that you meet with in this world are all the hell that you shall ever have. Here you have your hell; hereafter you shall have your heaven. This is the worst of your condition, the best is to come. Lazarus had his hell first, his heaven last; but the rich man had his heaven first and his hell at last, Luk. 16:19-25. "Woe unto you that are rich! For ye have received your consolation. Woe unto you that are full! For ye shall hunger. Woe unto you that laugh now! For ye shall mourn and weep," Luk. 6:24-25. But you have all your pangs and pains and throes here that ever you shall have; your ease and rest and pleasure is to come. "Blessed be ye poor: for yours is the kingdom of God. Blessed are ye that hunger now: for ye shall be filled. Blessed are ye that weep now: for ye shall laugh," Luk. 6:20-21. Here you have all your bitter, your sweet is to come; here you have your sorrows, your joys are to come; here you have all your winter nights, your summer days are to come; here you have your passion week, your ascension day is to come; here you have your evil things, your good things are to come. Death will put a limit to all your sins and to all your sufferings; and it will be an inlet to those joys, delights, and contentments that shall never have an end; and therefore hold your peace and be silent before the Lord.[1]

Get an assurance that Christ & pardon are yours and this will quiet the soul under trial.

Get an assurance that Christ is yours, and pardon of sin is

---

1. See my treatise called "Heaven on Earth."

yours, and divine favor is yours, and heaven is yours and the sense of this will exceedingly quiet and silence the soul under the sorest and sharpest trials a Christian can meet with in this world. He that is assured that God is his portion, will never mutter nor murmur under his greatest burden; he that can upon solid grounds say, "Nothing shall separate me from the love of God in Christ," will be able to triumph in the midst of the greatest tribulations, Rom. 8:33-39.[1] He that with the spouse can say, "My beloved is mine, and I am his," Son. 2:16, will bear up quietly and sweetly under the heaviest afflictions. In the time of the Marian persecution there was a gracious woman, who, being convened before bloody Bonner, then Bishop of London, upon the trial of religion, he threatened her that he would take away her husband from her. Said she, "Christ is my husband." "I will take away your child," said he. "Christ," said she, "is better to me than ten sons." "I will strip you," said he, "of all your outward comforts." "Yea, but Christ is mine," said she, "and you cannot strip me of him." Oh! The assurance that Christ was hers bore up her heart, and quieted her spirit under all.[2] "You may take away my life," said Basil, "but you cannot take away my comfort; my head, but not my crown." "Yea," said he, "had I a thousand lives, I would lay them all down for my Savior's sake, who has done abundantly more for me." John Ardley professed to Bonner, when he told him of burning and how ill he could endure it, that if he had as

---

1. "Who shall lay any thing to the charge of God's elect? It is God that justifieth. Who is he that condemneth? It is Christ that died, yea rather, that is risen again, who is even at the right hand of God, who also maketh intercession for us. Who shall separate us from the love of Christ? Shall tribulation, or distress, or persecution, or famine, or nakedness, or peril, or sword? As it is written, For thy sake we are killed all the day long; we are accounted as sheep for the slaughter. Nay, in all these things we are more than conquerors through him that loved us. For I am persuaded, that neither death, nor life, nor angels, nor principalities, nor powers, nor things present, nor things to come, Nor height, nor depth, nor any other creature, shall be able to separate us from the love of God, which is in Christ Jesus our Lord," Rom. 8:33-39.—H&F.

2. Acts and Monuments by John Foxe. So also John Noyes, Alice Driver, Mr. Bradford, Mr. Taylor, and Justin Martyr, with many more.

many lives as he had hairs on his head, he would lose them all in the fire before he would lose his Christ.[1] Assurance will keep a man from muttering and murmuring under the sorest afflictions. Henry and John, two Augustine monks, being the first that were burnt in Germany, and Mr. Rogers, the first that was burnt in Queen Mary's days, did all sing in the flame. A soul that lives in the assurance of divine favor and in its title to glory cannot but bear up patiently and quietly under the greatest sufferings that possibly can befall it in this world. That Scripture is worth its weight in gold, "The inhabitants of Sion shall not say, I am sick; the people that dwell therein shall be forgiven their iniquity," Isa. 33:24. He does not say that they were not sick. No. But that although they were sick, yet they would not say they were sick, because they were "forgiven their iniquity." Why should they forget their sorrows and not remember their pains nor be sensible of their sickness? Because the Lord had forgiven them their iniquities. The sense of pardon took away the sense of pain and the sense of forgiveness took away the sense of sickness. Assurance of pardon will take away the pain, the sting, and the trouble from every trouble and affliction that a Christian meets with. No affliction will daunt, startle, or stagger an assured Christian. An assured Christian will be patient and silent under all, "Surely goodness and mercy shall follow me all the days of my life: and I will dwell in the house of the Lord forever," Ps. 23:1-6. Melancthon makes mention of a godly woman, who, having been in much conflict upon her deathbed and then having been much comforted, broke out into these words: "Now, and not until now, have I understood the meaning of these words, Thy sins are forgiven," the sense of which did mightily cheer and quiet her. He that has gotten this jewel of assurance in his bosom will be far from vexing or fretting under the saddest dispensations that he meets with in this world.

---

1. Clarke's 'Martyrologie.'—G.

Dwell upon the benefit & profit that has redounded to your souls through affliction.

If you would be quiet and silent under your present troubles and trials, *then dwell much upon the benefit, the profit, the advantage that has redounded to your souls by former troubles and afflictions that have been upon you.* "In the day of adversity consider," Ecc. 7:14. Oh, now consider how by former afflictions the Lord has discovered sin, prevented sin, and mortified sin: consider how the Lord by former afflictions had discovered to you the impotency, the mutability, the insufficiency, and the vanity of the world, and all worldly concernments: consider how the Lord by former afflictions has melted your heart and broken your heart and humbled your heart and prepared your heart for clearer, fuller, and sweeter enjoyments of himself. Consider what pity, what compassion, what bowels, what tenderness, and what sweetness former afflictions have wrought in you towards others in misery. Consider what room former afflictions have made in your soul for God, for his Word, for good counsel, and for divine comfort. Consider how by former afflictions the Lord has made you more a partaker of his Christ, his Spirit, his holiness, his goodness, etc. Consider how by former afflictions the Lord has made you to look towards heaven more, to mind heaven more, to prize heaven more, and to long for heaven more, etc. Now, who can seriously consider all that good that he has gained by former afflictions and not be silent under present afflictions? Who can remember those choice, those great, and those precious earnings that his soul has made of former afflictions,[1] and not reason[2] himself into a holy silence under present afflictions in this manner: "Oh my soul! Has not God done you much good, great good, special

---

1. "For bodily exercise profiteth little: but godliness is profitable unto all things, having promise of the life that now is, and of that which is to come," 1 Tim. 4:8.—H&F.
2. Prove by good argument.—H&F.

good, by former afflictions? Yes. Oh my soul! Has God not done that for you by former afflictions that you would not have done for ten thousand worlds? Yes. And is God not, oh my soul, as powerful as ever, as faithful as ever, as gracious as ever, and as ready and willing as ever to do you good by present afflictions as he has been to do you good by former afflictions? Yes, yes. Why, why then do you not sit silent and mute before him under your present troubles? Oh my soul!" It was the saying of one, that an excellent memory was requisite for three sorts of men: first, for tradesmen; for they, having much business to do, many reckonings to make up, many irons in the fire, have need of a good memory. Secondly, great talkers; for they, being full of words, have need of a good storehouse in their heads to feed their tongues. Thirdly, for liars; for they, telling many untruths, have need of a good memory, lest they should be taken in their lying contradictions. And, I may add, for a fourth, viz., those that are afflicted, that they may remember the great good that they have gained by former afflictions, so they may be the more silent and quiet under present troubles.

Consider that your choicest & chiefest treasure is safe: your God, Christ, portion, crown, & inheritance.

To quiet and silence your souls under the sorest afflictions and sharpest trials, consider, *that your choicest, your chiefest treasure is safe:* your God is safe, your Christ is safe, your portion is safe, your crown is safe, your inheritance is safe, your royal palace is safe, and your jewels, your graces are safe; therefore hold your peace, "For I know whom I have believed, and am persuaded that he is able to keep that which I have committed unto him against that day," 2 Tim. 1:12 and "Henceforth there is laid up for me a crown of righteousness, which the Lord, the righteous judge, shall give me at that day: and not to me only, but unto all them also that love his appearing," 2 Tim. 4:8.

I have read a story of a man that had a suit at law, and when his cause was to be heard, he applied himself to three friends to see what they could do for him: one answered that he would bring him as far on his journey as he could; the second promised him that he would go with him to his journey's end; the third engaged himself to go with him before the judge and to speak for him, and not to leave him until his cause was heard and determined. These three are a man's riches, his friends, and his graces. His riches will help him to comfortable accommodations while they stay with him, but they often take leave of a man before his soul takes leave of his body. His friends will go with him to his grave and then leave him; but his graces will accompany him before God, they will not leave him nor forsake him; they will go to the grave and to glory with him. "Do good," says Paul, "be rich in good works," laying up in store for yourselves, "a good foundation against the time to come, that (you) may lay hold on eternal life," 1 Tim. 6:18-19.

In that famous battle at Leuctrum,[1] where the Thebans got a signal victory, but their captain, Epaminondas, a little before his death, demanded whether his buckler had been taken by the enemy, and when he understood that it was safe and that they had not so much as laid their hands on it, he died most willingly, cheerfully, and quietly. Well, Christians, your shield of faith is safe, your portion is safe, your royal robe is safe, your kingdom is safe, your heaven is safe, your happiness and blessedness is safe; and therefore, under all your afflictions and troubles, "There shall not an hair of your head perish. In your patience possess ye your souls," Luk. 21:18-19. But,

---

1. Rather Leuctra.—G.

Set yourselves in good earnest upon the mortification of your lusts.

If you would be silent and quiet under your sorest troubles and trials, then *set yourselves in good earnest upon the mortification of your lusts.*[1] It is unmortified lust which is the sting of every trouble, and which makes every sweet bitter, and every bitter more bitter. Unmortified sin adds weight to every burden, it adds gall to our wormwood, it adds chain to chain; it makes the bed uneasy, the chamber a prison, relaxations troublesome and everything vexatious to the soul. "From whence come wars and fightings amongst you? Come they not hence, even of your lusts, that war in your members?" Jam. 4:1. So say I, where does all this muttering, murmuring, fretting, and vexing, etc. come from? Do they not come from your unmortified lusts? Do they not come from your unmortified pride, and unmortified self-love, and unmortified unbelief, and unmortified passion, etc.? Surely they do. Oh, therefore, if ever you would be silent under the afflicting hand of God, labor for more and more of the grace of the Spirit by which you may mortify the lusts of the flesh, "For if ye live after the flesh, ye shall die: but if ye through the Spirit do mortify the deeds of the body, ye shall live," Rom. 8:13. It is not your strongest resolutions or purposes, without the grace of the Spirit, that can vanquish a lust. A soul disease, until it is healed, will fester, though we resolve and say it shall not be. It was the oil and the blood of the sacrifice that cleansed the leper under the law;[2] and that by these things was meant the blood of Christ and the grace of his Spirit is agreed upon by all. It was a touch of Christ's garment that cured the woman of her bloody issue, Mar. 5:25-34. "Philosophy," says Lactantius, "may hide a sin, but it cannot quench it; it may cover a sin, but it cannot cut off a sin." Like a black patch instead of

---

1. Augustine says, "If you kill not sin until it dies of itself, sin has killed you, and not you your sin."

2. Lev. 14:14-20.

a plaster—it may cover some deformities in nature, but it does not cure them. Neither is it the papists' purgatories, watchings, whippings, etc., nor is it St. Francis' kissing or licking of lepers' sores, which will cleanse the leprosy of sin. It is in the strength of Christ and in the power of the Spirit set without reserve upon the mortifying of every lust. Oh, embrace no lust, indulge none, but with resolve set upon the ruin of all! One leak in a ship will sink it; one wound strikes Goliath dead as well as twenty-three did Caesar; one Delilah may do Samson as much spite and mischief as all the Philistines; one broken wheel spoils the whole clock; one bleeding vein will let out all that is vital to life; one fly will spoil a whole box of ointment; one bitter herb will spoil the pottage.[1] By eating one apple, Adam lost paradise; one lick of honey endangered Jonathan's life; one Achan was a trouble to all Israel; one Jonah raises a storm and becomes lading[2] too heavy for a whole ship; so one unmortified lust will be able to raise very strange and strong storms and tempests in the soul in the days of affliction. And therefore, as you would have a blessed calm and quietness in your own spirits under your sharpest trials, set yourselves thoroughly upon the work of mortification. Ah, Christian, do you not know what a world of mischief one unmortified lust may do? Therefore, let nothing satisfy you but the blood of all your lusts.

Consider that all afflictions come upon you by & through that covenant of grace that God has made with you.

If you would be silent under your greatest afflictions and your sharpest trials, then make this consideration your daily companion, viz., *that all the afflictions that come upon you, come upon you by and through that covenant of grace that God has made with you.* In the covenant of grace, God has

---

1. Soup.—H&F.
2. Freight or cargo.—H&F.

engaged himself to keep you from the evils, snares, and the temptations of this world; in the covenant of grace, God has engaged himself to purge away your sins, to brighten and increase your graces, to crucify your hearts to the world, and to prepare you and preserve you to his heavenly kingdom. Consider also that by afflictions he effects all this according to his covenant: "If his children forsake my law, and walk not in my commandments; if they break my statutes, and keep not my commandments," Ps. 89:30-31. In these words, you have a supposition that the saints may fall both into sins of commission and sins of omission; in the following words you have God's gracious promise: "Then will I visit their transgressions with the rod, and their iniquities with stripes," Ps. 89:32. God engages himself by promise and covenant, not only to chide and check, but also to correct his people for their sins: "Nevertheless, my loving-kindness will I not utterly take from him, nor suffer my faithfulness to fail," Ps. 89:33-34. Afflictions are fruits of God's faithfulness, to which the covenant binds him. God would be unfaithful to his Word if, first or last, more or less, he did not afflict his people. Afflictions are part of that gracious covenant that God has made with his people. Afflictions are mercies, yea, covenant mercies, "I know, Oh Lord, that thy judgments are right, and that thou in faithfulness hast afflicted me," Ps. 119:75. Hence it is that God is called "the great and terrible God, that keepeth covenant and mercy," Neh. 1:5; because, by his covenant of mercy, he is bound to afflict and chastise his people. God is bound by covenant to preserve his people and not to suffer them to perish; and happy are they that are preserved, whether in salt and vinegar or in wine and sugar. All the afflictions that come upon a wicked man come upon him by virtue of a covenant of works, and so are cursed unto him; but all the afflictions that come upon a gracious man, come upon him by virtue of a covenant of grace, and so they are blessed unto him; and therefore he has eminent cause to hold his peace and to lay his hand upon his mouth.

Consider that afflictions reach only the base & the ignoble part of a Christian: his body & his outward man.

If you would be silent and quiet under afflictions, then dwell much upon this, viz., *that all your afflictions do but reach the worse, the base, and the ignoble part of a Christian, that is, his body, his outward man:* "Though our outward man decay, yet our inward man is renewed day by day," 2 Cor. 4:16. As Aristarchus the heathen said when he was beaten by the tyrants: "Beat on; it is not Aristarchus you beat, it is only his shell." Timothy had a very healthful soul in a body that was often infirm.[1] Epictetus and many of the more refined heathens, have long since concluded that the body was the organ or vessel, the soul was the man and merchandise.[2] Now, all the troubles and afflictions that a Christian meets with do not reach his soul, they do not defile his conscience, they make no breach between his noble part, his soul, and Christ: "For I am persuaded, that neither death, nor life, nor angels, nor principalities, nor powers, nor things present, nor things to come, Nor height, nor depth, nor any other creature, shall be able to separate us from the love of God, which is in Christ Jesus our Lord." Rom. 8:38-39. Therefore he has cause to hold his peace and to lay his hand upon his mouth. The soul is the breath of God, "And the Lord God formed man of the dust of the ground, and breathed into his nostrils the breath of life; and man became a living

---

1. 1 Tim. 5:23.
2. "For God, who commanded the light to shine out of darkness, hath shined in our hearts, to give the light of the knowledge of the glory of God in the face of Jesus Christ. But we have this treasure in earthen vessels, that the excellency of the power may be of God, and not of us," 2 Cor. 4:6-7; and again, "But in a great house there are not only vessels of gold and of silver, but also of wood and of earth; and some to honour, and some to dishonour. If a man therefore purge himself from these, he shall be a vessel unto honour, sanctified, and meet for the master's use, and prepared unto every good work," 2 Tim. 2:20-21.—H&F.

soul," Gen. 2:7; and of a divine offspring,[1] Heb. 12:9[2] and Zec. 12:1;[3] it is an immortal spirit. Souls are of an angelic nature; a man is as an angel clothed in clay; the soul is a greater miracle in man than all the miracles wrought among men. Now it is not in the power of any outward troubles or afflictions that a Christian meets with to reach his soul;[4] and therefore he may well sit mute under the smarting rod.

Keep up faith in continual exercise.

If you would be silent and quiet under the saddest providences and sorest trials, then *keep up faith in continual exercise*. Now faith, in the exercise of it, will quiet and silence the soul, thus,

1. By bringing the soul to rest satisfied in the simple enjoyments of God: "Men of the world," says the Psalmist, "have their portion in this life," their bellies "thou fillest with thy hid treasure: they are full of children, and leave the rest of their substance to their babes." But, he says, "As for me, I will behold thy face in righteousness: I shall be satisfied, when I awake, with thy likeness," Ps. 17:14-15.[5]

---

1. "I have said, You are gods *('elohim')*; and all of you sons of the Most High," Ps. 82:6. And in the New Testament: "The Jews answered Him, saying, We do not stone you for a good work, but for blasphemy, and because you, being a man, make yourself God. Jesus answered them, Is it not written in your Law, 'I said, You are gods *('theos')*?' If He called those gods with whom the Word of God was, and the Scripture cannot be broken, do you say of Him whom the Father has sanctified and sent into the world, You blaspheme, because I said, I am the Son of God?" Joh. 10:33-36.—H&F.
2. God is called "the Father of spirits," Heb. 12:9.—H&F.
3. Again, God is he who forms the spirits: "Jehovah, who stretches forth the heavens, and lays the foundation of the earth, and forms the spirit of man within him," Zec. 12:1. "Then shall the dust return to the earth as it was: and the spirit shall return unto God who gave it," Ecc. 12:7.—H&F.
4. "Be not afraid of them that kill the body, and after that have no more that they can do. But I will forewarn you whom ye shall fear: Fear him, which after he hath killed hath power to cast into hell," Luk. 12:4-5.—H&F.
5. "Trust in the Lord, and do good; so shalt thou dwell in the land, and verily thou shalt be fed. Delight thyself also in the Lord; and he shall give thee the desires of thine heart," Ps. 37:3-4.—H&F.

2. By drying up the springs of pride, self-love, impatience, murmuring, unbelief, and the carnal delights of this world.

3. By presenting the soul with greater, sweeter, and better things in Christ, than any this world can afford: "But now they desire a better country, that is, an heavenly," Heb. 11:16 and "But what things were gain to me, those I counted loss for Christ. Yea doubtless, and I count all things but loss for the excellency of the knowledge of Christ Jesus, my Lord: for whom I have suffered the loss of all things, and do count them but dung, that I may win Christ, etc." Phi. 3:7-9; "Eye hath not seen, nor ear heard, neither have entered into the heart of man, the things which God hath prepared for them that love him. But God hath revealed them unto us by his Spirit: for the Spirit searcheth all things, yea, the deep things of God," 1 Cor. 2:9-10.

4. By lessening the soul's esteem of all outward vanities. "If ye then be risen with Christ, seek those things which are above, where Christ sitteth on the right hand of God. Set your affection on things above, not on things on the earth," Col. 3:1-2. Do but keep up the exercise of faith, and you will keep silent before the Lord. "Faith is the substance of things hoped for, the evidence of things not seen," Heb. 11:1. There is no man who will remain so mute as he whose faith remains occupied with invisible objects.

Remain humble before the Lord.

If you would keep silent and quiet under the saddest providences and sorest trials, then *keep humble before the Lord*. Oh, labor every day to be more humble and more lowly and little in your own eyes. "Who am I," says the humble soul, "I am not worthy of the least mercy, I deserve not a crumb of mercy, I have forfeited every mercy, I have never improved a mercy." It is only pride that puts men upon contending with God and men;[1] a humble soul will lie quiet at the foot of God, it will be contented with bare commons:[2] "Every prudent man dealeth with knowledge," Pro. 13:16. As you see, sheep can live upon the bare commons, which a fat ox cannot. A dinner of green herbs is agreeable to the humble man's palate, whereas a stalled ox is but a coarse dish to a proud man's stomach.[3] A humble heart thinks none are less than himself nor worse than himself; a humble heart looks upon small mercies as great mercies, and great afflictions as small afflictions, and small afflictions as no afflictions; and therefore sits mute and quiet under all. Do but remain humble and you will remain silent before the Lord. Pride kicks and flings and frets, but a humble man still has his hand upon his mouth. Everything on this side of hell is mercy, much mercy, and rich mercy to a humble soul; and therefore he holds his peace.[4]

Hold fast these soul silencing & soul quieting maxims.

If you would keep silence under the afflicting hand of God, then *hold close and hold fast these soul silencing and soul quieting maxims and principles:*

> *The worst that God does is done to make within his people a heaven on earth.*

That the worst that God does to his people in this world is done in order to create within them a heaven on earth, in the

---

1. "Only by pride cometh contention," Pro. 13:10.
2. Food served at a common table or hall; here spoken of the knowledge of God revealed in his Word and received by those of a humble heart, Mat. 18:3-4 & "If any man teach otherwise, and consent not to wholesome words, even the words of our Lord Jesus Christ, and to the doctrine which is according to godliness; He is proud, knowing nothing, etc." 1 Tim. 6:3-4.—H&F.
3. A reference to: "Better is a dinner of herbs where love is, than a stalled ox and hatred therewith," Pro. 15:17.—H&F.
4. Augustine being asked, "What was the first grace?" answered, "Humility"; what the second? "Humility"; what the third? "Humility."

heavenly comfort within their hearts. He brings them into a wilderness, but it is that he may speak comfortably to them, Hos. 2:14;[1] he casts them into the fiery furnace, but it is that they may have more of his company.[2] Do the stones come thick and threefold around Stephen's ears? It is but to knock him the nearer to Christ: "And they stoned Stephen, calling upon God, and saying, Lord Jesus, receive my spirit. And he kneeled down, and cried with a loud voice, Lord, lay not this sin to their charge. And when he had said this, he fell asleep," Act. 7:59-60.

What God wills is best.

If you would be silent under affliction, then hold fast this principle, viz., *that what God wills is best,* Heb. 12:10.[3] When he wills sickness, sickness is better than health; when he wills weakness, weakness is better than strength; when he wills want, want is better than wealth; when he wills reproach, reproach is better than honor; when he wills death, death is better than life. As God is wisdom itself, and so knows that which is best, so he is goodness itself, and therefore cannot do anything but that which is best: therefore hold your peace.

---

1. "I will allure her, and bring her into the wilderness, and speak comfortably unto her. And I will give her her vineyards from thence, and the valley of Achor for a door of hope: and she shall sing there, as in the days of her youth, and as in the day when she came up out of the land of Egypt," Hos. 2:14-15.—H&F.

2. Our author is referring to the grace with which so many martyrs died in the fires of the Inquisition, some singing hymns, some preaching the Gospel, some pleading for forgiveness for their persecutors. John Hus dying in the fire in 1415, prayed beforehand: "Oh Holy Spirit, enlighten their deceived hearts, so that the truth of the holy Gospel may open their eyes and its praise be spread everywhere, for ever and ever, Amen." Hus the Heretic by Fra Poggius. Anne Askewe, burned at the stake in 1546, prayed, "Yet, Lord, I thee desire, for that they do to me, let them not taste the fire of their iniquity." Ballad composed by Anne Askewe in Newgate Prison, Select Works of John Bale.—H&F.

3. "For they verily for a few days chastened us after their own pleasure; but he for our profit, that we might be partakers of his holiness," Heb. 12:10.—H&F.

The Lord will accompany you in all your afflictions.

If you would be silent under your greatest afflictions, then hold fast to this principle, viz., *that the Lord will accompany you in all your afflictions:* "Fear thou not; for I am with thee: be not dismayed; for I am thy God: I will strengthen thee; yea, I will help thee; yea, I will uphold thee with the right hand of my righteousness," Isa. 41:10; "When thou passest through the waters, I will be with thee; and through the rivers, they shall not overflow thee: when thou walkest through the fire, thou shalt not be burned; neither shall the flame kindle upon thee. For I am the Lord thy God, the Holy One of Israel, thy Saviour," Isa. 43:2-3; Ps. 23:4-6,[1] Mat. 28:19-20.[2] These Scriptures are fountains full of divine consolation, the wells of salvation are full—will you turn to them and draw out that your souls may be satisfied and quieted?

The Lord has more noble & blessed ends in afflicting you than in the afflicting of the men of the world.

If you would be silent under your afflictions, then hold fast this principle: *that the Lord has more high, more noble, and more blessed ends in the afflicting of you than he has in the afflicting of the men of the world.* The stalk and the ear of corn fall upon the threshing floor, under one and the same flail,[3] but the one is shattered in pieces, the other is preserved; from one and the same olive and from under one and the same press is crushed out both oil and dregs;

---

1. "Yea, though I walk through the valley of the shadow of death, I will fear no evil: for thou art with me; thy rod and thy staff they comfort me. Thou preparest a table before me in the presence of mine enemies: thou anointest my head with oil; my cup runneth over. Surely goodness and mercy shall follow me all the days of my life: and I will dwell in the house of the Lord forever," Ps. 23:4-6.—H&F.

2. "Go ye therefore, and teach all nations, baptizing them in the name of the Father, and of the Son, and of the Holy Ghost: Teaching them to observe all things whatsoever I have commanded you: and, lo, I am with you alway, even unto the end of the world," Mat. 28:19-20.—H&F.

3. An instrument for beating corn from the ear.—H&F.

but the one is turned up[1] for use, the other thrown out as unserviceable: so, though afflictions do befall good and bad alike, as the Scripture speaks, Ecc. 9:2,[2] yet the Lord will effect more glorious ends by those afflictions that befall his people, than he will effect by those that befall wicked men. The Lord puts his people into the furnace for their trial, but the wicked for their ruin: the one is bettered by affliction, the other is made worse; the one is made soft and tender by afflictions, the other is more hard and obdurate; the one is drawn nearer to God by afflictions, the other is driven further from God, etc.

The best way to have your own will is to resign
yourself to the good will & pleasure of God.

If you would be silent under your afflictions, then you must hold fast this principle, viz., *that the best way in this world to have your own will is to rest in the will of God and quietly to resign yourself to the good will and pleasure of God.* "Trust in the Lord, and do good; so shalt thou dwell in the land, and verily thou shalt be fed. Delight thyself also in the Lord; and he shall give thee the desires of thine heart. Commit thy way unto the Lord; trust also in him; and he shall bring it to pass. And he shall bring forth thy righteousness as the light, and thy judgment as the noonday," Ps. 37:3-6. Luther was a man that could have anything of God, and why? Why, because he submitted his will to the will of God; he lost his will in the will of God. Oh soul, it shall be even as you will, if you will be swallowed up in the will of God.

---

1. Crushed in the press.—H&F.
2. "All things come alike to all: there is one event to the righteous, and to the wicked; to the good and to the clean, and to the unclean; to him that sacrificeth, and to him that sacrificeth not: as is the good, so is the sinner; and he that sweareth, as he that feareth an oath," Ecc. 9:2.—H&F.

God will make times of afflictions special
manifestations of divine love & favor to you.

Lastly, if you would be silent under the afflicting hand of God, then you must hold fast to this principle, viz., *that God will make times of afflictions to be times of special manifestation of divine love and favor to you.* Tiburtius saw a paradise when he walked upon hot burning coals. "When I said, My foot slippeth; thy mercy, Oh Lord, held me up. In the multitude of my thoughts within me thy comforts delight my soul," Ps. 94:18-19. "And when they had laid many stripes upon them, they cast them into prison, charging the jailor to keep them safely: Who, having received such a charge, thrust them into the inner prison, and made their feet fast in the stocks. And at midnight Paul and Silas prayed, and sang praises unto God," Act. 16:23-26. "When they had called the Apostles, and beaten them, they commanded that they should not speak in the name of Jesus, and let them go. And they departed from the presence of the council, rejoicing that they were counted worthy to suffer shame for his name," Act. 5:40-41. And so, I affirm this by a cloud of witnesses and have now come to a close. Ah, Christians, as you would be quiet and silent under the smarting rod, hold fast to these principles, and keep them as your very lives. But,

To silence your soul under the afflicting hand of
God, dwell much upon the brevity of man's life.

Lastly, to silence and quiet your soul under the afflicting hand of God, *dwell much upon the brevity or shortness of man's life.* This present life is not *vita, sed via ad vitam*, it is not "life, but a journey[1] towards life." Man's life, says one, is the shadow of smoke, yea, the dream of a shadow: says another; man's life is so short that Augustine doubted

---

1. That is, a way or road. Christ calls himself the way: *"ego sum via et veritas et vita,"* "I am the way, the truth, and the life," Joh.14:6, and it is upon this path alone that we must make our journey to life.—H&F.

whether to call it a dying life or a living death.[1] You have
what is but a day to live in this world, and perhaps you may
be now in the twelfth hour of that day; therefore hold out
faith and patience. "What is your life? It is even a vapour,
that appeareth for a little time, and then vanisheth away,"
Jam. 4:14. Your troubles and your life shall shortly end
together; therefore hold your peace. Your grave is going to
be made and death begins to call you off the stage of this
world, although you have a great deal of work to do—a
God to honor, a Christ to close with[2], a soul to save,[3] a race
to run,[4] a crown to win, a hell to escape,[5] a pardon to beg, a
heaven to make sure,[6] yet you have only a little time to do

---

1. Augustine, Confessions.
2. Come together with: "Serve the Lord with fear, and rejoice with
trembling. Kiss the Son, lest he be angry, and ye perish from the way, when
his wrath is kindled but a little. Blessed are all they that put their trust in
him," Ps. 2:11-12.—H&F.
3. "Doth not wisdom cry? And understanding put forth her voice? She
standeth in the top of high places, by the way. Now therefore hearken unto
me, Oh ye children: for blessed are they that keep my ways. For whoso
findeth me findeth life, and shall obtain favour of the Lord, etc." Pro. 8:1-3,
32, 35-36.—H&F.
4. "Wherefore seeing we also are compassed about with so great a cloud of
witnesses, let us lay aside every weight, and the sin which doth so easily beset
us, and let us run with patience the race that is set before us, Looking unto
Jesus the author and finisher of our faith," Heb. 12:1-2.—H&F.
5. "How shall we escape, if we neglect so great salvation; which at the first
began to be spoken by the Lord, and was confirmed unto us by them that
heard him," Heb. 2:3.—H&F.
6. "According as his divine power hath given unto us all things that pertain
unto life and godliness, through the knowledge of him that hath called us to
glory and virtue: Whereby are given unto us exceeding great and precious
promises: that by these ye might be partakers of the divine nature, having
escaped the corruption that is in the world through lust. And beside this,
giving all diligence, add to your faith virtue; and to virtue knowledge; And
to knowledge temperance; and to temperance patience; and to patience
godliness; And to godliness brotherly kindness; and to brotherly kindness
charity. For if these things be in you, and abound, they make you that ye
shall neither be barren nor unfruitful in the knowledge of our Lord Jesus
Christ. But he that lacketh these things is blind, and cannot see afar off, and
hath forgotten that he was purged from his old sins. Wherefore the rather,
brethren, give diligence to make your calling and election sure: for if ye do
these things, ye shall never fall: For so an entrance shall be ministered unto
you abundantly into the everlasting kingdom of our Lord and Saviour Jesus
Christ," 2 Pet. 1:3-11.—H&F.

it in; you have one foot in the grave, and will you now cry out in your affliction? Will you now mutter and murmur when you are entering upon an unchangeable condition? What extreme folly and madness is it for a man to mutter and murmur when he is just going out of the prison and his bolts and chains are just now knocked off! Why, Christian, this is just your case; therefore hold your peace. Your life is but short, therefore your troubles cannot be long; hold up and hold out quietly and patiently a little longer and heaven shall make amends for all:

"For I reckon that the sufferings of this present
time are not worthy to be compared with the
glory which shall be revealed in us."
Rom. 8:18.

"By manifestation of the truth commending ourselves to every man's conscience in the sight of God."
2 Corinthians 4:2

HAIL & FIRE

Hail & Fire is a resource for Reformed and Gospel
Theology in the works, exhortations, prayers,
and apologetics of those who have
maintained the Gospel and
expounded upon the
Scripture
as the Eternal Word of God
and the sole authority in Christian doctrine.

For the edification of those who hold the Gospel
in truth and for the examination of every
conscience, Hail & Fire reprints
and republishes, in print
and online,
Christian,
Puritan, Reformed
and Protestant sermons and
exhortative works; Protestant and
Catholic polemical and apologetic works;
Bibles histories, martyrologies, and eschatological works.

Visit us online: www.hailandfire.com

26288661R00134

Made in the USA
Lexington, KY
24 September 2013